ATLANTIS & LEMURIA

THE LOST CONTINENTS REVEALED!

BY TOM T. MOORE

Other Publications by

Tom T. Moore

The Gentle Way:
A Self-Help Guide for Those Who Believe in Angels

The Gentle Way II:
Benevolent Outcomes, the Story Continues

The Gentle Way III:
Master Your Life

First Contact:
Conversations with an ET

For print books, visit our online bookstore at www.LightTechnology.com.
eBooks are available on Amazon, Apple iTunes, Google Play, and Barnes & Noble.

ATLANTIS & LEMURIA

THE LOST CONTINENTS REVEALED!

BY TOM T. MOORE

For more information about special discounts for bulk purchases, please contact Light Technology Publishing Special Sales at 1-800-450-0985 or publishing@LightTechnology.net.

ISBN-13: 978-1-62233-037-9
Published and printed in the United States of America by:

PO Box 3540
Flagstaff, AZ 86003
1-800-450-0985 • 928-526-1345
www.LightTechnology.com

CONTENTS

This book is dedicated to all the people who have posed questions about Atlantis and Lemuria during the past seven years. I especially wish to thank Helen Keahi in Hawaii, whom my guardian angel Theo says was one of my trusted staff in my migration life from Atlantis. She posed many questions and organized much of this book.

Mantej Kalsi in the UK submitted over 500 questions. Jim Connell in Florida submitted a number of questions and organized some chapters. Anne-Marie Barrett organized several chapters, as did Cyd Carlson in Colorado.

Thanks to my son, Todd, I was able to keep my newsletter running, which is where many of these questions were posted. Finally, thanks to my wife for keeping our business going while I spent weeks and months putting this book together. I could not have done this without everyone's assistance and support!

PREFACE

In this book, you'll read questions sent to me from all over the world from people who read my weekly newsletter. I pose these questions in my meditative alpha state to Theo — a "golden light being," who I believe is my guardian angel — and the soul of Earth, commonly referred to in modern times as Gaia. Gaia is, or has been known as, Mother Earth, Terra, Dìqiú, and Prithvī in different parts of the world. These entities have told me they will answer any question, but I have to ask specific questions, not general ones.

I began asking questions for this book seven years ago. I've had lots of practice doing this with my spiritual friends and loved ones. I've also been told that I have done this for many lifetimes, as you'll read later in this book. So keep yourself open to this information. Everyone has filters in place from being taught that certain things are true or not true by families, friends, schools, and religious institutions. It is sometimes quite difficult to break out of the boxes you have put yourselves in when you don't even realize you are in one.

As you read, you'll learn why I became so interested in both the continents of Atlantis and Lemuria, but here is a little hint:

Gaia, why is it part of my soul contract to write the book on the history of these two continents?

Because you were intimately involved, Tom, and had more lives on both continents than anyone alive today. And it is time for people to learn more about your world history.

INTRODUCTION

Sixty thousand years ago, two additional continents existed, each about 10 to 12 percent larger than the continent of Australia. One was located in the Atlantic Ocean between North America and Africa: Atlantis. The other was located in the Pacific Ocean: Lemuria, or Mu. Why are they no longer there?

Scientists have estimated that the sea levels of the world are 300 to 400 feet higher than they were in the ancient past.[1] Ruins of a city have been found submerged off the west coast of Cuba,[2] another on the coast of Spain,[3] and there's a submerged road off the coast of Bimini in the Bahamas.[4] Giant ruins of a civilization have been discovered under the sea near Yonaguni-jima, Japan.[5] Legend has it[6] — and most legends are rooted in actual events, I've discovered — that the Atlanteans destroyed the remaining eight islands that warred

1. Benjamin Strauss and Robert Kopp, "Rising Seas, Vanishing Coastlines," *New York Times*, November 24, 2012, accessed June 8, 2015.
2. BBC News, "'Lost City' Found beneath Cuban Waters," December 7, 2001, accessed June 8, 2015.
3. NBCNews.com, "Lost City of Atlantis Believed Found off Spain," March 14, 2011, accessed June 8, 2015.
4. Found by divers in 1968, Bimini Road is located near Bimini Island in the Bahamas. The half-mile long underwater formation is posited to be remains of Atlantis (http://en.wikipedia.org/wiki/Bimini_Road).
5. Masaaki Kimura, a marine geologist at the University of the Ryukyus in Japan, believes submerged stone structures lying just below the waters off Yonaguni-jima are actually the ruins of a Japanese Atlantis (http://news.nationalgeographic.com/news/2007/09/070919-sunken-city.html).
6. Plato, *Dialogues of Plato*, translated and edited with analyses and introduction by Benjamin Jowett, Cambridge Library Collection — Classics (New York: Cambridge University Press, [1871] 2010).

against each another after the continent was destroyed by earthquakes 18,000 years earlier, a result of it sitting in the middle of the Mid-Atlantic Ridge. The Lemurians also sank their continent during a climatic war 5,000 years after the last islands of Atlantis were destroyed.

Plato wrote about Atlantis in his Timaeus and Critias dialogues around 360 BC.[7] These works have been covered extensively in other books, so we won't dwell on them except to ask later where Plato obtained his information. And Edgar Cayce, known as the "sleeping prophet," received extensive information about Atlantis and Lemuria.[8]

The Atlanteans and Lemurians were just like you and me. If you can imagine the differences in daily life between, say, the people of North America and Europe or Asia, then that will give you an idea of the sophistication these two societies achieved over 50,000 years. We have not yet caught up to their advancements in energy and medical treatments. Later, you'll read that the few Atlantean survivors (and those who migrated prior to the final destruction) traveled in all directions, including Egypt, Guatemala, and the Yucatán, where they integrated with the much less developed populations.

Can you imagine the displacement and rise of water levels (and accompanying tsunamis) engulfing all the coastal towns around the world, wiping out any trace of their existence when the two continents sank? The largest religions of the world relate the story of Noah and his ark.

Archaeologists keep identifying civilizations older than the last one discovered, so we cannot dismiss all legends as old wives' tales. Let's begin our exploration in ancient times — before Adam and Eve existed — with the existence of these two continents and how they became inhabited 60,000 years before they destroyed themselves.

TIMELINES

This is an excerpt from my book *First Contact: Conversations with an ET*. It will help explain what timelines are — basically parallel worlds that scientists have long theorized about.

My guardian angel says that each soul fragment has twelve parallel, or simultaneous, lives on Earth. He calls it the twelve timelines. There are

---

7.   Ibid.
8.   Frank Joseph, Edgar Cayce's *Atlantis and Lemuria: The Lost Civilizations in the Light of Modern Discoveries* (Virginia Beach: A.R.E. Press, 2001).

twelve "yous" who were born on different frequencies. Just imagine twelve matrices.

The timelines are divided into fours and then subdivided into twos, with the lower timelines at lower frequencies as compared to the upper timelines. Therefore, timelines one through four, five through eight, and nine through twelve are grouped together with smaller changes in frequency but with a fairly large jump between four and five and eight and nine.

Timeline twelve is nonphysical and is considered the perfect life by our souls. All others are compared with timeline twelve. Then the timelines are subdivided again, with one and two, three and four, five and six, seven and eight, nine and ten, and eleven and twelve closer in frequency to each other.

We are on timeline six — basically in the middle frequency — so there are versions of ourselves having harder lives living at lower frequencies, and the versions above are having easier lives at higher frequencies.

This might be confusing, so let me give you a personal example: On timelines one through eight, I attended Texas Christian University and received a Bachelor of Business Administration in finance. On timelines nine and above, I majored in English and became a science-fiction writer, later writing spiritual books. On timelines one through eight, I went through the ROTC officers' program in order to pay for my schooling and spent two years in the Army. On the upper timelines, I did not participate in ROTC, as there was no Vietnam War. They settled their differences with little conflict.

On the upper timelines, I married my college sweetheart, we moved to Colorado, we divorced, and I remarried and had children. On the lower timelines, my college sweetheart sent me a Dear John letter while I was in South Korea and married someone else.

On timelines one to eight, I married my wife of today, but on the lower four of those timelines, we divorced eighteen years ago and both remarried. I'm still married to my wife on timelines five through eight.

Thirty years ago, my wife and I sold our international tour business and I started an international film and TV program distribution company, but on the lower timelines, I remained in the tour business. In 2005, I experienced congestive heart failure. It was caught just in time on these timelines, but I died on timelines one and two.

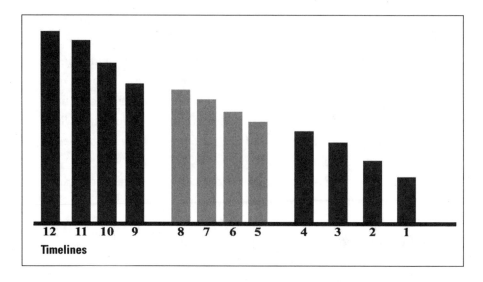

12 11 10 9   8 7 6 5   4 3 2 1
Timelines

Figure 0.1: A simple chart displaying the relations between timelines and frequencies for the purpose of this discussion.

Figure 0.1 should give you at least a basic idea of how different our lives can be depending on which timeline we're on.

THE EARTH DIRECTIVE
Antura, Gaia, and Theo

Were there twelve timelines in Atlantis?
Yes, they existed then.

If the ETs communicated with all twelve timelines, why weren't the ETs able to see the writing on the wall much sooner?
The best way to describe it is that they had blinders on. They did not understand at that time how and what they were doing would interfere so dramatically with your human development. It was too late when they realized where things were headed, even on the upper timelines. You were thick in the middle of the third focus, and so the ETs made the decision to withdraw, as they saw their efforts to assist your growth were being used to defeat the other side. They learned the hard way that you needed thousands of years more to learn how to get along together.

Antura, did your force field devices protect you during the Atlantean days?
Yes, the devices were the same as they are now. Bear in mind that was only

a little over 1,300 universal years, and there have been only few changes made to our equipment in that amount of time. There were some adjustments or improvements, not many.

Were you limited in the time you could spend on the planet?

It was more of a fatigue issue. Even with force field devices, the amount of time we wished to spend in the third focus weighed heavy on those who were doing work at that time. It was refreshing to return to a fifth-focus mothership.

What were the ETs trying to accomplish then?

They were trying to assist, as we would any other new society we have first contact with. But in the case of the Explorer Race, it was impossible, as you have much shorter lives and you're veiled from knowing your true selves. This was difficult for us (meaning Federation-type people) to comprehend. Those people only wanted to increase their power. They could not see the future past the end of their noses, you could say.

Was the contact with the extraterrestrials major, or did the extraterrestrials figure these would destroy themselves, so they kept their distance?

Good question. They kept a certain distance, as these people were in a process of breaking up their continent with destructive rays. The extraterrestrials wanted to have nothing to do with the situation after they saw it was hopeless.

How long before the island sank (around 10,500 BC) was the Earth Directive instituted?

It was several hundred years in Earth time. The ETs could foresee the path the Atlanteans were on and ordered all parties to disengage. It was quite perplexing, you understand, to those leaders who had been involved with the ETs, as they could not be told the reason for their departure. You might say they felt as if they were left adrift at sea. So to answer your question, it was not at the last minute or even in the past few years. Their path was seen well in advance, and the ETs knew they had interfered too much, so they withdrew.

It took some time in Earth years for this to come about, as there was much discussion about what should and should not be included. The ETs formulated a plan that would be in place for thousands of Earth years; therefore, they wanted to get it right. Yet even with all the discussion, they left off what the Zetas found a few thousand years later — abducting people when their souls allowed it.[9]

Antura, are there connections between ETs and the Lemurians?

---

9. Tom T. Moore, *First Contact: Conversations with an ET* (Light Technology Publishing: Flagstaff, Arizona, 2013).

Yes, it is the same as with the Atlanteans. However, when the Earth Directive was created, they were left to their own devices, and destructive behavior developed earlier than with the Atlanteans. As we have discussed, the Lemurians lasted another 5,000 years, give or take a few. Every society on Earth had some ET connection at that time, and we were guilty of making a mess of things, which is why we had to withdraw.

Were they aware of the Earth experiment?

Yes and no. Some were quite aware of the Earth experiment, but the general population was not. It was kept from them, as their leaders did not think they would understand. There was a lot of contact with the ETs during those times, but there was not much relating of their history.

Are any of the ETs who visited Atlantis — either here now or coming soon — still alive or would they have transitioned or retired?

There are a few, but they have mostly retired. You were told previously that your next life would last well over 1,000 universal years, which is over 10,000 Earth years.

When we start having public contact with ETs, will they correct or broaden our view of history regarding Atlantis and Lemuria?

They will answer those questions if asked. It is up to those who are contacted to ask questions, and the questions will be on a wide variety of subjects. Your history and their involvement definitely will be one of the topics of discussion.

KEY TERMS

Adam man and woman — the final human model (body) settled on for the Earth experiment

Adama — Tall, pale-complected Lemurian. He was the leader of the underground city of Telos, located under Mount Shasta, California, at a slightly higher focus than Earth.

Agartha — (sometimes Agartta, Agharti, Agarta, or Agarttha) is a legendary city that is said to be located in the Earth's core. It is related to the belief in a hollow Earth and is a popular subject in esotericism.

akashic records — the records for every single soul fragment's lives on Earth

Antura — an extraterrestrial member of Tom's soul cluster who has had over 800 lives on Earth

Aryan — principle island of the Sons of Belial faction of Atlantis

Atlantis — ancient lost continent located in the Atlantic Ocean between North America and Africa, or Oz

balancing life — You have to have a balance of good and bad lives during the average of 600 to 800 lives on Earth. This is for your soul's learning, as a soul fragment must experience everything Earth has to offer — from wonderful lives to lives with great challenges.

Bosnian Pyramids — A group of pyramids discovered near Sarajevo dated back 26,000 years with miles of tunnels connecting them. The biggest is approximately 30 percent larger than the Great Pyramid of Giza.

bucket list — Every soul fragment must have every single experience Earth has to offer during the 600 to 800 lives they have on Earth.

crystal power — the energy derived from crystals on Atlantis that powered every conceivable device

Earth Directive — a directive agreed on by the Federation of Planets that forbade further interference in Earth affairs

Earth experiment — the experiment requested by the Creator to veil humans so that they would create in new ways and to eventually bring small amounts of negativity to other planets after first conquering it themselves

Edgar Cayce — American psychic known as the "sleeping prophet" who gave extensive readings, including many on Atlantis and Lemuria

Explorer Race — Earth humans who volunteered to help ascend Earth and will go to the stars one day to assist other societies in raising their vibrational levels

extraterrestrials (ETs) — beings originating outside of Earth

Federation of the Planets (Federation) — a group of 200 planets formed after the original Star Wars who are not only our protectors but also contributed DNA to the Adam man and woman

first contact — when ETs contact a planet for the first time and offer future assistance, typically done thousands of years before a society reaches an advanced stage of development

focus — a common dimensional reference, such as the third focus (dimension) or fifth focus

Golden Gate City — the principle governing city of Poseidia

guardian angel (GA) — A whole-soul golden lightbeing that cares for thousands of soul fragments during their Earth lives. They prefer the term "servants of the Creator."

Law of One — one of the two factions that inhabited Atlantis

Lemuria (Mu) — an ancient lost continent, located in the Pacific Ocean near Japan, that sank in a war between the five countries on the continent

Master Kryon — a spiritual master channeled by Lee Carroll

most benevolent outcomes (MBOs) — prayers sent to the Creator via your guardian angels

moving Earth — Earth was moved from the Sirius B star system to our solar system as part of the Earth experiment to be in a remote part of the galaxy.

Nibiruans — habitants of the planet Nibiru, who are on probation with the Federation for enslaving humans to work their mines and having a nuclear-type war between their own factions on Earth

Poseidia — the principle island ruled by the Law of One faction of Atlantis

Oz — north Africa

Reveals the Mysteries — An American Indian shaman who lived in the 1600s in the western part of North America. He was the first being Tom communicated with in 2005 and is one of the soul fragments in his soul cluster.

Sons of Belial — one of the two factions that inhabited Atlantis

soul cluster — a group of six to twelve soul fragments living on Earth as part of the Earth experiment

soul contract — the soul path decided and agreed on by all soul fragments prior to living on Earth to experience the greatest challenges, learning, and success for souls to raise their vibrational levels at a much faster rate

soul fragment — a fragment of a soul living on Earth and other planets

space-time continuum — the four-dimensional continuum of one temporal and three spatial coordinates in which any event or physical object is located

Still Water — Tom's name when he was a shaman during the 1600s, as told to him by the shaman Reveals the Mysteries

Strabo — A Greek geographer, philosopher, and historian — as well as one of Tom's past incarnations. Strabo's works are still studied in modern times.

Theo — an angelic entity and Tom's guardian angel — or servant of the Creator, as he likes to be known

Therans — People who lived on Thera, about 200 km southeast of Greece's mainland. A great volcanic eruption destroyed much of the island. What remains has been named Santorini, now a popular tourist destination.

Telos — the Lemurian city beneath Mount Shasta, California, that exists at a higher focus

the Gentle Way — a modality Tom was inspired to create 200 years before the Atlantean islands destroyed themselves in a horrific war

the Things — Mutated human models created by ETs. The Atlanteans finally fixed their DNA after thousands of years of neglect.

timelines — Also know as parallel worlds. There are twelve timelines, as described in the *First Contact* chapter excerpt.

transition — Commonly known as death. The body transitions when the soul fragment leaves the body as the cord attaching it to the body is severed.

universal year — Ten Earth years equals one universal year.

veiled — All humans living on Earth and other planets are blocked from knowing about their past lives. The Creator of the universe desired this as part of the Earth experiment.

Chapter 1

HUMAN ORIGINS
Theo and Gaia

Theo, please explain human origins.

Several of the ET civilizations collectively gave you your DNA after much experimentation with all sorts of bodies. This went on for many thousands of years in your time; however, they had the ability to jump ahead in the future to see how these creations developed and were able to handle themselves. So much tweaking went on for centuries. They did this in consultation with their spiritual advisors who were directed by the Creator in what to accomplish. When the Creator of the universe comes calling, you listen, and when the Creator asks you to do something — certainly you have the option of not doing — usually you do as the Creator requests.

When did the first thought-form humanoids appear?

Thought-form humans actually appeared much earlier than what you think — more than 2 million years ago. Keep in mind this was still allowed much later, as the timelines were in place. You could say they were testing the space-time continuum. This is a very complex subject, as it seemed on one hand that thought-form humans appeared in a number of time periods, which they did, but always for specific reasons. Some were just putting their toes in the water, and others were testing the space-time continuum to make sure it would work.

Were the thought forms described by Edgar Cayce in his writings about Atlantis[1] in the shape of humans, orbs, or what?

---

1. Edgar Cayce's Association for Research and Enlightenment (A.R.E.), *The Edgar Cayce Readings*, Readings 257-207, 262-119, http://are-cayce.org/ecreadings/Default.aspx (membership required).

Yes, thought forms had a variety of shapes, as you can imagine, because they were just that — thoughts. They were not physical yet, so there was no need to be a certain shape, although as they grew closer to being physical, they took on a completely humanoid form. In the early stages, they probably looked closer to the shape of an orb, but again, as they took on the thought forms of humans, their images grew closer and closer to that of a human being.

Edgar Cayce said there were humans on Earth 10.5 million years ago.[2] Did you service any clients then?

Yes, I did, but only a couple.

Were they embodied physically at that time?

Yes, they were.

There were humans on Earth 10.5 million years ago?

Humans, yes, but not with the same brain capacity as you have today. The Adam man and woman had not been decided on at that time. Still, they were ensouled by those who wished to get their feet wet. You were one of the first, and as was typical at that time, you did not last too long. Yet you still gained valuable experience in that short life.

Okay, then please help me understand the seeming contradiction when Edgar Cayce said that on the continent of Atlantis there were humans who were barely physical.[3]

Yes, this is a little difficult to understand. Humans had been physical for millions of years, but new souls in their first Earth lives were still permitted at that time to experience physicality without being birthed. This was so they could get their toes wet, to use your vernacular. It was to give them a feel for what an Earth life would be like but without all the dangers.

Still, there came a time when, even with their partially solid lives, they had to go all in. This process ended not too long after that. All souls taking part in this experiment had to be humanly conceived and birthed through a woman's birth canal.

Was there a line waiting of souls who volunteered for these lives?

Definitely. The souls were anxious to get started, which was why they were allowed to ensoul the early humanoids in order to get a feel for the land and living conditions.

So obviously the ET scientists had several million years of knowledge on how to do all of this, correct?

Yes, they had knowledge but not so much on the practical side. Which is why they made a number of mistakes.

---

2.   Ibid. Text of Readings 5748–2.
3.   A.R.E. website, Readings 364-13, http://are-cayce.org/ecreadings/Default.aspx.

. . .

ABOUT ADAM AND EVE

Gaia, does the term "Adam and Eve" refer to a specific couple, a class of beings, or what?

"Adam and Eve" is a class of beings. There were Adams and Eves in each of the root races, you could say, all over the world. Bear in mind that there were several groups of humans of the same race deposited at different points on a continent, thereby ensuring that one or more of these clans, we shall call them, survived. Naturally, this took several thousand years. So to answer your question, there weren't two people named "Adam and Eve"; it only references the type of being who was finally settled on for Earth inhabitation. The "Adam and Eve" stories are allegories.

Did the Earth experiment begin with Adam and Eve or before?

Before, you could say. It was agreed on several million Earth years ago, and then it went through many experiments to find the right body and mind to handle all of the challenges. But the big kickoff, or formal ribbon cutting, did not occur until the introduction of the Adam and Eve seedings.

Were the first souls seeded on Earth specialists in adaptability? How were they chosen?

Souls such as you were willing and able to jump into the water, shall we say, and did so beginning over a million years ago. These souls desired to begin the Earth experiment. Were they specialists in adaptability? No. Many floundered their first time on Earth, and I'm speaking about the ones who chose to incarnate early. As you well know, there are people incarnating now in your modern times who also flounder but for different reasons.

The souls for Atlantis and Lemuria were not seeded at the same time several million years ago?

No, the seeding of these two continents came later. They were not part of the initial seeding.

When the Adam man and woman were seeded on the Atlantean and Lemurian continents, were they each seeded north, east, south, and west with just fewer seedings on the Lemurian continent?

That's correct. That's why it took much longer for the Lemurians to develop since the society that seeded the Lemurians wished to take it slower than those who seeded the Atlanteans. Therefore, when the First Destruction — or the pole shift came [see chapter 8] — there were fewer people on the coast of Lemuria who perished than on the coast of Atlantis. The population of Atlantis was already at 1 million, give or take a few. It was not even one-tenth of that in Lemuria.

THE TWELVE TIMELINES

When did the twelve timelines begin? Was it when Earth arrived in the solar system or when the Explorer Race was created?

There you have it. Your souls, in setting up the experiment (naturally with input from the Creator), also created the space-time continuum. There was no need for it before the souls taking part in the experiment were ready to begin ensouling first the humanoids, which was quite long ago — millions of years.

The use of timelines was in place well before the first Adam man and woman models. After all, the ET scientists who created the Earth experiment were being provided with a lot of information from the scout crafts monitoring the different models they had created.

Why would the twelve timelines be needed in those simple lives?

The timelines were needed before the Adam man and woman were established and agreed on. The ensoulments, which were done before that time, were for you and others to get the feel of the land — a trial run, if you will. From that point forward, there had to be twelve timelines in order to maximize your lives on Earth, no matter how simple they were even then.

BODY TYPE TRIALS

If ETs created the Adam man and woman, was this well after we first appeared on Earth and were, at times, not quite physical?

Yes, this was well after you first appeared, as we have previously covered how these bodies did not have the same brain capability the Adam man and woman have now. The archaeologists are discovering these bodies in remote regions, such as Africa. The testing of these bodies went on for a couple million years before the Adam man and woman were finally introduced as the final models. Various ETs tested all sorts of bodies, many that have never been discovered, but you can include Cro-Magnon and Neanderthal in that group, plus the "Things" that existed for thousands of years on the continent of Atlantis.

Were there large populations of other body types besides Cro-Magnon and Neanderthals that existed before the Adam model that archaeologists have yet to discover?

There were several. I knew we would cover this a little more for the book, but still, we need to limit the questions.

I'll try, although it is a little confusing when you mention "humans" but are including all the models before Adam man and woman. What were the populations of the Cro-Magnons and Neanderthals — over 1 million or over 5 million?

There were definitely more than 1 million each; however, your archaeologists have found little evidence. Cro-Magnons cremated bodies at death, and the Neanderthals simply killed and ate the older members when they could no longer take care of themselves.

Were there more than 5 million Cro-Magnons?

Use that number, as that was close to their population at the peak of their existence.

How many Neanderthals were there at their peak?

It was a little less, but much more than the archaeologists have estimated. It had to be a large group to be part of the experiment with that type of humanoid body, you see. Because of their cannibalism, their numbers never grew. Their bodies required more food, so that was a controlling factor too.

Then who created them?

It was your friendly Arcturians. They wanted to see how a muscular humanoid would adapt to primitive conditions. They were a warrior race at one time.

Were the Cro-Magnon and Neanderthals ensouled?

Yes, they were. This was part of your early appearances to get the feel of the planet in preparation for all of your Adam man and woman lives. Your souls even ensouled the very early, what we call, Lucy-type models in which the brain capacity was pretty low. The Cro-Magnon and Neanderthal models had to be ensouled too, and there were plenty of volunteers to ensoul these models as part of learning about life on Earth.

Why did the Cro-Magnons die out? Did the ETs somehow stop their ability to procreate?

In a way, they did. Many lost their lives in the floods [detailed later], and for those who were left, it was quite easy for the ETs to engineer their demise in humane ways that you have not discovered yet.

What was wrong with the Cro-Magnon model? Why did the ETs decide on round eye sockets for the Adam man and woman models but not square, as was the Cro-Magnon?

This would take a lengthy discussion, but the body type was tweaked in a number of different areas, many of which were internal. Your archaeologists can only look at the bones and hypothesize as to their makeup and then gather information of things around them. The ETs found over a long period of time what was working and what would prevent this model from achieving all Creator wished the Earth human to accomplish.

Suffice it to say, there are a number of models yet to be discovered where several thousand would be needed, at a minimum, in order to gain sufficient information. You perhaps had the idea, along with most people, (including your archaeologists) that there were just a few humanoids. But the ET scientists had a field day in testing different body types over hundreds of thousands of years. The early models were quite rough, hence the creation of the Things with sometimes hideous appearances.

The Adam man and woman were chosen only after many models were tried, watched over several thousand years in many cases, and then allowed to die out. There is no record of these trial bodies, as these took place millions of years ago in Earth time. Due to the space-time continuum, ET scientists did not have to wait in real time, we'll term it, but could hop from the creation every one hundred years or so to see what was working and what wasn't.

Scientists are positive we descended from apes, especially as they note how similar our DNA seems. A number of remains of the early humanoids lead to that theory.

Yes, they can draw those conclusions, but that's not how it happened. May I repeat that your ET brothers tested many body types? They would try one model, then come back for it in, let's say, a few hundred years to see how the model had adapted. As time on Earth now has been sped up for your learning, so it was then by a factor of ten. They could even stay nearby and critique the form. Much study and research went into the development of the Adam man and woman.

Were there any groups in Europe or Asia that reached the numbers of the Cro-Magnon model?

Yes, one other, but that body type has yet to be discovered. We will leave them for a future conversation.

THE MODEL HUMAN

Please explain more about the Adam man and woman. They were introduced at an early time on the continent of Atlantis, but were they simultaneously introduced as different races all over the world, or had they already been introduced?

The Adam man and woman were introduced to Atlantis at that early time, and the same model, if you will, was introduced in other places then as other races. There were other models in existence, but they did not have the same brainpower. These early models were ensouled millions of years earlier so that the kinks would be worked out on the hominid model while giving souls an early taste of life on Earth.

The real breakthrough was when the Adam man and woman model was agreed on by your Federation ET forefathers, and the master plan went into effect to have different races introduced all over the world at almost the same time. The other models were left to die out, such as the Neanderthals, as the

Adam man and woman were given a much greater brain to cope with all the conditions Earth offers.

Was the model tweaked first in Africa before its introduction in Atlantis?

Yes, but only by a few thousand years of your time. As soon as the final model was agreed on, all continents received the new model.

Does the fact that early humanoids were seeded with ET DNA have anything to do with the Garden of Eden story and snakes?

No, not really. This story came long after the manipulations of the humanoid DNA as your friendly ETs experimented with what would work best. Of course, the Pleiadians were heavily involved, and many other societies contributed DNA to make Earth humans the best they could to survive and flourish.

The story of the Garden of Eden and the snake came much later and has to do with continued manipulation by the ETs who regarded your world as a source of minerals — primarily gold — and used the humans for drudgery work in the mines. To go into detail would take us hours, as you can imagine. People have written books about this period. Zecharia Sitchin's[4] books were somewhat accurate, but a lot was speculation.

Are archaeologists accurate in their estimation that there were people living 700,000 years ago in Egypt?

It was actually much longer than that. Carbon dating and so on shows that humans existed long before the current major religions of the world claim. These findings will seem small in comparison to what will be discovered in the next few years.

Were the Adam man and woman created to look similar to the people of the Pleiades and other human-form worlds?

Adam and Eve were seeded by a combination of worlds in which humans look similar to you today. Each world put some of their DNA into you — what they considered their best attributes — to help you survive living short, veiled lives, relearning each time you were born. So they mixed up the best DNA cocktail they could create and seeded it in the Adam man and woman.

When the Adam man and woman models were decided as the best to cope with life on Earth, did the ET societies get together and say, "Okay, this is Adam and Eve. Let's all start manufacturing the bodies with differences in skin color and other slight modifications"?

Yes, everyone agreed, as the major players — the Pleiadians, Sirians, and Arcturians — basically ran the show with contributions of a smaller nature from all

---

4. Books by Zecharia Sitchin: *The 12th Planet* (New York: Stein and Day, 1976); *The Stairway to Heaven* (HarperCollins, 2007); *The Wars of Gods and Men* (HarperCollins, 2007).

the other planetary societies. This was not done willy-nilly, you could say. Therefore, a number of bodies were created to populate the various parts of the world.

Were different races purposely put in extreme temperature climates to test their capabilities to withstand extreme temperatures regardless of their skin colors?

Exactly. Your ET fathers and mothers wanted to make sure every extreme temperature could be handled without more layering of skin. Much thought went into creating the ideal man and woman.

Did Cro-Magnons or Neanderthals ever inhabit the continent of Lemuria?

Yes, at one time the Cro-Magnons did, but not the Neanderthals. Like the continent of Atlantis, they were created elsewhere. The Cro-Magnons flourished for a time and then the Adam-seeded man and woman slowly took over.

Was there more than one alien society that populated Atlantis?

Yes, but several of those experiments did not work out. The Adam man and woman were seeded there too, so they eventually flourished.

When the ET scientists were creating the Adam man and woman, did they use a particular process or form to create these bodies? In other words, was it sort of a mold, or were there laser-type machines that followed a pattern to create each body?

More of the latter. It was a very sophisticated way of punching in the data and having machines create the body forms using the DNA figures given in the supercomputers, as we'll call them for your purposes.

After the Adam man and woman were decided on, how many were populated around the world?

Several thousand of each race was seeded. And to answer your next question, they were populated as full adults, as it would have been impossible for them to survive had they been deposited in each location as newborns. For a while, they kept their memories of who they were, but this gradually faded, especially as they created their own babies in the normal fashion. That's how legends were passed down of coming from the stars. Initially they knew from where they originated.

Was this done on board the spaceship, and then were they deposited on Earth two by two or in groups?

Yes, very small groups ensouled so that they knew where they originated from and their purpose. With this knowledge, they did not stand around looking forlorn and wondering what to do. They knew they had to find shelter and clothing if they were in colder climates and so on.

Then no structures were built for the Adam man and woman when they were first introduced?

There were none whatsoever.

How fast could one of these bodies be formed?

Quite fast — in just a couple of minutes — as we're talking about machines that, even then, were millions of years ahead of your current machines. Although, I will say, you are catching up fast.

I assume that the scientists who created these Adam men and women have long since transitioned?

Yes. Like everyone else, they were not immortal, so they transitioned, and since their souls' main interest was science, most of them are back tweaking their work or working on other projects.

Did the ET scientists populate the North American continent, or was the continent populated just by migration?

No, parts of the continent were populated by the ETs, but they were small groups. The migration occurred much later.

Then there was no transport, let's say, from Africa to Atlantis. The bodies for each were created separately?

That's correct.

· · ·

THE HUMAN RACES AND CULTURES

Theo, what were the blood types of the Atlanteans, Lemurians, and ancient Indians?

All humans began with the same blood type, but it was decided by your ET ancestors that more variety was needed. So different blood types were introduced. As you are not familiar with all the blood types, it would be difficult to give you those specific blood types for these ancient people. Definitely, they were different, yet they combined as people migrated or were forced to relocate.

Where were the five races established on Earth?

The black race was naturally seeded in what is now known as Africa. Great studies have already been done there of skeletal remains of the early models and then later your current Adam man and woman. The white, or Caucasian, race was established in Scandinavia. The yellow-skinned people were naturally established in what is now China. The brown-skinned people were seeded in what is now Asia, and the red-skinned people were originally in North America and northern Asia. Of course when Atlantis was populated, there were red-skinned and brown-skinned people in Lemuria.

Where did the Aryans [Indo-Iranian/European race] originate?

They originated quite a few thousand years ago, much earlier than scientists have been able to prove. They were one of the established ET clans, and they were one of the first to be set in Northern Europe to see how they would fare in colder conditions.

Hopefully it was summertime if they were placed there with no clothes.

That's correct. But they were made aware that this was a colder country, and they needed to clothe themselves and build shelters before the onslaught of winter.

Was this a Pleiadian group?

No, but from another Federation member.

Where did the Vikings originate?

They originated from one of our robust humanoid groups, which is part of the Federation. They wanted to give their experimental humans a war-like trait to see what the results would be.

Were there multiple establishments of these races, or was it just one colony that grew from there?

There were multiple colonies. Part of the reason was to ensure that these races would flourish.

Were the Etruscans and Hungarians seeded in Italy originally, or did they come from central Europe or where?

I don't wish to give too much away for those who study the origins. They can discover more through studying DNA and such; look toward central Europe. Your ET scientists seeded a number of various locations in Europe, and this particular group seeded just a few — slightly different in makeup but still the Adam man and woman model. Therefore, that should tell you these people originated 60,000 years ago, not just 5,000 or so as has been estimated. This group migrated for various reasons until they found the warm shores of Italy, which had inlets for their boats and areas to farm.

Was Lemuria seeded at the same time as Atlantis?

It was seeded a little later than Atlantis but not too much. The population was initially smaller than Atlantis's, so it took longer to grow compared to Atlantis's. This continent was an ideal setting for thousands of years. It was only in the later stages that wars erupted.

Did they communicate in their home planet language, or were they veiled from knowing, and if so, how did they communicate?

Yes, they were allowed to have that communication, which is why today you see such diversity in languages. Still they were pretty basic, and they evolved over a long period of time. The ETs also needed to be able to communicate with them too. Yes, they had their translators, but it was easier to have a basic language to communicate with them.

Did the Atlanteans or Lemurians have twelve-strand DNA?

No, it was not available to them. They had their limits, just as you have in today's world. There will come a time when you add to the strands. Again, this is difficult to discuss, as you do not have a science background, the knowledge of the fundamentals of the DNA strands, as they are very complex.

As the Atlanteans and Lemurians were the Adam man and woman template, I assume they had the same emotions we have today, but what about the ancient societies that came before them? Were they all humanoid, and did they have the same emotional makeup as today?

Those are interesting questions. Yes, the Atlanteans and Lemurians had the same emotional makeup as today. The other ancient societies (which there are no records of) had an emotional package, shall we call it, similar to yours. They were not part of the Explorer Race. Therefore, they ranged up and down the scale, you could say, just as your ET cousins, aunts, and uncles do. They can be very low-key or quite mercurial.

How many years have people had blue eyes, as some people say it is around 7,000 years?

It is much, much longer than that. People have had blue eyes for perhaps a million years. The genetic code was introduced back then. Your records just do not go back any further, so that's why that number is used. It has nothing to do with fact.

Were any Atlanteans blue-eyed, or did they vary in color?

There was a variance in eye color, blue being one of them.

ANCIENT TIMES

Scientists theorize that landmasses originated from a supercontinent that split apart. However, nowhere does it take into account the existence of Atlantis or Lemuria.

Yes, but they did exist. Scientists could only make projections from what current maps show. They did not take into account the possibility that other parts of this supercontinent also existed. If they add the extra land in, they would see it fits too.

So you are saying there was a supercontinent?

Yes, continents have been splitting apart for eons and are now colliding against each other again.

Why do the depths of the Atlantic and Pacific Oceans vary so much?

Perhaps this answer might seem a little simple, but it has to do with plate movements. As your scientists speculated, the continents were more like a single landmass. The landmass needed to be split in order for the Earth experiment to work, with different looking people sowed, shall we say, on each landmass. The landmasses, which split and formed the Atlantic Ocean, left a shallower ocean depth than that in the Pacific. It was always that deep. The continent of Lemuria existed.

Nowadays, as the North American landmass moves to the west and the Asian landmass moves to the east, great pressure is brought along the Ring of Fire, as each landmass moves farther into the Pacific Ocean, slowly filling its depths.

So the difference between the depths of the Pacific and Atlantic is because of the preexisting landmass?

That's correct.

ALIEN ARTIFACTS

There was what appeared to be a computer chip found embedded in a rock 450 million years ago (see fig. 1.1). Was there a race of people that far back?

Yes, but they were not part of the Earth experiment, as you guessed. They had long since moved on, leaving behind a couple remnants of their existence, and the rock is one of them.

Was it 450 million years?

Yes, Earth was still quite young in its development and not really too suitable for habitation. Again, they moved on.

To whom did the iron cup (see fig. 1.2) belong to that was found inside a piece of coal reportedly dated 300 million years ago?

It belonged to an off-world group that eventually moved on, as Earth was quite volatile at that time. You can see this from the iron cup deposited into what became coal. It was not very safe, so they went on their way.

Figure 1.1: What appears to be an alien chip was discovered in Labinsk riverside of Hojo in the Kuban region in Russia, embedded in an unusual stone (http://www.ancient-code.com/researchers-find-a-250-million-year-old-micro-chip-in-russia/).

Figure 1.2: In 1912, Frank J. Kennard discovered the iron cup in a large block of coal while mining in Wilburton, Oklahoma (http://www.ancient-code.com/iron-cup-discovered-inside-a-piece-of-coal-that-is-300-million-years-old/).

There seems to have been more than one group that inhabited Earth at one time and moved on.

This is true. Earth appeared attractive to others numerous times in the past, but they either moved on of their own free will or were asked to leave later.

Did these groups appear before Earth was moved here?

That's true too. There were many groups of people, not always humanoid, who were out exploring, and this planet seemed to meet their needs for a time. But when Earth was moved here, there was still the occasional group that would discover it and plop down their tents, so to speak.

Then the very early groups were not body types being tested by ET scientists?

Not that early. The testing started several million years ago when the space-time continuum was put into place. After that, they were either warned away, or in the case of the people in Antarctica, were mostly wiped out when I shifted the poles.

EARLY ANIMAL SPECIES

What wild animals first inhabited Atlantis and then Lemuria? Were there dinosaurs on each continent or just Atlantis?

Dinosaurs only inhabited Atlantis. The stories are wrong about dinosaurs inhabiting Lemuria. That's not to say they did not have their share of other carnivores, but they only had to deal with large lizards, plus an array of other more typical wild animals. Some inhabited the continent that no longer exists. They had bears, just as the Atlanteans did, along with a form of tiger. Both continents had wolves, which were eventually domesticated after many centuries.

What about dragons?

Yes, more so on Lemuria than Atlantis, but there were a few. Both had their share of exotic birds that were also carnivores. There were mountain lions and a few others from the feline family as well. Tom, you had to put up with them in one of your previous lives.

How long ago was that?

Well over 1 million years, but they lasted long after you transitioned. They disappeared due to a shift in poles before the final destruction in Atlantis. But the memory of those creatures was burned into the brains of the humans left living at that time, so the stories were passed down over and over again from father to son, you could say.

EARLY LIFE IN ANTARCTICA

Did the pole shift of the first destruction cause the destruction of the society inhabiting Antarctica, or was there another pole shift thousands or millions of years before Atlantis?

No, they were gone long before Atlantis. Even during the days of Atlantis, there were no written records of their existence. As the ice melts in the warming trend, you will see remnants of this society.

What part of Antarctica was inhabited?

There were a number of towns and cities on this continent. Many will be discovered in the interior in the future. Bear in mind that the coastal towns that existed when the water level was lower are now underwater. Within the next five years, they will begin discovering these settlements from an ancient time. Archaeologists will come to this continent in droves to discover what lies beneath this ice sheet. Some of the settlements will be barely below the surface, as they were coastal settlements.

Archaeologists will eventually discover large remnants of cities. Keep in mind that this continent was not always locked in ice. It was verdant before the axis rolled, which was done to give this continent a rest, as it was heavily populated at one time many thousands of years ago. It was modern even by your standards so that each discovery made here will seem even more fantastic than the last.

Who were these people?

They existed a long time before the Atlanteans and Lemurians. You have no written record or even legends about these people.

How many people lived on the continent at its peak?

Several million people lived on the continent. It was well populated until the polar shift. Many died at that time; only a few escaped.

Did the Brunhes-Matuyama magnetic reversal event[5] occur 781,000 years ago, and was it a slow or fast action? Did this cause the destruction of the society on Antarctica?

Yes, your scientists are fairly accurate in reading the changes in the layers

---

5. Named for the scientists who identified the geologic event, the Brunhes–Matuyama reversal, which was when Earth's magnetic field last underwent reversal (http://en.wikipedia.org/wiki/Brunhes–Matuyama_reversal).

of earth. This caused the destruction of the society living on Antarctica at that time. A few were able to survive, but the event occurred quite suddenly, and people were not prepared to handle the severe climate change. They were warned it was coming but did little to prepare or leave.

Did any of their souls join in the Earth experiment?

No, this group wanted nothing to do with the Earth experiment after having their lives cut short by my reversal of poles.

Why did you reverse them?

It was to set up the continents in preparation for the Earth experiment. You could use the analogy of setting up a Monopoly game board. In this case, everyone taking part had different starting points.

ANCIENT HUMANS

Was there ever a continent, or island, or place called Hyperborea?[6] If so, when was it inhabited?

Yes, this place, like many more in legends, is based on fact. The Hyperboreans lived in the northern areas of Earth before I shifted the poles. It was sunny almost every day of the year, very fairly idyllic, but the people as a whole did not progress. So they were allowed to leave as I moved the alignments of the poles. They were not part of the Explorer Race; however, legends of their existence have lasted through modern times. They were put there by a race or society of ETs neither you nor most of humanity is familiar with.

Were the Greek gods and goddesses from Atlantis?

They were from some of your former planets. They seemed like gods and goddesses to others because of their great abilities.

Did they work in the ancient copper mines reported to exist in the Great Lakes area? If correct, was this before the Atlanteans?

Yes, quite some time before their arrival. So we are speaking about ancient mines.

That would predate the Adam and Eve model?

True, but there were other beings alive, including the Cro-Magnon and the Neanderthals.

Who worked them?

Your friendly Nibiruans (a multidimensional off-world council connected

---

6. In Greek mythology, Hyperbolea is considered a fabulous realm of eternal spring located in the far north beyond the land of winter (http://www.theoi.com/Phylos/Hyperborea.html).

to the planet Nibiru) worked them. It was during one of their swings through the solar system. They needed not only gold but copper as well. They had devices to easily find the metals. Then it was simply a matter of rounding up sufficient bodies and forcing them to work in the mines, who were already present in fairly large numbers when they arrived. These were simple tribal-type people. They easily subjugated them to work in their mines.

How long did this go on?

It went on for several hundred Earth years. This is why they are on probation with the Federation.

They fought among themselves too?

That's correct, using nuclear-type weapons. They wiped out thousands of humans.

Where did the Caucasian race originate?

They originated in Europe. They had fair skin, and quickly had to learn to adapt to the colder, wet climate.

Were all the different Adam and Eve models always placed as full adults?

Yes, as life was too harsh for them not to be. And to answer your next question, no structures of any type were built for them. They had to fend for themselves. You call this "hitting the ground running." Life was very short for these "subhumans" (we will call them this for your purposes) — just long enough for the scientists to see how the bodies adapted.

Was the world back then as we have imagined it? Was it like a jungle, or were some people put in jungles, others in desert conditions, others in harsh cold, and so on?

Exactly, as they had to test the bodies in all types of conditions to make sure they could adapt.

Who was the golden race of giants? Did they exist before the creation of the Adam man and woman models?

Yes, they did. These gentle people came from another star system, stayed awhile, and then moved on after it was explained to them that Earth was to be part of an experiment for the Creator.

How tall were they?

Well over seven feet, topping out at ten feet. They were enormous.

AMAZON WOMEN

Was there ever a strong matriarchal society on Earth?

Yes, there were several. The most well known were the Amazon women.

Most of them only lived from 100 to 200 years before they were conquered and their leaders disposed of.

How much of the legend of the Amazon women is true?

Legends are born of real events but embellished along the way. There was a group of women warriors many eons ago who were quite fierce.

Was this before Atlantis and Lemuria?

Yes, even before that, so we are speaking of truly ancient history here.

Where did they exist?

In a land now covered by ice many thousands of years ago.

Was it true they cut off one breast to hold a shield better?[7]

That was an embellishment.

Was their height taller than most men?

Again, a little embellishment there. But they were taller than most women, so they were quite imposing to the men of that day and time.

So they did not exist in the early days of Atlantis or Lemuria?

No, they were long gone by the time the Adam man and woman were seeded in those continents.

VIRAL WARFARE

Where did viruses originate? Were they used in ancient warfare? Did the Earth people develop them or people from off planet?

Viruses have always been on Earth. It is an old wives' tale that they were introduced from outside. That said, yes, they were used in ancient warfare, as it was known how to contain them. This form of warfare was eventually forbidden, but over many years, it slipped from those who had experience using them for any purpose.

At one time, some viruses were introduced by the Nibiruans. That was all part of their war. Other viruses were developed and some used in an ancient time before Atlantis and Lemuria. Some viruses were created but never used.

Please understand we are talking about hundreds of thousands of years of history here. Even though you have no records, it does not mean these people did not exist. Records are kept generally by conquerors, and when warring factions destroy themselves, there is no one left to write the history. Stories are passed down by survivors, if there are any, which become legends. Therefore, when you bring up a subject such as viruses, there are multiple answers

---

7. Learn more about this theory at http://en.wikipedia.org/wiki/Amazons.

according to which period you are referring to, and this question cannot be answered with a simple yes or no.

Were they used in Atlantis and Lemuria?

No, this was quite some time before. Keep in mind that viruses could be treated with the healing crystals in Atlantis, and the Lemurians had advanced to a point where viruses were controlled and, you might say, nonexistent. Earth groups and ETs used these long before that. It was part of the previous destructions. Millions died. Yes, that figure is correct, but of course there are no records of these folks except in ancient mythology.

THE BOSNIAN PYRAMIDS

Edgar Cayce referred to a continent as "Og."[8] Was that South America or another continent?

It was not South America but another continent.

Would it have been Australia?

There you have it. Og was Australia.

Are the mounds or hills in Bosnia near Sarajevo reported to be pyramids by Dr. Semir Osmanagich[9] actually pyramids, or are they natural formations?

No, certainly these are pyramids that the gentleman discovered. They have been overgrown by vegetation from thousands of years of neglect after being abandoned. Slowly Dr. Osmanagich will discover more about this complex of pyramids, as he has much assistance from the local area. These pyramids date much further back than currently believed, so there is much left to discover over the next twenty-five years or so. He will learn that the Bosnian Pyramids of both the Sun and Moon are taller than the largest Giza pyramid, and they are over 25,000 years in age, making them the oldest pyramids found to date.

Can you comment on the energy beam reported as coming out of the Bosnian Pyramid of the Sun?[10]

The more they explore these pyramids, the more mysteries they must solve. There is energy — a beam emitting from the large pyramid. There is definitely a connection there with its purpose to be determined by the scientists involved

---

8. A.R.E. website, Report of Readings 294-193, http://are-cayce.org/ecreadings/Default.aspx.

9. Learn more about the Bosnian Pyramids at www.BosnianPyramidoftheSun.com.

10. An international team of physicists has detected an energy beam coming directly through the top of the Pyramid of the Sun site in Teotihuacan, Mexico. The energy of the continuous beam measures 4.5 meters in radius and 28 KHZ in frequency. Read more: http://scienceray.com/astronomy/impossible-energy-beam-detected-at-bosnia-pyramids/#ixzz3fJsYUtXK.

in the research. They found healing chambers, as they speculated. There will be many more intriguing discoveries over the next few years. The healing chambers are contained in the miles and miles of tunnels connecting all the pyramids. Each summer, they have several hundred volunteers from all over the world continue the excavations.

What was the purpose of the Rock Wall (see fig. 1.3) in Rockwall, Texas, and how old is it?

Here you have an example of a society many thousands of years old, as this wall dates back much further than your modern history. Reports that the wall is seven stories high yet completely covered with dirt are correct. There now needs to be carbon dating and excavations to determine the use of the wall. What did it protect? Why are there miles of wall and not just one enclosure?

As you have pointed out, the Rock Wall has been ignored, but it is an archaeological treasure and would attract tourists should anyone begin serious excavation. The people of Rockwall should be encouraged to do what is being done in Bosnia: Ask for volunteers to help uncover the wall. Amazing artifacts will be discovered.

The Rock Wall in Rockwall, Texas, appears to have ancient markings. Please explain.

The wall is made up of materials that are that old, but the wall itself only dates back to the time when the waters had receded all the way to the north Texas area. The middle of the country had no water, as had been the case previously. So the people who lived in this area constructed the wall to protect themselves from the fluctuating ocean levels, as there were storms very similar to today's hurricanes, which originated off what is now the Gulf of Mexico.

The wall was built earlier than the Adam man and woman models, so delete them from consideration. The wall was built by one of the earlier models, not

Figure 1.3: Found by farmers digging for a well in 1852, the rock wall measures roughly 3.5 miles wide by 5.6 miles long. R. F. Canup excavated part of this wall. Digging 8 feet down, he eventually unearthed about 100 feet of the wall. This was enough to convince him that it was the masonry wall of an ancient city.

by an ET race. They only occupied this site for a couple of centuries, as the ocean continued to recede from this area. So they migrated farther south.

Is this wall over 1 million years old?

That's correct. A group of people you have absolutely no records about lived there and eventually moved on as the waters continued to recede. They wanted to be near the ocean and have the ability to sail and move about. So this town was occupied for just a couple of centuries.

One day in the future, more artifacts will be found. But keep in mind the city is pretty far below the surface of this town. It will take some fairly deep excavations to find remnants. Just look at the Bosnian Pyramids with three feet of dirt and shrubs and trees in only 26,000 years.

Were the beings who built the Rock Wall part of a different humanoid group we have yet to discover, and were they large in number?

There were several thousand in this group. They had a brain capacity somewhat similar to the Cro-Magnons. Heights were just a tad lower, and these beings were quite capable of defending themselves. They were hunters and gatherers who also planted some crops. They wanted to be near the ocean so that they could constantly fish.

How did they die out?

Like many humanoids around the world, they drowned when the waters came rushing in.

What about the copper miners in North America [Michigan]? How large were their numbers?

They were a fairly large group, larger than the Rock Wall people. They were three to four times the number, but they were not quite as intelligent as the Rock Wall men and women since they were a little earlier model.

Did the Nibiruans use the Adam man and woman to work the mines, or were they the earlier Cro-Magnon, Neanderthal, and other models?

All the above, as don't forget, the Nibiruans came every 3,600 years or so. The tales of the enslavements came from their later visits.

To summarize, over millions of years, different models of humans were created before the ET scientists finally settled on the Adam man and woman model 60,000 years ago. All the different races of the world were seeded to begin the Earth experiment using this model.

Chapter 2
THE RISE OF ATLANTIS
Theo, Gaia, and Antura

Theo, would you please compare the size of Atlantis to present-day Australia?

Atlantis was a little bit larger than Australia, about 10 percent.

Was the continent of Atlantis connected at any point to North America or Europe?

No. It was never connected to the coast of Europe, and it ran parallel to the coast of North America at its closest point, approximately 100 miles. The coast of Atlantis was irregularly shaped. North America was barely populated, and it was quite easy for the Atlanteans to have a settlement as far as Arkansas to mine crystals. Thanks to the crystal power, they were also able to travel long distances across both continents. The space between Atlantis and North America was a little wider until it almost joined near the tip of Florida.

ATLAN BEGINS

Was Atlantis known as Atlan in the early days?

That's correct. It only took on the more formal name, Atlantis, in later centuries.

Was there a clarion call across the universe to seed Atlantis?

No, not in the way the question was asked. Keep in mind that the spiritual leaders were informed that the Creator desired to commence the Earth experiment, so great work went into developing the perfect human to handle extreme temperatures among many, many attributes. Therefore, the clarion call, if you will, was to develop the Earth human. During this time, the planetary societies also learned the reasons for the experiment. Atlantis was just part of the equation. Lemuria was seeded along with other parts of the world. This was considered a grand design.

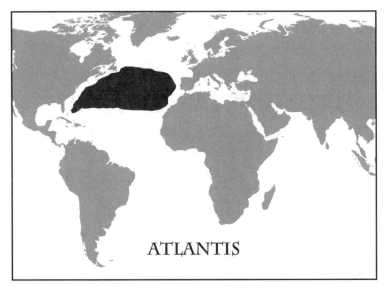

Figure 2.1: Atlantis was larger than Australia and sat between North America and Europe.

Who seeded the Adam man and woman on Atlantis, Lemuria, and elsewhere?

It was a combination of off-world cultures who look very much like you. They each contributed DNA to the experiment so that your bodies would be hardy enough to survive being veiled and so that you could make your own way with no prior knowledge allowed to assist you. Each life was (and always has been) seemingly your first and only one so that only we guardian angels, as you call us, were allowed to assist you in any way.

Were the Atlanteans aware of how the ET scientists had seeded their continent, and were they aware that other continents had been seeded too?

They were aware, as there was much communication between the ETs and Atlanteans. They were much more aware of their history than you are today.

How long did the Atlantean people exist, for 57,000 years, more or less?

They were in existence a couple of thousand years or more before the meeting to rid the world of dinosaurs. Use 57,000, and keep in mind the colonies that were seeded there were small. But you might say they proliferated, as each generation doubled in size to well over 1 million people before the First Destruction [see chapter 8].

Did the Law of One and Sons of Belial exist that long ago?

No, the two factions were created several thousand years later. Bear in mind that survival was the primary goal of the people at that time, as they still had to contend with beasts roaming the continent.

How far did Atlantis progress before the First Destruction?

They had achieved a great deal during those several thousand years. Naturally, there were cities and states, villages and farms — all the typical progress you would expect over several thousand years.

Did they discover the use of crystals during that time?

Oh yes. It fueled, you might say, their development as they were able to power all of what you might imagine, including heating their homes and factories. It really spurred their development before the giant earthquakes and tsunamis of the First Destruction.

Edgar Cayce wrote that some Atlanteans lived for hundreds of years?[1]

Yes, but that was more at the beginning of their occupation of this continent and the years lived slowly contracted as they became denser. This was really in the very early years of Atlantis, not when there was a large population. They lived extremely long lives at first in the early days, and their years gradually shortened, whereas your lives are gradually lengthening. In the early days, they would live several hundred — even a thousand — years, but that decreased over time. Still, they lived longer than you do today.

They had the healing centers, so they did not have all the diseases you have today, nor did they have the Big Pharma, as you call them, to shove harmful drugs down their throats, causing more harm than good.

Was Atlantis in a third focus or higher?

No, it was in a third focus, almost the same as you are now. Of course, they failed to move on, as wars and animosity to those who were different or had different religious beliefs destroyed them.

Did the Atlanteans have red skin?

They were a red-skinned people, similar to the American Indian.

Were all the people the same race or different races on that continent?

Good question. The red-skinned race was prominent, but there was some mixing of races as others came to Atlantis in their travels or were brought there by the Atlanteans, both with and against their will. Soldiers would return with wives and children just as this occurs in your times. The Mediterranean people were also dark-haired and dark complected. The Atlanteans never conquered Scandinavia, although there was contact and commerce with them. There was not a race of blond-haired Atlanteans.

---

1.   A.R.E. website, Text of Reading 1968-2 F 29, http://are-cayce.org/ecreadings/Default.aspx.

Was Atlantis finally inhabited by migration of some sort, let's say, from North America or even from the European side, or were people dropped there by ETs?

It was both. The people of Atlantis were red-skinned for a reason. They were connected to the red-skinned people who lived on the coast of North America, who subsequently perished, leaving no trace due to the tsunamis. Understand that these were simple farmers and hunter-gatherer types. It would take thousands of years of development before they became more sophisticated.

The American Indians are red skinned. Are they from Atlantis, or do they just have the same red skin as the Atlanteans?

As has been surmised and studied by your anthropologists, they came from Asia across the then-existing bridge and flowed down through North America. They were not part of the Atlantean survivors. Bear in mind that the Atlanteans commingled and basically disappeared with the people in the Yucatán and other parts of North America when Atlantis disappeared. This was thousands of years ago, and much combining was done during the years that followed.

Are they descendants of the Atlanteans, who over thousands of years reverted to primitive ways of living?

No, they were created by your ET ancestors, just as the Atlanteans were. They came across the bridge, but there were others established across the continent, as the land was fertile and would support a population. Yes, there were those Atlanteans who fled to the Americas but more to the south. The land along the coast was subject to tsunamis.

THE BEINGS OF ATLANTIS

Were Goliath and giants connected to Atlantis regarding their stories?

No, at least not all of them. The Goliath giant was quite an abnormality during its time [thousands of years later]. He was well over 6' in height when most of the people at that time were only around the 5' mark due to their diets. So he obviously seemed to be a giant, and his masters fed him well. As far as giants in general, there were some on the continent of Atlantis in the early days of Atlantis, but they mostly died out during the first period of Atlantis.

Were Cro-Magnons living on the Atlantean continent?

Yes, some were, but very few, and they lived in the early days of inhabitation, not later.

What about Neanderthals?

No. They were created elsewhere.

Did the Atlanteans encounter the Neanderthals as they explored, since they seemed to be alive at the same time?

Yes and no. They were alive at the same time, but the Atlanteans left them alone in their explorations, as they were a more primitive native people and quite rough around the edges. They would just as soon try to murder and eat the Atlanteans, so they were left to their own devices.

Was there any interbreeding with the Homo sapiens?

Not too much. They were regarded as a food source.

Did Atlantis have mountains, and if so, were they high enough for snow?

Yes, there were mountains and streams just as there are on most continents. The mountains were high enough in some places to have snow. That led to the normal recreations associated with that type of environment. You must understand that the continent of Atlantis was much larger than, say, the islands of Japan, even though when the Second Destruction came about, large islands were the result as the continent started breaking up. Millions of lives were lost when the continent broke up into islands.

As the continent of Atlantis sat on top of the Atlantic Ridge, did they use steam for warmth and for other purposes, such as heating their caves?

Yes, there were hot springs in certain parts of the continent, but the only use of the springs and steam vents was to heat homes and baths. Therefore, it all depended on the location.

Who was the feathered serpent?

A mystical being in their folklore based on spaceships the people had seen.

Did the Atlanteans ever have a shift as we did in 2012?

No, they actually sank deeper into the third dimension, but that was the plan. Remember, they started out almost nonphysical, and then they had lives during which they adjusted to the third focus.

TOM'S LIVES IN ATLANTIS

Theo, in past communications you have told me that I had lived 100 to 200 lives on the continent of Atlantis. Can you be more specific with the number, and over what time span were these lives?

Ah, an interesting time of growth for you. Let's see if you can receive this number — 187 is pretty close. The time span was over 50,000 years, so they were not bunched up, as you say "one after another."

Did I have a life on Atlantis earlier than, say, 60,000 BC?

Yes, a little earlier, not much.

Were the majority of my lives during the past 50,000 years of its existence?

Yes. The earlier lives were for you to get the feel of the land and its potential.

This continent, as you can imagine, grew from a fertile, unused land to one with tribes and such, and then to one that was scientifically on par with your lives today. That's why they gained such advances in science and the arts and all phases of life, as they had many, many generations to progress, just as people have progressed greatly in the past 2,000 years in your modern age. They used crystals to power everything that you have still not discovered. On a subconscious level, you have tried to stay away from the use of large crystals, as subliminally you remember what a catastrophe that use brought on.

What appearance did I have in that early life on Atlantis? Was I short, stocky, hairy, or what?

You were short in stature, just as the others, as they used a machine to construct the bodies. You had a lot of body hair, and your ET creators felt this was needed to keep you warm. Over time, this was modified and people started to project different appearances.

Did the body types of the Atlanteans change in each epoch? If so, what was their appearance?

They remained fairly consistent in their appearance over those thousands of years and epochs, as you call them. They were a red-skinned people of average to shorter height, and they had the same brain capacity as you do today. There were slim Atlanteans and those who were very fit, as they had their games. It was understood that a body needed exercise, so many people walked, although as they progressed, it is like today — less walking and more riding. Because there were wars between the two sides, the soldiers were quite fit too. There was little to no obesity unless there was something wrong with their health. If so, people went to the healing centers, which used crystal lights, and they were much more successful at treating people than today's drugs.

What was the average height of the Atlantean men and women?

They were a little shorter than today. The men were about 5'6" to 5'8" on average, and the women were more in the range of 4'11" to 5'2".

• • •

THE AGE OF DINOSAURS ON ATLANTIS

Gaia, what dinosaurs were around when ensouled humans and Homo sapiens started to appear?

There were quite a few of these beasts present on Earth when the first ensouled humanoids appeared. There was just about every variety known. They were not killed off by any outside force, meaning a meteorite — as has been suggested by scientists. So not only were they around during the time of the first ensoulments, but they were also around when modern humans were well established.

They had to contend with many of these species. Some were harmless plant eaters, as has been deduced by your scientists, and some were meat eaters and fierce competitors for food who preyed on the humans themselves. They were wiped out by events that took place, but I will let them work on that mystery for a while longer. They would feel cheated if I just gave the answer. That's part of your learning process, which will serve you well when you go out to the stars.

Was the Atlantean continent free of dinosaurs?

They were so well advanced that the beasts had no room to forage and died off there long before the end of Atlantis. But on other continents with much fewer people, they ranged and hunted at will. You might compare it to the tigers, which roamed India, and the villagers were part of the prey. Therefore, they had to be sharp-minded to survive. It was the same dealing with the large, voracious dinosaurs.

When did dinosaurs roam the continent of Atlantis?

They roamed Atlantis well before the First Destruction. When you have a continent inhabited for over 50,000 years, you will have this problem. So this happened fairly early in their timeline and was resolved after the Atlanteans advanced to crystal power.

Did I ever run across dinosaurs during any of my lives on Atlantis?

You did in the early days of your first lives on the continent; they still existed. You even died a couple times from your run-ins with these creatures, so you had a very healthy respect for them in the lives in which you existed at the same time. Of course, these early lives there served as your basic boot camp, to use a military saying. You were one of the first souls to have lives there, so it was a pretty rugged, basic existence.

Did people hunt them?

Yes, you and others were very quick to catch on to how to trap them and kill them. Even then, people were lost. The plant eaters were no match for you, but the carnivores, as has been depicted in your movies, were a handful. Naturally there were people who had experienced this firsthand in their past lives and drew subconsciously on their experiences to write books and movies.

How were dinosaurs still roaming the continent of Atlantis 60,000 years ago, or am I somehow off on my times as they supposedly died out hundreds of thousands of years ago?

No, you are not off, as these large fellows disappeared from many regions of the world but not all. Atlantis was not the only place they continued to roam. Dinosaurs were decimated several times in history, but they would come back and flourish again, depending on the area and how dense the foliage was for not only eating but also hiding from the carnivores. Your archaeologists have yet to stumble on these leftover remnants of their existence, but they will in time.

So they existed at the time Atlantis was populated with humans, and the humans, including you, had to deal with them — not always successfully. That's another Earth experience, the one on the bucket list that says you must deal with wild animals.

Wasn't Atlantis, at least part of it, in a colder climate, sitting up on a latitude equal to that of Newfoundland today?

Yes. They had a wide range of temperatures, as the continent extended all the way down to what is now the Bahamas today.

Wouldn't the dinosaurs have kept to the warmer climate?

No, not all, as they ranged up and down — at least some of the species. Then you had other large animals, so they had their hands full for a long time.

What types of dinosaurs were there during that first life?

Many you're familiar with, and there are still species of dinosaurs your archaeologists have not yet discovered. Just look at the sixty-five-ton behemoth they recently unearthed. There are plenty more where that one came from.

You said it was not just an asteroid that killed the dinosaurs. Was there a comet that also led to their demise, or what series of events doomed them?

No, I realize there is speculation regarding a comet in the distant past, and certainly a couple have come closer to Earth than the ones seen in your modern history, but there was not one so close as to cause the demise of dinosaurs or other living beings.

With that said, there are some specific events that led to their demise:

1. Humanity was involved, as there were a couple of societies that had the power to kill the dinosaurs, and contrary to public opinion, there was a fairly large population of people during those times not only on Atlantis but in other societies as well. Some banded together to kill these creatures, as there were people frequently killed by the voracious flesh eaters.

2. An asteroid[2] caused the climate to change for a time.

3. There was a pole shift that caused many of these creatures to die. I have natural cycles, and the shift in poles wiped out a number of dinosaurs.

4. There was a great change in the weather in which it became intolerable

---

2. As posited by the Alvarezes, the mass extinction of the dinosaurs was caused by an asteroid impact on the Yucatán Peninsula (http://en.wikipedia.org/wiki/Alvarez_hypothesis).

for the creatures to continue to exist in their natural habitats. They were unable to escape when there was no food for them.

So, you see, there were a series of events — not just one as has been speculated by your scientists. The Pleiadians will bring up this bit of history for you when they arrive. The history lesson will include actual videos of the wide variety of dinosaurs living on Earth.

• • •

LEMURIA

Theo, what shape would you say Lemuria was?

Somewhat like a small potato, but that does not accurately describe the shape. The shape is difficult to describe.

How close was Lemuria to present-day Japan?

Quite close, as of course you've seen photos of the underwater ruins off the coast of Japan.

Was Japan part of Lemuria?

Yes, part of it was but not all.

Was its eastern edge to the west of what is now the Hawaiian Islands?

Yes, but not by much.

• • •

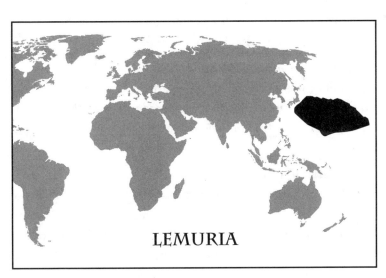

Figure 2.2: Lemuria, shaped like a potato, was quite close to what is now Japan.

Gaia, was the shape of Lemuria more like Australia, or did it have a decreasing tail as did Atlantis?

It had a decreasing tail, but just a little different from that of Atlantis. It did not extend down as far as the landmass of Atlantis did before the Second Destruction. It was approximately 10 to 12 percent larger than Australia is today. The islands were connected to the countries they were closest to. At that time the islands were mostly inhabited by the people indigenous to the land. They were left pretty much on their own.

Was it more in the center of the continent and not to one side?

Yes, more centered. It was much shorter than the tails of any of the other continents, including the tail of Atlantis.

Was Lemuria one big continent? Was it connected at one time to the northern or southern part of Japan, and is there any portion of Japan still above the ocean that was connected?

Yes, but as with all continents, it had a few islands close by. These islands were not part of the continent and are not generally included in a discussion of Lemuria. It was connected in more than one place, but those points went underwater when the continent of Atlantis sank. Still toward the southern end of Japan, those ruins of a costal fortification of Lemuria are underwater. This was so early in their development that the Lemurians had plenty of land and had no desire to migrate there. They considered the people living in Japan primitive at that time. The Lemurians were a kind and gentle people for thousands of years.

But the Japanese islands were quite large. I'm surprised that more people from Lemuria did not inhabit the area.

Yes, but that's the way it was. It was not until the end that people escaped to Japan and to what is now China. Japan was looked at as backward.

Hawaii is or is not a remnant of Lemuria?

No, it is not. It was a large island, not far from the shores of Lemuria, that shrank in size to multiple islands when the seas rose over 150 feet as Lemuria sank. It was visited many times by the Lemurians, a quiet haven away from the strife.

What about Tahiti? Was it part of Lemuria?

No, it was not. It was too far to the south. Remember that there was much more land before the ocean rose. The people inhabiting it were mostly obliterated when the tsunamis rolled through. They were much too close to the Lemurian continent and, like Hawaii, bore the brunt of the tidal waves.

So the tail of the continent did not extend down that far?

No, it did not.

Where did the Tahitians come from?

They were the survivors of the tsunamis, just not many who inhabited the islands. Only those who lived or were higher up when Lemuria sank survived.

Did both Atlantis and Lemuria have four seasons?

Atlantis did farther north. As you recall, you were told that the tail of the continent extended down to what is now the Bahamas. That section of the continent, before the Second Destruction, experienced almost no winter, just rain and cooler temperatures. But to the north, they had all four seasons.

Lemuria was slightly different. Its tail experienced the flow of what would have been hurricanes, but they were knocked down to just heavy rain by Lemurian technology. The northern section experienced all four seasons.

• • •

THE ATLANTEAN MOON

Antura, did Earth have two moons back in the days of Atlantis, or was this before Atlantis was populated and really existed as a society?

Yes, there were two moons in the days of Atlantis, and one of them exploded, which was caused by a scientific experiment gone awry. Needless to say, that soul took on quite a bit of karma that is taking thousands of years to balance.

What was the period when it was destroyed? Was it 1,000 or more years before the Second Destruction?

It was more — about 2,000 years before the Second Destruction.

So 30,000 years ago, more or less?

It was about 31,000 years ago.

Was it the Law of One scientists or the Sons of Belial scientists who destroyed it, or were both working together at that time?

No, it was the Sons of Belial who made the mistake and blew up the satellite. It caused great strife between the two, as you can imagine. People all over the continent were heartbroken at the loss of the satellite and also how it affected all the power grids at that time. They had to establish many more relays, which were called "posers," to fill in the gaps of energy that were lost.

Then the second moon was a satellite, not an actual planetary-type body?

Yes, it was a satellite.

Therefore, it acted as some sort of power relay?

The satellite was put up by the Atlanteans to act as a power grid or source. It reflected energy to ground stations, which had very sophisticated ways of converting the energy to power.

Why wouldn't we still see fragments of this satellite today?

Most fragments were slowly drawn into Earth's orbit and burned up, and others went far out into space.

Did the Atlanteans or ETs design it?

It was designed with a lot of help from the ETs.

Did the Arcturians assist in its construction, and if so, why?

Yes, they assisted the Atlanteans, as the benefits were deemed benevolent at that time. The Arcturians had no idea how the Atlanteans and especially the Aryans would mess things up. They were mortified.

How was it launched — by the ETs or some vehicle or giant crystals?

It had to be carried aloft using what you would call a strong tractor beam from a mothership.

Was it five miles in diameter?

Almost exactly five miles in diameter, and it reflected light quite well, which was why it was easy to see in the night sky. And it was in a low orbit too, which made it look larger than it actually was.

Did I have a life during the time the moon crashed?

Yes, of course you did. You would not have wanted to miss that time.

Was I living a life as a Law of One person or a Son of Belial?

It was the latter. You had a balancing life at that time and were one of the bad guys. You were an influence then, but you did not cause the satellite to crash. You helped move the people along who directly caused it.

Antura, how close was the Atlantean moon's orbit to Earth?

It was not as close as, say, our ship is that is taking constant measurements, [fifty miles above Earth]. But it was much, much closer to Earth than, say, your Moon, which is why a five-mile wide structure would appear quite bright in the evening sky at that time. The idea of its orbit being around the same height as your international space station would be about right within a few miles. As the space station is visible to the naked eye and is only a few hundred feet long, you can imagine how a large structure with a reflective surface would appear. Therefore, it was high enough in the sky to not be dragged down by Earth's gravity, but not too far, so it appeared quite large to the naked eye.

Was it metal, crystal, or ET elements?

No, the elements were all Earth metals, but it had a crystalline surface, which as noted made the second moon quite visible and bright.

Would the Atlantean artificial satellite moon have appeared brighter than Earth's Moon?

It appeared slightly less bright than Earth's Moon. As you know, when Earth's Moon appears over the horizon at night, it can seem immense, whereas the Atlantean satellite moon remained in the sky in one position day and night. It was necessary to remain perfectly stationary so that all the energy could be focused and reflected from one spot. There was no need for it to encircle Earth as your Moon does.

Did the pyramids feed off it, did the satellite feed off the pyramids, or was there no connection between the pyramids and the satellite moon?

There was a natural connection, but it served more as a transponder of energy from the crystals back to the surface to run many machines, certainly flying machines.

• • •

POSEIDIA

Theo, was the island of Poseidia located at the same latitude as Newfoundland, or was it located near the Bahamas?

No, it was near the north. The tail of Atlantis slowly narrowed down toward what is now known as the Bahamas. Therefore, the largest portion left of Atlantis after the Second Destruction [more in chapter 8] was in the north, Poseidia. It also had the largest population.

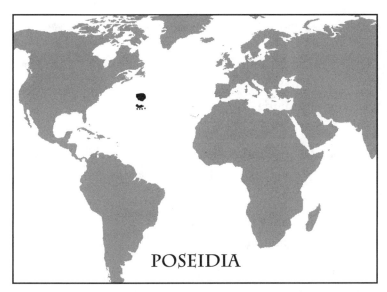

Figure 2.3: Poseidia, Aryan, and the four smaller islands below them were the portion of Atlantis that was left after the Second Destruction.

Was the shape of Poseidia long and slender like Cuba, or was it round?

It was round in shape.

Was the cluster of islands, including the Atlantean island Aryan, on the same latitude of, say, where New York is today?

It was located a little below that, more on the level of Washington DC and a little farther to the south.

I had envisioned them being a little more to the north.

That was their approximate location for your purposes. Keep in mind that the Atlantean continent originally extended all the way down to the Bahamas. After the Second Destruction, only the three islands remained near Poseidia and the other five islands were closer to the middle, you might say.

Was the population of Poseidia (the size of Cuba) under 15 million or over?

The population was slightly over 15 million at its peak.

Why were there not any other islands under the control of the Law of One?

Because they were driven from their homes to find refuge on Poseidia over a number of years. At one time, they coexisted, but just as you see in the Middle East today, one religion pushes the other out. This is a problem you will solve one day. It is a carryover from the Atlantean days that was not solved then, so you must now solve it, and you will. This is similar to soul contracts in which when you do not solve a challenge in one life, it will keep coming back until you do.

Were the ruins found in the marshlands of Spain the same size or a miniature version?

As you guessed, it was much smaller. There were fewer people who lived there, so the appearance would have been similar but not the same size, more on a scale of one-quarter the size of the original. Naturally, that one was flooded with the sinking of Lemuria.

Were the islands below Poseidia longer in shape or round in appearance?

Those islands were a mixture. Remember that these islands were what was left of the continent, and they would have a more rugged appearance than, say, a Caribbean island today.

Was Aryan more or less than 30,000 square miles?

Less than 32,000 square miles.

Is there an island today it would compare to?

Yes, check the Caribbean islands. Hispaniola [home of the Dominican Republic and Haiti] in the Caribbean is the closest in size at 29,530 square miles.

What are your comments about mapmakers or those who study maps offering the opinion that the former continents could have fit together with nothing in the middle?

Atlantis and Lemuria existed, and both took up space. The mapmakers basically tried to put together a puzzle without two of the pieces.

Please name the islands left over in the present that were originally part of Atlantis?

The Bahama Islands were remnants of the Atlantean continent. They remained afloat, and there are traces of the civilization buried beneath the sands of the islands. The tsunamis created by the sinking wiped out much of what existed there before. The Florida Keys were in existence at that time but not really attached.

Then Key West, Florida, was not originally part of the Atlantean continent?

Parts of it were, the very edges of the continent.

I thought the islands were located in the west.

No, if you look at a map, they string out from the east. They were not so much part of the continent as located nearby, so the Atlanteans inhabited them. Dig deep enough on those islands, and you'll find remnants.

What about Bermuda and the Canary Islands?

Certainly, they were remnants.

Were the islands off the New Hampshire and Maine coasts also remnants?

Definitely, as all of these were remnants even before the final sinking of the islands left from the Second Disaster, when much of the continent broke apart. Naturally, when it happened, they were almost wiped clean by the resulting tsunamis, so it took a few thousand years for them to come back. But they hold the old Atlantean energy signature, which people visiting those islands notice to be different. There are ruins deep beneath the surface that will be found someday.

So Poseidia was the largest island, not Aryan, and it had the largest population?

That is absolutely correct.

Did Poseidia have, or was it large enough to have, mountains, lakes, and streams?

Yes, the island was home to several million people, so there were your typical farms, and it had mountains, lakes, and streams. The people of this island could have resided there for thousands of years, but their leaders were just as corrupt as those who ruled the smaller islands that made up or were controlled by the Sons of Belial. Those leaders caused the Third — and final — Destruction.

THE GOLDEN GATE CITY

Was there an actual City of the Golden Gates in Poseidia?

Yes, it was a beautiful city at one time, and it had a large port entrance.

I assume it was initially formed after the Second Destruction?

You're correct there. As you remember, the seas rose when the major part of the continent sank, so all the ports in the world were wiped out by the rising water and the tsunamis, and new ports were formed.

Plato described Atlantis as a city of concentric circles with moats and canals. Was he describing the City of the Golden Gates or all of Atlantis?

He was limited in his comprehension and understandably so. The City of the Golden Gates was just part of Poseidia. This lasted for several thousand years before the Final Destruction.

Was the City of the golden gates the capital or just a port city?

It was the major city for the island. It would be like a combination of New York and Washington, DC. It was important as a commercial center and also a seat of power.

Were there actual golden gates, or why was the city named that?

Yes, there were magnificent golden statues and such that were quite impressive to anyone entering the harbor. It was a showcase.

How tall were the Golden Gate City's statues at the entrance to the rings?

They were enormous for that period, about 45 feet high. They were quite imposing.

Were the statues men or some mythical animal?

Good question. They stood vertically, not on four legs, more warrior-like in appearance.

Were they gold colored?

Yes, they were. They were not made of gold, but gold plated, so they shone with lights on them at night. Very impressive!

Did Poseidia's Golden Gate City face the south?

Yes, it did. The depictions of the city were fairly accurate as to the shape. The size is another matter, as some depictions are closer than others.

How large was the portion of the city that was divided into concentric rings? Was it over, let's say, five square miles?

Easily. It was quite large. This was a massive project when it was built.

•   •   •

THE RINGS AROUND THE GOLDEN GATE CITY

Gaia, please confirm how large the Golden Gate City was, as my understanding of square miles might leave something to be desired. Was it as large as, say, Manhattan, or smaller?

Just a little larger, not by much. There were concentric rings [as shown in figure 2.4]. So the length was shorter and wider, shall we say.

Were there offices and government buildings located on the concentric rings, or did people live there too?

There was apartment-type housing. Several thousand people lived and worked on the concentric rings.

Across from the outer ring, were there buildings and housing on the other side?

Yes, but as you can imagine, that housing was more for the workers, and they would have to take ferries to work each day, sometimes three if they worked in the center rings. It was quite a commute in those days. But just as today in a place such as Manhattan, it was much more expensive to live there. So there were a lot of commuters on trains. There were also a number of farms on the main part across from the islands. Just as today, it was not as hectic as being in the city.

Am I correct in thinking that the buildings were much shorter than today's buildings?

Yes, there were fewer people, so most of the buildings were no higher than eight to ten stories.

Was the city constructed — the waterways — using crystal power?

Exactly. The crystal rays allowed construction to proceed at a rapid rate. They had an earthen dam across the sea entrance as they excavated the canals.

Was the innermost ring elevated on a hill, or was it flat?

It was a little elevated, but then the tallest buildings were also on the inner ring, so this ring seemed elevated above the others.

Were there any bridges between the rings?

No, each was separate. They had ferries to shuttle people to and from each island.

Were the rings too far apart, or were bridges just not developed yet?

No, it was more a choice of design. They felt bridges were not aesthetically beautiful, shall we say. And you could say this gave them some protection from anyone trying to conquer or invade. They did not count on the rings being destroyed by crystal ray guns. No one could imagine anyone being so heartless.

Were the distances between the rings from 607 feet to 1,820 feet?

You are quite close on your figures. Naturally, the largest distance was between the outermost ring and the rest of the island. Between the second and

Figure 2.4: Depiction of the lost continent of Atlantis.

third rings, the distance was halfway between your numbers, about 1,214 feet, and was close to the actual distance between the first and third rings.

Was the population of the Golden Gate City over 1 million?

Yes, about 3 million, which was quite large in those days.

So the population was not over 3 million?

No, that was the maximum size the concentric rings could handle, which was fairly densely populated, and the wealthy had individual residences on the rings slightly similar to the luxury residences along the waterways of Miami, just not as opulent.

AYRAN

Gaia, were any of the islands of Atlantis close enough to each other to have bridges connecting them?

No, several of the islands were controlled by the Sons of Belial, but they were not so close as to have bridges spanning them. They used what would be the equivalent of ferries to move people back and forth, and the military used aircraft.

So were Aryan and the other four islands approximately 350 to 400 miles to the south of Poseidia?

You're correct. It was slightly less than 400 miles to the south. That places the five islands on about the same latitude as Washington, DC.

Was Aryan the northernmost island in the group of five?

Yes, it was. Your vision of the island and the others in the cluster is pretty close to how they appeared.

How many people lived in the largest city of Aryan, and was it a port too?

Yes, it was a port city with a population of a little over 2 million people.

I visualized Aryan with a semi-circle of the other four islands below it. I take it that it was not as dramatic in appearance as the Golden Gate City?

It had an elaborate city center, but they did not dig canals around it, as the Law of One people did for their city. It was a little more garish. It had the appearance of many port cities in the world today but with smaller buildings.

What did the Sons of Belial look like?

They were all red skinned. The Aryan tribesmen were located in northern Europe.

But how did both have the same name?

They were named by the Atlantean explorers who encountered them. They noted their hardiness and ability to fight.

What was the population of the largest island for the Sons of Belial — Aryan, I understand?

Yes, it was several million but certainly less than Poseidia.

Was it more than 5 million?

Yes, they were more densely populated, so their numbers rose to 9 million.

What was the size of this island? Was it two-thirds the size of Poseidia?

It was slightly less but not by much.

Would it have been the size of, say, Hispaniola?

Poseidia's approximate size was 43,000 to 44,000 square miles. It is very close to two-thirds the size of Poseidia.

What about the populations of the smaller islands?

They totaled another 5 million between them.

THE GREAT FLOOD

Was there a time on Earth when humans experienced the forty days and forty nights of rain?

Yes, there was a time in your history — much further back than the biblical references indicate — when the weather patterns were disrupted and there were deluges of rain and snow. These stories were passed down through hundreds and then thousands of years and adopted, you could say, by each society and their religions.

So the story of Noah and his Ark did not take place in the past few thousand years?

It happened years before and for a different reason. Keep in mind the great tsunamis caused by the sinking of Atlantis. Millions of people lost their lives. Only those who, fortunately, lived away from the coast — and few did — were able to survive. Noah was guided to build a boat, which saved him and his family plus a number of animals.

Was Noah caught up in the Second Destruction or the Third Destruction?

It was the Third Destruction. The weather became quite unstable, and the tsunamis caused great destruction to the Mediterranean area where Noah lived with his family.

Was it the eastern part of the Mediterranean?

Yes, that's where he and his family lived.

Did he and his family live in what is now Turkey?

We would prefer allowing that to remain a little mystery, as there are a number of religions with their own beliefs who have their own story of Noah. A little mystery should remain.

To clarify, did the story of Noah originate with the Atlantean Third Destruction or Lemuria's sinking 5,000 years later?

This might be a little confusing, but the story of Noah actually originated during, or shortly after, the Third Destruction. When the islands sank, it caused the weather patterns to become unstable for a time, and there were those forty days and nights of rain, plus the rise in the ocean level of forty feet. The Atlanteans' use of ray guns during their fighting caused the atmosphere to become unstable, and then came the wall of water rising over forty feet, covering coastal lands where millions of people lived at that time.

Noah was advised of this before it came and built the boat for his family and livestock and other animals. So the story of Noah is quite ancient — much more so than people realize — which is why even you had trouble understanding when it occurred.

That puts the story of Noah at around 12,500 years ago. To use a saying in the film business, "That story has legs!" Was Noah's boat already floating when the rapid forty-foot rise in the ocean level occurred, or did it float with the arrival of the forty-foot increase?

Noah's boat was built in a low-lying area that flooded from the torrential rains and the rise in sea level as each island sank. The boat began to float when the islands sank and raised the ocean level over the course of just a few days. The water level did not rise all at once, but as each island was destroyed, it caused the ocean level to rise a few feet more.

When the Third Destruction occurred, did the water pouring through what is now the Straits of Gibraltar force the water to rise higher initially and then settle back to forty feet?

No, I understand how it might seem to do that with the tsunamis, but there was only the exceptional rise as the waves of water flooded into the Mediterranean basin while the islands sank. Beyond that, there was no appreciable rise of, let's say, twenty or thirty feet. It was strictly the tsunamis that came crashing through that accompanied the rise in sea level.

The Hindu religion has a story about a man, a boat, and animals quite similar to the story of Noah but by a different name. Was there a second person like Noah, or was this the same person? Therefore, should I expand the area in which he lived?

No need to widen the area. The story traveled to India via trade routes as people recounted the story of Noah around their campfires. India, don't forget, had its share of coastal flooding as several million people drowned when the continent of Atlantis sank. The waters rose again another forty feet when the islands sank. Therefore, the story of a man surviving with his family and even with animals would have been one of those stories that would travel far and wide. So, yes, it was the story of Noah, with his name lost or changed for Indian tastes. There was not another person who did the same thing.

How many members of his family sailed with him?

He sailed with his two sons and daughters and their families, along with his wife.

Didn't Noah have a son who was not married until after the Ark landed?

Yes, he had one son who was not married when they floated away. He was the youngest and still had not chosen a wife. It would be a while before he found a girl who survived the floods.

What animals did he take, and were any different from today?

Here the story was embellished over the centuries. He took a number of animals with him but they were domesticated animals, not the wild ones attributed to him, Don't forget that the Noah story says the entire Earth was inundated, so all the animals had to be added in to make the story believable. Therefore, he had herds of animals both he and his extended family owned in the boat with them. There were also bird estuaries on board.

I assume they brought extensive food provisions on board for their family and for all the animals?

That's true. He was advised in his dreams and communications that they would need to survive some time on board the boat.

Did he have any weapons on board the boat?

They were mostly just farm tools. He was a simple farmer who was given divine inspiration and messages to build the boat. The stories of Noah and his family being ridiculed are fairly accurate. His neighbors called him the equivalent of "Crazy Noah." They all perished in the tsunamis.

When the floods came to the low-lying area, you said his boat was lifted up, but wasn't it already afloat from the rapid rise in sea level?

That's correct. It was difficult for the people who passed down this story to understand there was this rise in sea level accompanied by a change in atmospheric conditions forming huge storms — hurricanes, if you can visualize — that swept across the Mediterranean with a deluge that carried Noah and his boat along.

How large was the area flooded by the rains of forty days and forty nights? Did the waters recede, or did they remain for some time?

The area flooded was fairly wide, as the rains were preceded by a rise in the sea levels over a period of days while each island sank into the ocean. Thus, you first had the tsunamis and rise in the sea levels and then the rains came. We are speaking about the Mediterranean now and not some other place, as the storms flowed from west to east.

The torrential rains brought as much as one foot to two feet more, and the swollen rivers and streams overflowed and flooded the farmlands and such so that they were under an extra ten to twenty feet of water. Anyone in these areas — as I said, most lived by some water source — was swept away in the floods.

Noah's Ark was able to withstand the winds and rain for several weeks. Afterward, it took weeks for the waters to recede. The waters on the coast stayed at that higher level. So to summarize, the flooding lasted for several weeks after the rains had ceased.

The story goes that his Ark eventually settled on Mount Ararat in Turkey. Is that correct?

That's true. But all traces of the boat have disappeared.

Did the Ark land on top or lower?

It landed on a lower elevation of Mount Ararat. Landing on top was an exaggeration of the people who passed along the story.

Were there any people left alive in that area?

Yes, there were survivors in that region, as certainly there had been people who survived the storms who lived away from the coasts that were able to take shelter. Only those with sufficient supplies were able to withstand the storms that were constant until the atmospheric conditions improved. That's where the story somewhat breaks down, as they could not understand how the families proliferated and grew. It simply was because many people who lived away from the coast on farms and in villages at higher elevations were able to survive, but all those along the coasts perished.

So after landing the boat, they set out to reestablish themselves with farms again?

Yes, the population was quite sparse, so there was plenty of land with streams and such for their crops.

Chapter 3
DAILY LIFE ON ATLANTIS AND LEMURIA
Theo

Theo, did the people of Atlantis, Lemuria, and Oz have first, middle, and last names like we do in the West?

No, names were quite different in that time.

Could they be compared to anything today?

Yes, but there was a wide variety of names depending on which continent you were on.

Let's take Atlantis first.

Yes, they used lengthy names, with the family name first and then the given names.

Lemuria?

Slightly the same, but with variations, as their names would be somewhat compared to, let's say, Japanese and Chinese names.

Oz?

The name structure they use today dates back to their beginning, and there was a wide variety of names, as the continent was so large. This would apply to Lemuria too, as there were different countries on the same continent that differed greatly from each other.

THE ROLE OF WOMEN

Were men and women considered equals?

No, not even then, as women were subjugated depending on the belief system they chose. You have come a long way in the equality of women in this time, further than the Atlanteans ever achieved.

There were women in temples who performed many jobs, but the power remained with the men, who did a terrible job — as you can imagine. They eventually caused the complete destruction of what was left of their continent.

Did most women buy their food for their families at stores and shops, or was it more prevalent to use the open-air markets?

This varied from society to society and time to time. But as a general rule, women went to the open-air markets, which contained not only fresh fruits and vegetables but also all types of meat and fish. They enjoyed getting out and shopping and meeting their friends at these markets. It was a social time. In the cities, there were more shops, such as butcher shops, and stores that specialized in specific foods.

Did the Atlantean and Lemurian women crochet, knit, and sew?

Oh yes, these skills are quite ancient, dating back to the days when the Adam models were first introduced. These people had memories of where they came from. They had to wear certain types of garments in the colder weather, so they were instructed on putting skins together. Then, over thousands of years as they learned about yarn and so on, they learned how to join them together. They had great artisans in these techniques, just as you have today.

You could say there is nothing new under the sun, as once these skills were learned, they were retained on a soul level and used in more modern times or were passed down through generations. It was just not recorded because men did not think such things were important enough to write about; it was women's work.

Did most people purchase their own clothes, or did they make them?

It all depended on economic status. The women were quite proficient in making clothes for their families. If they could afford it (and this was a certain status symbol), they bought the clothes at stores and shops instead of purchasing the material to make them.

Did women use laundromats, have washers and dryers, or wash by hand?

They used all of the above. It all depended on their economic status. Their washers and dryers were not as developed as today's. You might compare them to the earlier days in your time when the washers used rollers and people hung their clothes out to dry. They had free energy, but they were less concerned in the male-dominated society of trying to make things easier on women.

The Atlantean society was especially chauvinistic while the Lemurian countries were a little less so for several thousand years, until they deteriorated as they approached those end years of wars. Still, the women of Lemuria were like their counterparts, the Atlanteans, in not having inventions that were more modern to assist them in their housework.

Did women write, paint, and sculpt at home?

Some did if that was their interest. They were quite busy going shopping for the night's supper, as they enjoyed fresh vegetables and meats. Their refrigerators were not up to your modern standards, so you could compare markets to the many open-air stands of today's in Europe and Asia. They were also responsible for getting the children off to school and looking after them when they returned. A woman's work is never done, you see. Still, if the desire was there they would find time to enjoy creative pursuits.

LOVE AND MARRIAGE

Was marriage universal? If so, was it generally a monogamous relationship, or were there polygamists?

There were both, depending on the age. Monogamy was the prevalent form of marriage, but there were polygamists. They had fewer laws, so a man could have multiple wives should he choose.

How were the Atlantean families structured? Did they marry?

Yes, they had family-structured units just as you do today. Their marriage ceremonies were quite different, depending on their beliefs at that time.

How did they select their mates?

It was similar to today in that respect. The men and women could socialize together at their temples and schools. Naturally, there were matchmakers even during Atlantean times.

Did they tend to marry early or later in life?

They married fairly early, typically in their teens. It depended on the beliefs, which of course changed over thousands of years. Still they married, on average, at a younger age, especially in the latter years of the civilization, as there were wars and constant conflicts between religious factions (Atlantis) or countries (Lemuria). When you look at your World War II, you see many young men and women married seemingly impulsively. But of course, those were soul contracts for brief unions if the young men did not come back from the war.

But you said their life expectancy was greater than ours today?

Yes, so they would change mates occasionally. It was unusual for mates to stay together throughout their whole lives.

I assume Lemuria had marriage ceremonies of some sort?

Of course they did. They were elaborate affairs if the families could afford it. The marriage celebration is an ancient tradition dating back before Lemuria and Atlantis existed.

What were the average ages of the couple who married?

The couples were quite young, similar to that in Asian countries today.

Were there arranged marriages as there still are today?

Yes, this was an ancient tradition that lived on long after Lemuria sank. This was the norm, but there were different beliefs even then, so there were those who married out of love.

FAMILY STRUCTURE AND RESPONSIBILITY

Were their families generally large or small?

Small. They did not believe in having as many children as a body could produce. Therefore, their population never exploded as yours has. Consider that they existed for 60,000 years (the population certainly shrank with each destruction), but the population never would have reached the density your population has in such a short time. Each family would have one to (at most) three children, not more. Rarely would the family be larger than two, and that would be because of twins.

Did both societies have birth control?

Yes, both had learned how to control births.

Did the Atlanteans and Lemurians have abortions?

Yes, again, according to belief systems. But these were much more rare, and it was done more for health reasons than for lack of wanting a child. Their birth control methods were much better. They had methods of not fertilizing the eggs until a woman wished to have children.

In Atlantis and Lemuria, were children raised mostly by the parents or by the community?

There were many different methods of raising children over the 50,000-year period of time each was in existence. But the prevalent method of raising children then (as it is now) was by the parents, but like today, extended families stepped in when a parent or both parents died. The children, though, on average, left home a little earlier, and their schooling was shorter. Plus they tended to marry younger.

As there were fewer distractions during those times for both societies, I would assume that families had more time to spend together?

Affirmative. Things were not as rushed as they are today. Children did not have computers, smartphones, and video games to occupy their time as they do today. Evenings were spent eating a nice, relaxing dinner, telling stories, playing various games, or taking walks around the parks and greeting friends and neighbors. Perhaps you could compare it to the early 1900s in the United States.

Did both the Atlanteans and Lemurians have gardens, or was this not possible because most lived in apartments?

Land was set aside for individual gardens, somewhat similar to those plots of land in the United Kingdom you've seen. There was plenty of land, so they were not so crammed together. They could adopt a plot of land even in the green spaces next to the apartments and grow flowers and such. For the most part, women did not work outside the home, so they could spend time on a garden each day during the warm months, depending on what section of the continent they lived in.

Were the Lemurian and Atlantean children spanked as part of their discipline?

Yes, it was one of several methods used. But children were not as hyperactive as they are today, because they ate healthier foods without the additives and heavy amounts of sugar that children consume today.

We have covered that people of Atlantis and Lemuria married more than once, so did they have divorces?

Not exactly the same as you, but yes, there was a way to separate. Bear in mind that men were much more in control in those days, similar in some ways to certain religions and sects today.

Was divorce, or separation, acceptable in both Lemuria and Atlantis, or were they different?

They had wide differences according to their beliefs. Some beliefs were like you have today, such as believing the union should last forever. Others were more liberal, and it was quite easy to end a marriage. Therefore, this cannot be answered with one or two responses, as there was such a divergence in beliefs. This changed and evolved over thousands of years.

What was the rate of divorce in each society?

This is a question almost impossible to answer due to the differences in beliefs and the passage of thousands of years. Overall, it was much less than today. People were not as stressed then. Life for thousands of years was much simpler than today. Yes, there were soul contracts to divorce, but if their beliefs forbade it, then it was mostly the women at that time who shouldered mental, verbal, and physical abuse. You are making great strides in this area during recent times. You have a long way to go, especially in your more restrictive societies, but we can see a slow but steady improvement.

Was there physical and sexual abuse during those times as there is now?

Yes, this has not changed, as soul contracts were at work here. If someone abused his or her mate or children in one life, it had to be balanced in another. Even now there is balance being made for some people who had lives back in Atlantis and Lemuria. Balancing can occur in any period.

I would think there is less balancing needed from the Lemurian lives, as you have said they lived very peacefully — in almost a utopia, it sounds — for thousands of years?

That's true. Had they been able to maintain that balance, the continent of Lemuria would still be in existence today. This was a very slow but gradual deterioration in their relationships. It was not something that occurred overnight.

You humans today are going in the opposite direction — from great conflicts to smaller conflicts and eventually no conflicts, ultimately achieving the ability to honor all beliefs.

Did the Atlanteans have pensions for the older people?

The Atlanteans had a form of pensions up until things started going downhill.

Were these pensions from their governments?

That's true. They could receive all the medical care they needed, and families would take care of most of the pensioners, we will call them.

Was it common for extended families to live together on either continent?

It was quite common, although a little more common (as you might guess) on Lemuria, but even the Atlanteans would not neglect their mothers and fathers. Lemurians were much more family oriented, as the elderly lived with their children, similar to what you see today in Asia. That way of life continues to this day. Most people lived in the equivalent of a basic condominium, where there was typically a room set aside for elderly parents.

Were there assisted living centers if for some reason they could not live with their children or the children were unable to care for their elderly relatives?

Yes, but this was rare, as most women then, on both continents, did not work unless their economic status demanded it. They had socialist governments that provided housing for the elderly if needed.

But there was a smaller percentage of elderly parents who lived with their children?

Yes, there were many who lived with families, but for those who could not or would not, there were facilities somewhat similar to your retirement centers. Still, they were different and not as elaborate as many are today.

The Sons of Belial would not have lived similarly to the Lemurians?

No, there was a great difference over the ages, and it also depended on their economic status. Today you have a range of living styles according to your economic status. There are many people today who do not own a bed. They just sleep on the floor. It was the same back in those times. The majority of the Atlanteans had furniture while the majority of the Lemurians lived more casually.

"MAN'S" BEST FRIENDS

Did dogs and cats originate in Atlantis or before?

Dogs and cats have been with you since your original Adam and Eve days. Their soul group created these beautiful creatures at the behest of the Creator, who knew the Explorer Race needed animal companions to assist you in a variety of ways over hundreds of thousands of years. They were created as was the Adam and Eve model human. In fact, they preceded the Adam and Eve model human just a bit, so they were present when both Atlantis and Lemuria were seeded. Then it was up to the humans to domesticate them; as you can imagine, it is not always an easy process. They were looked at as a food source until the humans discovered their attributes.

Did they come from Sirius A or B?

Yes, they did. I'll let that revelation be made by your ET cousins in the future.

Were there any other animals that either of these peoples kept as pets?

The dogs and cats were introduced to humans at a very early stage and were domesticated for different reasons — hunting and then taking care of "varmints," to use your terms here, in and around their homes, as they went from living in crude dwellings to longer lasting structures. There were people who kept exotic animals, just as you do now, but it was not common. Keep in mind that the Things sort of went under the category of pets. They were not looked at as humans, but people would grow attached to them. This especially came true after the Things were ensouled. Then there was action taken to correct these genetic failures.

FASHION

Did the people on Atlantis mostly dress in tunics or robes, as we call them, or did the fashions evolve into modern types of clothing as we have today?

The people of Atlantis evolved from primitive loincloths and such through the stages of robes and tunics to modern wear, at least their concept of modernity. The priests and other officials continued to wear the fine robes and such in public appearances, but the rest of the population wore clothing more appropriate for work — loose fitting shirts and slacks for men and dresses for women. Many of the styles that have been present in your modern times first appeared during the days of Atlantis, and the designers of today — some of them at least — spent one or more lives in Atlantis.

They evolved as we did from tunics to regular clothes — pants, shirts, dresses, and such?

Yes, quite similar to today. Tunics came and went and the fashion was much more like today, with pants, shirts, blouses, and dresses prevalent. Naturally, over thousands of years, the styles changed. There were those who were fashion designers then who are incarnated today continuing with their lives, which were cut short many times due to war.

Did the women of both Atlantis and Lemuria wear dresses and pant suits, or did they wear robes?

Here it is difficult to answer, as we are looking at more than 50,000 years of existence for both, and you must simply look at how the fashions have changed so dramatically over the past few thousand years in modern times. You would have to take it one hundred years at a time to discuss what people were wearing. I can say there were certainly many times when women's dresses looked similar to today's fashions.

What were their clothes made of?

The clothes were made of cotton fabrics, very similar to today's clothes. The styles varied from year to year just as they do now. They did not have jeans; they wore stylish pants and dresses. Bear in mind that this society was quite old, even though more advanced in some areas than you are today. They bought their clothes in shops and department stores similar to today.

At times in our history, certain cultures dressed with women's breasts exposed. Was this common for both societies, or was this strictly according to beliefs?

You can say all of the above and more, as they went through their periods when it was seen as fashionable for women to expose their breasts. Then as certain religious beliefs developed, it was seen as a sin — verboten. Toward the end for both societies, women covered their breasts.

Did the women have to wear veils and robes because of religious beliefs at any time?

Yes, but this was, again, during certain times and was not something constant.

Was the dress for the beach similar to today's, with swimsuits for both men and women?

Yes and no, according to the society. Some allowed nudity and others were quite conservative with the women wearing what would be considered old-fashioned swimsuits today.

Did both men and women wear boots?

Yes, coverings for the feet were an early development for any society. Shoes, boots of all kinds, and sandals were worn.

Did women wear stiletto heels at anytime on both continents?

The heels were not nearly as high as today's. Two to three inches was the maximum height. Their shoes were much more comfortable.

What colors were popular — the same as today?

Yes, more the basic colors, although this varied greatly, even over the span of one hundred years.

Did mourners at funerals wear black as is mostly done today?

This varied from society to society and belief to belief. Yes, there were those who wore black, and others would wear certain colors denoting flowers and almost the colors of a rainbow. It all depended on the beliefs in the afterlife.

Would an Atlantean be able to recognize the difference between the Laws of One people and the Sons of Belial since they were all the same race?

Yes, it was by dress. Each side had their own style of dress to separate them from each other.

Did both societies have a form of umbrella?

Quite so. If you have rain, people are going to invent ways to stay dry, including umbrellas and rain gear of all sorts, depending on the season and the part of the continent where they resided. Obviously, a person living at the southern end of the continent would not dress the same when they traveled to the northern part of the continent.

Did the Atlanteans wear a lot of jewelry?

Yes, quite a lot — silver, gold, precious stones, the whole gamut. That is something else that has not changed over the centuries.

Will gold prove more important to us in the future for other than a measurement of wealth and for its uses in jewelry?

Quite so. It is one of those commodities you need to take care of, and we know you will due to its rarity. But you will find other uses for it in the future. It has properties as a conductor of energy, and there are healing qualities they used in the healing temples. Gold has other capabilities your scientists will rediscover in the future.

RETAIL AND DINING ESTABLISHMENTS

Theo, did the Atlanteans have what we call department stores with clothes, shoes, and so on?

Yes, they did. These stores were fairly large, perhaps not as large as yours today since you have more densely populated areas. There were stores with multiple items of merchandise for sale, just as you have today.

Did they have the concept of a mall with multiple stores under one roof, or were stores mostly open on a street?

No, they were mostly open to foot traffic on a street. Bear in mind, because the population was much less than today, they had more room for these stores to be facing the street. There were the larger multi-merchandise stores, but for the most part, individual stores and shops serviced the population.

Did the stores have façades like the European stores on boulevards, like Asia, or modern with manufactured panels as we have today?

They were more your brick-and-mortar façades. They had nice window displays as you have today. All stores must display their goods for the public to see.

Did people pay by cash, or did they have checking accounts (both Atlantis and Lemuria)?

This varied over thousands of years, so let's say at their highest degree of development, they used checks. But cash was the preferred form of payment. Paper credit was an invention of recent times.

Did they have restaurants?

Most assuredly. They enjoyed the company of friends and would have lavish dinners. Sometimes it would just be a family affair.

Did people in restaurants pay a gratuity, or was it included in the bill as is done in many countries today?

It was almost universal that an amount was added to the bill for the wait staff in those days.

Were all the restaurants in both Atlantis and Lemuria sit-down, or did they have the equivalent of fast food drive-throughs?

They had mobile stands that offered food because few people had cars. Cars were owned by the government and the wealthy. Everyone else tended to take public transportation of various types. You are ahead of them in having restaurants that can serve fast food, but then you also have chemicals and processed foods that cause health problems of all types.

Were there bars in restaurants, or were they separate in those days?

Regulations were much more relaxed, so if a restaurant wished to have a full bar, they could do so. If they chose to just offer wines and ales, then that was just as acceptable.

Did women work in the bars and restaurants on both continents?

Definitely. This was permissible and was considered normal for a certain class of people. Naturally, the more well-to-do families would never consider the idea of their female children doing this work.

Did the Atlantean continent, its islands, or Lemuria have prohibition at one time or another?

That depends on whether you mean just alcohol or drugs people take, a modern decision. Both societies were liberal with their use of alcoholic drinks such as wines, beers, and other spirits. There was some drug use then, but usually people did not become addicted as they do now. If someone on Atlantis became addicted, he or she could visit one of the healing centers and use crystal therapy. On Lemuria, a person could visit a different type of healing center, and it would still be quite effective. Both societies were ahead of you in that department.

What about cannabis?

Again, lightly used. Both societies were quite aware of its healing qualities, so it might have been part of a treatment. Recreational use was not very widespread. There were no laws prohibiting its use, so there was no psychological thrill of doing something against the law — no fun, you might say.

SPORTS AND ENTERTAINMENT

Theo, what type of sports did the Atlanteans and Lemurians participate in?

Typical ball games that, as you have noticed, males especially love. They were not the violent games like American football you have today, just spirited contests between teams —soccer rather than the rougher American football. They had different rules, but the concept was the same. Many more sports were similar to the Olympic style games, such as running, jumping, and so on. This included all sorts of skilled ball games, along with such things as swimming, a form of skiing, and games similar to chess.

Basketball?

Yes, but again different sets of rules.

Baseball?

Affirmative, but with a different set of rules and the balls were a different size.

Did billiard games such as pool and snooker exist in Atlantis and Lemuria?

There were ball games, just not the table games of today.

Did golf exist in Atlantis or Lemuria?

A crude form, you might say, but it would be hard to recognize it as such.

What about martial arts?

Yes, a form, quite unique for each continent.

Was fitness part of the culture in Lemuria?

People were much more fit. They took part in games and lots of outdoor exercises. Gyms were almost nonexistent. They ate a much more balanced diet than the Western world does today, so there was little obesity. People enjoyed walking in parks and in cities and playing outdoor games.

Were there hot tubs and swimming pools in Atlantis and Lemuria?

Cities had public pools, and everyone enjoyed visiting the lakes, the coasts, and the oceans. There were fewer private pools than you have today.

Did both continents have snow during the winter seasons?

Yes, although each continent has its own topography. They had ski wear, although not as developed as today, plus winter recreational activities such as sledding. Their skis were not as highly developed as yours are today.

Did either or both Atlantis and Lemuria have boat races, and if so, were they sailing or motor?

They had what you term these days sailing regattas. There were many types of yachts similar to what you have today. Motor races were almost nonexistent in both Atlantis and Lemuria, due to the limitations in their energy sources. There was no way to turbo charge these engines to perform at a higher level, so they were limited.

Did they have some form of water skiing?

No. A few people had sled-shaped devices they could tow, but actual water skis were not in use then.

Were there scuba divers on both continents?

Affirmative. That was a sport everyone could enjoy, and there were also professional divers.

Did the Atlanteans have horses?

They had horses, and they would race them, so this was one of their pastimes.

Did the Lemurians also have horses?

No, horses were not introduced to this continent. It was decided by your ET uncles and aunts for that society not to have this animal on the continent. Such decisions, I might add, are done with much thought, just as you can see today in which Australia has certain animals no one else has on any other continent.

How old is yoga? Did it date back to the Atlantean and Lemurian times?

Forms of yoga have existed for many thousands of years. It is much older than the estimated 5,000 years you have heard of. It was passed down from generation to generation as an exercise for the whole body without the need for such things as weights or machines of any kind. Tied into this was meditation; both went hand in hand.

It was used more extensively in ancient Lemuria, but the Atlanteans had their own form of yoga. It is something that ancient people were inspired to do as they explored the use of their bodies and what the human body was capable of doing. Therefore, it had a very early introduction.

Did they have card games and gambling?

Quite so on both accounts. They were very active people. Another form of recreation to them was war games, much as it is today. Still it was different from yours.

What form of dance did they have on the continents of Atlantis and Lemuria?

Quite a large variety, as we refer to the fact that these continents were inhabited for thousands of years. Therefore, each had tribal dances in their early days, which evolved to many forms, just as you have today. There was a form of ballet, as you can imagine those souls whose main interest was the art of dancing would wish to explore all forms of dance, even then.

Their music tended to be of a lighter form than, say, what is called head banging now. They did not have rock-and-roll back then, but they did have some forms of faster dancing. They did not have the electronic instruments you have today. So there was a large variety of dancing, according to the music being played — a slow dance or a fast one. The dance varied widely not only from culture to culture but over many centuries.

Was the music simple, or did they also have complex orchestrations?

Both. They had developed to the point that they had orchestras, as it is but a step from small groups to those groups joining together to make a variety of musical arrangements.

Did both societies have plays, and if so, were they performed indoors or outside in some form of amphitheater?

You could say all of the above here, depending on the time. Both had large amphitheaters as well as auditoriums for the inclement months of the year.

Both societies enjoyed stories of love and mystery. Naturally, the plays became more political as the different countries of each society warred with each other.

Did they have parades of any sort to celebrate specific dates, past events, or the return of soldiers from wars, and so on?

Yes, these were pleasant experiences. Most of the largest parades celebrated seasons and harvests and such, but there were military parades and parades to celebrate past events. They were not as elaborate as some of the parades these days.

Did they have the equivalent of televisions?

Oh yes. They were advanced enough to have this equipment. Televisions were much less important during those times than today, as the people loved live shows. The TVs contained mostly boring programs put on by their respective governments.

What other forms of entertainment, besides music, were there in Atlantis?

They had a form of movies, which you were involved in as a producer and director and actor. That's another reason why you volunteered for this life, as you had the prior experience. Many of the forms of entertainment you have today were first realized on the Atlantean continent with different variations. They did not sit around all day, as depicted in some of today's paintings, in togas listening to a harp.

They had motion pictures?

Yes, in a slightly different form, but the presentation looked about the same.

Exactly what did I do?

You were what would be termed today a producer and director. It was close to what they do now. You also were an actor in one life, so you had a well-rounded understanding of the business you're in now.

How long would films play at the cinema for both the Atlanteans and Lemurians?

Equally about the same, less than a week, and sometimes just a day or so, depending on how much push it was given. Films overall had not reached the artistic and technical levels that films at this time have achieved.

Did Atlantis and Lemuria both have zoos?

They had smaller enclosures not nearly as nice as most zoos are today. Even though these civilizations lasted thousands of years, having zoos that are more elaborate only came at the height of their civilizations and were not as well done as today. Animals were not treated as well then as they are today. To cage an animal, as you must know, is very sad to see. These are prisons. At least in modern times they are better taken care of — in modern countries.

I assume there were famous writers who were Atlanteans and Lemurians?

Yes, there were writers who became famous, but of course all was lost with the destruction of the continents.

Did the Atlanteans and Lemurians have vacation times as we do in modern times?

Yes, they did, as both societies were sophisticated. They would take time away from work just as is done today, and they would travel.

Were beach resorts quite popular?

They had beaches, mountain resorts — all the normal pursuits. And I might add, the vacations typically were longer than those you take today.

Did both continents have souvenir and gift shops at the vacation spots?

Yes, of course. People have for eons wished to have mementos of their vacations and to provide gifts for various remembrances. They were no different from you today.

Did the Lemurians have all the entertainment choices that the Atlanteans had?

Definitely, but as was explained before, their dances, music, and all other forms of entertainment were different, as their cultures were quite different. It even varied widely on the Lemuria continent due to the differences in religions. There is nothing new under the sun, as humans have explored every type of religion and belief system over thousands and thousands of years.

Did both the Atlanteans and Lemurians have all the forms of art we have today?

Yes, whether the art was in the form of paintings, statues, metal work, or any other form of artwork you can imagine, there were humans who wished to express themselves through creating art. Naturally, over thousands of years, this art took many forms, and they went through periods that in one century one type of art would be popular and then in a few years something else would gain interest.

LEMURIAN AND ATLANTEAN DWELLINGS

Theo, how were the Atlantean houses and buildings constructed — normal wood or metal frame and then wood, brick, or stone exteriors?

Yes, exactly. This form of construction is very old, you see. Of course, in the very early days of inhabitation, they went through their own periods of huts and so on. Once they progressed to a higher level, they lived similarly to how people live today, similar to the differences in, say, the way the Japanese or Europeans live differently from those in the United States.

Were the Atlantean and Lemurian houses square, round, or pyramid-shaped?

Again, we have to answer in the affirmative, as there were a variety of buildings. In both societies, only the wealthy had houses, and when someone has a lot of money, as you know, they tend to get creative in the places in which they live. Most people lived in square-shaped buildings, in simple apartments. If they were a little more well to do than their friends, then the apartments would be more nicely decorated with expensive rugs. Neither society used carpets as you do today.

Did the buildings or houses have multiple levels?

There were only just a few in each society.

Were there many houses?

Not many. These were more for the upper classes.

What about the sizes of the apartments or houses?

Most were small dwellings. There were many apartments with large green areas surrounding them so that people could go out and enjoy the grass and trees and play sports.

Were the apartments the Atlanteans and Lemurians lived in rental units, or were they like the condominiums we have today?

It was more the latter. Most people of those times did not have the funds to purchase a whole house. Those were for the more elite and wealthy business and government people. But the average earner could afford to purchase a unit in an apartment complex. Naturally, this varied over thousands of years.

Were these complexes usually two or three stories, or were they high-rises?

Very few high-rises existed on either continent. So the buildings were usually two or three stories in height. They were not as luxurious as your condos today, but because they had free energy, they could invest in these units. They could decorate them to their own tastes; there was variety in the paint used in each unit along with what was hung on the wall and so on. The rental units were obviously much more plain in style, just as they are today.

Did they purchase them with bank loans, or did they just pay a certain fee per month to the builder?

They took loans from banks. There were bankers back in those days, just as there are now, but on a much smaller scale. They were mostly locally owned, and in some instances, people could afford houses with the money they made and from the loans.

Did they also have radios and modern kitchen appliances?

Not exactly the same as here. They had a type of radio, but they weren't very advanced in kitchen appliances. The Atlanteans had the Things to do the menial work, so there was no real demand to invent timesaving devices for the kitchen.

Were their living rooms similar to those we have today with chairs and couches?

Quite so. In the early days, they had mats to sit on, and then they graduated, we will say, to furniture.

What were the outside walls made of for both societies — brick, wood, stucco?

There were all three at one time or another. Brick was the primary material for all the office and retail buildings. Wood was mostly for houses and apartments, very similar to today.

What type of flooring did they have — wood, tile, or what?

They used a variety of flooring in both houses and apartments in both societies. Wood was most commonly used, along with tiles of different colors and shapes.

What materials did they use for the ceilings?

Lightweight particle or plywood boards.

Were many buildings equipped with sunroofs?

They were not prevalent and used sparingly.

What materials were used for roofs in each society?

Asphalt was not used. Slate-type materials were used.

What material was used for insulation in the Atlantean and Lemurian houses, buildings, and apartments?

Normal insulation was used for the houses and buildings. There was insulation, just not based on the fiberglass of today. The insulation was more of a papier-mâché type.

How were the homes and buildings heated?

By tapping into the heat of the inner earth, as compared to the gas and electricity now used for heating. They used electrical currents but in a completely different way.

Was the power to light homes and businesses on Atlantis provided free of charge?

Yes, there was no charge for the power. Each house or business had its own receptacle, as there were no electrical lines as there are today.

In the Atlantean homes, did they sleep on mattresses similar to ours, or did they sleep on mats or something else?

No, they had in the latter years, mattresses, but they went through the stage of sleeping on mats, as you call them. They were equal in many ways to the level of advancement you have today; however, you have surpassed them in many ways as well, just not in the use of crystals.

What were their mattresses made of — feathers, foam, water?

They were made primarily of feathers. You are ahead of them today in making mattresses more comfortable.

Did both societies have frames for the mattresses or were they on the floor?

The Atlanteans tended to have frames for their beds while the Lemurians preferred the floor.

So neither used mats?

Correct, except in earlier times.

Did they have futons?

Not really.

I assume the houses were decorated with mirrors and artwork?

Yes, and metal art pieces too.

They did not have crystal windows, did they?

Perhaps in a few of the expensive houses they existed.

Did the Atlanteans or Lemurians have garages or tool sheds as we do?

Not the same. In the cities, we mentioned that most people lived in apartments. Only the wealthy people had houses, and there were work areas for those who were hired to take care of the houses.

It was different on the farms since, naturally, they needed places to work on the equipment, to repair broken machinery, and much more. Farmers were pretty handy with tools as compared to the city folk. It all depended on their soul contracts as to what their interests were. Again, we are speaking of thousands and thousands of years, with many disasters befalling, especially the Atlanteans and anyone who lived on the coasts when they experienced the rising water levels and tsunamis.

Chapter 4

FORMS OF COMMUNICATION AND SOCIAL INTERACTIONS

Theo and Gaia

Theo, did the Atlanteans have a written language as we do, or was it in the form of hieroglyphics?

The Atlanteans had a written language. They were quite advanced in communication with letters — not Roman, though.

Were the letters Japanese, Chinese, or Arabic?

They were a combination. They influenced all three languages. But they were unique and complex at the same time.

Did they write left to right or right to left?

They wrote left to right.

Did they have bound books as we have today?

Oh yes, they were quite sophisticated after thousands of years with books and other reading material, even computers of a type.

Were their computers more basic or more sophisticated than ours today?

"Different" would be a better answer. They were designed for functions different from the personal computers you have today. The general population did not use them, only governments and other institutions.

Will we ever discover the Atlantean language written anywhere?

Not in your lifetime. Perhaps someday it will be discovered in the ruins.

How did they communicate with other races they met in their travels — by physically learning the language, or did they have some type of translating devices? Were they telepathic?

They were not telepathic. They tended to pick up other languages and had schools as you do today that would teach the languages for those involved in international trade and explorations.

Were there written languages on Lemuria?

Yes, of course. Again, they had made great strides in their development. The only fly in the ointment was their inability to get along with each other.

• • •

Gaia, did the Japanese language originate in Lemuria, and did the Korean language originate in China?

The Japanese language is an offshoot of one of the three major Lemurian languages. We have not covered the fact that Lemuria had more than one language, but it did. Your language changed over hundreds of thousands of years to what it is in the present day, and it will continue to evolve as all languages on Earth do. For example, the Korean language evolved from one of the Chinese dialects, and it also took on its own personality, we will call it, over many centuries.

Were there two languages in Atlantis or did everyone speak the same language?

Everyone spoke the same language until the two groups completely split, and then the language evolved separately as there was little contact, so this increased the differences between the two and forced them further apart.

• • •

Theo, how did the Atlanteans and Lemurians greet one another?

This varied, as you can imagine, over thousands of years with the different cultures. Just look at the different forms of greetings you have these days, and all of these types of greetings were used by the Atlanteans and the Lemurians. It included bowing, grasping hands in several different ways, hugging, kissing on the cheeks, and even fist bumping, as used by your younger folks today. The old saying, "There is nothing new under the Sun" even applies to greetings.

Did both the Atlanteans and Lemurians have their own form of swearing?

Oh yes. Swear words date back to the very beginning of the Adam and Eve models. There has been much to swear about over these thousands of years. It is universal.

RECKONING TIME AND SPACE AND VALUE

How many days constituted a week on the Atlantean and the Lemurian calendars?

Some calendars did not even subdivide into weeks, although they would have their days of rest and worship. The months were divided by the moon phases as compared to the one you use today.

Did the Atlanteans, Lemurians, and people of Oz use the same calendar?

Definitely not. They all kept a basic calendar of seven days, but that's where the similarities end. Each had a separate day to remember their gods and to work, along with different national days. You can see this today where the Chinese have separate calendars, one used by Western societies and one used by Middle Eastern countries. But to answer your question, they calculated their days quite differently.

How did the Atlanteans calculate their calendar? Did they use a special event or formation of the country, as their calendar had to be ancient with so many years of existence?

Yes, but they were more interested in the present and did not dwell on the past.

Did the Atlanteans have a twelve-month, thirteen-month, or some other form of calendar, or did they not have anything?

They were quite sophisticated in this area, as they had many thousands of years to develop a sophisticated calendar, perhaps more accurate than what you have today.

But was it based on twelve or thirteen months?

Not exactly, but certainly days were part of it just as it is in modern times.

Was it lunar in scope?

There you have it, much closer to a lunar calendar, but it was still different from today's.

How did they measure things?

Their measuring devices were a little primitive compared to today.

Were things weighed using the energies of both societies, or was it simpler?

A little simpler, but you are fairly close, as far as scales are concerned, to what is in use today.

Did they have celebrations to mark the return of winter, spring, and summer?

Yes, they celebrated the return of spring, the planting season, and then the harvesting. Those were much more important than, what we term, the artificial start of your new year.

CURRENCY

Did the Atlanteans have a form of currency? How did they pay for items, unless everything was free?

No, they were an advanced society, and people used a form of currency to purchase everything needed for a home, just as is done today.

What form of currency did they use?

They had various denominations of coins, worth more than today's coins, and some paper money.

Could both the Atlanteans and Lemurians take out loans? If so, did they charge simple or compound interest?

Yes, they did have a form of loans not too dissimilar from today, as the bankers of those days would have other incarnations doing the same work if that was their soul interest. They used a simple interest then. It was not as complicated or onerous as today's. This was for both societies.

Was there poverty during, let's say, their best years?

Small pockets, not as widespread as today.

SOCIAL CONSTRUCTS

Did women and men both consume alcoholic beverages?

Yes, although tastes varied extensively throughout time, just as you have seen in modern times where wines and beers became more popular than the heavier spirits.

What was the typical age a young person was allowed to drink in Atlantis and Lemuria?

Younger than today — twelve to fourteen as a general rule, but this varied over thousands of years.

As teenagers go through puberty nowadays and find ways to rebel, what did teens in those times do?

It was different, as they were not schooled as long, so even though they were going through puberty, their realities were that they had to start to work and have families at an earlier age. No time to goof off, to use an old expression. Still, they had their fun times. They were not as rebellious as teens today, as they were not pumped full of all the harmful chemicals from your foods consumed and prescribed drugs. Again, their healing centers took care of any problems that arose safely and humanely.

Were there the usual crimes we encounter today — thievery, assault, and even murder?

Yes to all of those crimes. Atlantis was a violent place to live at times. It was not always the peaceful picture it has been painted. There was much crime against other faiths. That's another reason people were attracted to the Gentle Way. None of your flock had the problems that the other people living at that time had. You could equate it to the Sunnis and Shiites of today in Iraq. At times, they lived together quite peacefully and at other times quite the opposite.

Since I had a number of lives on Atlantis, was I aligned with both groups?

Yes, of course you were. You had to experience the yin and yang — the duality of those times. So you were both a good guy, shall we say, and a very bad guy during those thousands of years. I'm using your terminology, as you had contracts to play those parts.

Did the Atlanteans have individual cars and trucks?

Most Atlanteans had access to good public transportation, so only wealthy people owned automobiles. They had trucks, but those were owned by corporations.

What were the top speeds of their automobiles?

As they relied on free energy devices, their average speeds were less than today's and their top speeds were no more than the 50 to 60 mph level.

Did both Atlantean and Lemurian women drive or only men?

This varied, according to whatever religion was popular during the ages when there were cars, but most assuredly, men drove much more than women. There were fewer cars, and they were used more for businesses and governments. Both societies had good public transportation.

Did they have bicycles in each society?

For a fact, that was the favored transportation for most people when they would go short distances for various reasons.

What side of the road did the Atlanteans and Lemurians drive on?

That depended on the country and even the time as the road systems developed. Right was the predominant side, but several countries used the left side — more in Lemuria.

Did they have stoplights or roundabouts?

They had both, as they had plenty of room to build the roundabouts. Stoplights were much more prevalent in the cities and major town centers.

Did either the Atlanteans or Lemurians have public telephone booths?

Yes, they have not progressed as much as you have today with your smartphones. They had the ability to communicate, but they needed public facilities, as you used to, when they needed to contact someone.

Did both have phones in their homes?

Yes, they did — certainly in the later years.

How tall were the tallest buildings?

They were no more than ten to twelve stories in height. There were not as many people per square mile as there are today, so there was not a need to build up vertically.

Did they have elevators?

Most assuredly.

Did they have tattoos?

Yes, but not widespread.

Theo, did either or both Atlantis and Lemuria have the following:

Facials?

Yes, people liked to be pampered back as far as Adam and Eve models existed.

Massages?

Again the same.

Tanning?

No, this is a recent phenomenon that is slowly dying out due to the harm doctors are pointing out to your skin and the higher risk of melanoma.

I assume those in hot countries, such as the desert areas, learned quickly that they must enclose or cover most of their bodies to keep from burning.

Quite correct.

Hair dye?

Yes, this was done on both continents at times. It all depended on whether having gray hair was in. But women would dye their hair for different looks, just as is done today.

Exercise gyms?

No, this is something created in modern times primarily for those with sedentary lifestyles in large urban areas. People were much more active in the past.

Yoga?

A form of it was done in Lemuria and carried over as people there used it to enhance meditation.

Meditation?

Yes, both continents saw the benefit of quieting one's mind to receive not only physical benefits but spiritual and mental too. You do understand that there are many forms of meditation, but you asked a general question, and generally, the answer is yes.

Holistic practices?

For a fact — again, more in Lemuria than Atlantis, but even there you could find these practices.

Did either have cruise ships for their pleasure?

No. There were limits on the crystal power for the Atlanteans, and people remained fairly close to the continent, except during the time when they colonized or conquered the simple people inhabiting the Mediterranean. They had some very nice sailing ships.

• • •

Gaia, did Atlanteans and Lemurians enjoy the beach as much as we do in modern times?

Most assuredly so. This has been so for as long as the Adam man and woman have been on Earth. Not only could they find food from the waters, but also the sand was warm and a place to rest over many thousands of years of existence for both continents. We have previously discussed their swimwear. But family outings to the beach were just as common in those times as they are today.

Were dolphins present then?

Absolutely. They could interact even more with the dolphin population than they can today. They recognized them as intelligent creatures and did not slaughter them then as is done today.

EDUCATION

How many years did a student go to school in Atlantis?

Schooling was a little different from today. They didn't go as long as children go today, closer to eight or ten years. There were not as many breaks as you have today for vacations and such. They had holidays tied into their religions and some public holidays. Only those with a scientific aptitude continued with their education to be taught about crystal power. And there were those who joined the military.

Were the schools public or private? Were some religious based?

They were public. They were taught their religions at home and in other gatherings. The religious buildings were not as massive as today's.

Were children taught in the same ways in both Atlantis and Lemuria?

No, there were significant differences. There was a lot of "home schooling" in Atlantis. In Lemuria, the opposite was true. They felt that children needed the interaction with other students, but they spent some time teaching meditation and practiced in school. The home lives for children were similar. There was playtime and the enjoyment of just being a child.

Their educations could take a longer time, as they were not as rushed as you are today nor were their schools so structured. The crystal power in Atlantis had many uses, including transferring knowledge to people. There was much they could learn and absorb, according to the child's interests, right from home using this crystal power.

What were schools like in Atlantis and Lemuria?

In Atlantis, a little similar to today, which we will take up first. They had teachers and the size of the classes were a little smaller than today — around fifteen or so on average, as there were much fewer people during those centuries.

How did Lemuria differ?

It was even more casual, you could say, until the nations started warring with each other, and then the emphasis was on preparing the children for military service. Their population was much smaller. You could equate it to Israel today, and everyone was required to serve. After service, they would still be in a reserve unit.

Did they have a preschool for the younger children?

No, they had not yet developed preschools.

Was their curriculum the typical reading, writing, and arithmetic?

Yes, much closer to the simpler times of your youth. However, their language was seemingly more complicated than English — at least the writing, so it took longer to learn.

Did the children play as children do today?

Yes, that has not changed over thousands of years. Children have remained the same, and they need activities, so yes, they even had recesses when they would play. Children will be children.

Did they have the playground equipment of today?

No, it was much simpler. They had swings and equipment that they climbed over. Many of their activities would involve games of a sort, including ball games.

Were the ball games similar to today's?

Yes, a similar game to football or soccer. Round balls have been in existence for many thousands of years.

Did both the Atlanteans and Lemurians have sex education?

Yes, things were much more open in those days. They discussed sex with the family and in school. Remember that they went to school for fewer years than you do, and they typically married and started families at an earlier age.

What roles did the parents play in their education?

Much less than today, as the children were not so taxed with learning as they are now.

Was telepathy used more during Atlantean times than now in the present?

No. Telepathy was used about the same. But in Lemuria, it was used to a higher degree than now. Still the percentage would be low, actually no higher than 20 percent, and that was before the societies living there started to degenerate. There were schools that taught their students how to communicate in this fashion.

JOINING THE WORKFORCE

What was the legal age to work in both Atlantis and Lemuria?

This varied over the centuries, but on average in their later years, it was still lower than the age today. Even in today's times, you have children working in sweatshops and in mines and such. It was not too different in those times, although a little more benevolent. As both societies' children did not attend school for as long a period of time as in modern-day First World societies, they tended to begin work at an earlier age of, say, between twelve and fourteen, depending on their education, just as it is now. Toward the end, they were required to go into the military, as not only the Atlanteans but also the countries of Lemuria warred with each other. They used much propaganda to incite the population to hate the others.

Did they have pensions and labor unions?

No, those are modern-day creations. Older people were much more inclined and accepted to live with their children. They were not as cut off, as is the case with many modern families.

Did families on both continents typically live close to work?

This varied so much over the years, as there was an extensive network of trains and other public transportation such as the trams, streetcars, and buses everyone could use. People then were like today, wishing to live in certain parts of the country and certain sections of the city, so they thought nothing of a commute using public transportation. There were people who lived so close to their work that they could walk in almost any kind of weather.

How did their public transportation compare to today's?

Their public transportation would have been considered as equal or even above what you have now. Public transport was what everyone but the few elite people used, so there were many forms of public transport.

How often did the Atlanteans and Lemurians have mail service, or did they have to go and pick it up?

Their mail service was excellent for quite a bit of each society's existence. It normally was similar to today where you receive it six days a week. Obviously, it varied over several thousand years, but this was the way most people — the common people — communicated during those times. They had telephones, but fax-type machines were normally only used in businesses and governments. Service was even good in rural settings.

Was there a large number of mail carriers?

Exactly. Mail was delivered in a variety of ways, just as it is now, including by foot, in postal boxes in the apartment complexes, and even from water vehicles.

For both continents, were there fewer police officers as a percentage of the population than there are in more modern times?

That's true. As mentioned before, they had fewer crimes, as people with the potential for violence were treated when they discovered this in tests. But also as noted there was always the specter of family arguments of all kinds and physical and verbal abuse of women, which would get out of hand, resulting in the police being called. There was the occasional murder, which was likely connected with domestic violence. It was rare for there to be perpetrators who would murder someone not in their own family.

Did all the governments on Atlantis and Lemuria provide fire and ambulance service?

These units would compare quite favorably to modern-day fire services. They had fewer volunteer services compared to today.

Were there door-to-door sales clerks in both societies?

Yes, this was similar to your time period many years ago when people would go door-to-door selling such items as those needed for the household — brooms as an example.

How easy was it for people to start their own companies? Was there a lot of red tape?

No, there were few restrictions compared to now, but companies as a whole were small in comparison to today's companies. There was free energy, and it was quite easy to start shops, stores, and restaurants. There were companies, just as there are today, that supplied goods and weapons for the government. They just did not have thousands of employees as you do today.

WOMEN AT WORK

Did women work in both Atlantis and Lemuria, or were they just supposed to take care of the home? I realize this is general, so please expand as you need to.

When considering that these societies existed for around 50,000 years each, you must understand that times were ever changing and evolving. In both societies, women were always in charge of the household, no matter how modest it might have been. That's no different from today, as keep in mind these people were the same in structure and biology as you today. Sometimes in modern times, they seem almost foreign to you, but they were not. They were human.

Therefore women, just as today, became pregnant and had children, although not as many as some women have today, and they took care of the home. However, depending on their economic status, they worked in many jobs — nurses, as an example, along with restaurant jobs and so on. As a general rule, men were even more chauvinistic than they are today. This was more common in Atlantis than in Lemuria where the feminine side was much more prevalent for many thousands of years until there were more and more conflicts between the countries that made up the continent. Overall, women worked outside the home in these societies, but almost never were they in charge of large companies or governments.

Which jobs were common for women to work outside the home?

Most were not looked at in high regard if they had to work outside the home. It was, as has been stated before, a male-run society. Still, women were needed as secretaries in businesses, nurses in hospitals, workers in restaurants, and so on. But they were never — or almost never — in managerial positions.

* * *

OCCUPATIONS THEN AND NOW

Theo, please comment whether the people on Atlantis and Lemuria worked in the following occupations:

Bricklayers and carpenters?

Certainly, these trades were quite important.

Bus drivers?

More on Atlantis, but Lemuria had some public transportation.

City council members?

Yes, as both societies had villages and towns and even cities, and they had a variety of ways that they governed. You could list every way of governing, as both had long histories.

Civil servants?

They came along with the formation of the towns and villages.

Dentists?

Yes, as long as there are people with teeth, those teeth will need to be repaired or pulled. There was less need for dentists than there is today because of their healthier diets.

Factory workers?

Naturally there would be a need for people to work in the factories. They had the automation you have developed in modern times.

Famous explorers?

Over thousands of years, you can imagine how many people wound up on the list of explorers. They explored most of the continents and oceans of the world, bringing back information and knowledge to the people at that time. Their names would mean nothing to you today. Yes, there was great exploration over 50,000 years of civilization, but you have long ago surpassed them in your explorations as, bear in mind, none of them reached space.

Hair stylists and barbers?

This is another profession almost as old as people living on Earth.

Importers?

Very little was imported. Both continents had sufficient resources so that they were able to supply almost all they needed. May I remind you that the sizes of the continents were larger than Australia is today and much more verdant than Australia's interior.

Jewelers?

Almost as long as there have been precious metals and stones, there have been people who worked with them.

Lawyers?

Yes, there were people who specialized in the legal aspects of the day, naturally more so toward the end. These people were involved in representing those who went afoul of the law in those days.

Massage therapists?

Yes, including those who specialized in physical therapy for those with broken bones and so on.

Disc jockeys?

They were almost nonexistent in those days.

Meteorologists?

Here they were more advanced than you are today, as they had learned how to control the weather.

Morticians?

Not the same as today. The way they were buried is not the same as today, as they used cremation much more. All this varied according to the religious beliefs that were in vogue at the time.

Newspaper reporters?

Oh quite so, and you can imagine that the two factions we've discussed before had their own publications greatly slanted to their own viewpoints.

Nurses?

Yes, as stated above.

Nutritionists?

Neither side called them that, but there were people studying what were the best foods to eat. They had fewer obese people as noted before, as their diets were much better than today.

Opticians?

Yes, this was in the later stages.

Pawnbrokers?

Yes, there were people and stores that acted as pawnbrokers. There was also a lot of barter too.

Plastic surgeons?

There were no doctors who specialized in this field, as they had other energies to improve or keep the looks of people at that time. If there was an accident, then all sorts of healing would be implemented, but reconstructions were sometimes needed.

Real estate agents?

Yes, on both continents, but they were different from today. It was not as organized.

Restaurant chefs?

There have always been people who would feed you for a price — whatever the form of payment was in that particular time.

Royalty — queens, kings, emperors, empresses?

These folks existed at times but not all throughout history.

Secret agents?

Yes, of course there were spies. There is nothing new under the sun, you could say, as spies and secret agents have existed all the way back to tribal days. Being a spy is another on that bucket list. So in the times of Lemuria and Atlantis, there were many occasions as you might imagine during which each country, or set of rulers, would employ these agents to spy on their enemies.

Stenographers?

Yes, used naturally in business.

Stockbrokers and traders?

No, they were not quite the same. The companies, we will call them, were smaller, not the huge conglomerates you have today. None were even one-tenth the size of even the smaller conglomerates today. Most were privately owned. Therefore, there was not the constant transfer of stocks that occurs in today's world. Very few companies had holdings in other companies. Things were slower then, not nearly as fast-paced as today. The states had their own operations for using the crystal powers, so there were not public utilities the same as you have today.

Trash collectors?

Yes, but there was not the huge amount of garbage per person generated as there is today. The people were not as wasteful. You are slowly learning to conserve.

Truck drivers or train engineers?

Yes, many of the things you have today existed before on one or both continents.

Veterinarians?

They existed in the later stages when people were much more civilized. There has always been a need to take care of our animals, and it was no different then, just that the treatments were more advanced than today's.

Were there auctions?

Of a sort, not quite up to today's standards, but they had occasional auctions of various types.

As my soul cluster is known as teachers, were we schoolteachers back then in Atlantis and Lemuria?

You had many lives as different types of teachers, but your soul cluster liked to get in and learn how to do something so that you could eventually teach it well. Therefore, you had many lives of learning trades, science, and so forth, of where you could be of service, and that included the various spiritual beliefs of those times. They had their own religions, perhaps not as extreme as today, but something for everyone. Atlantis and Lemuria were destroyed by science and greed, not so much by religion.

THE LAW OF ONE AND THE SONS OF BELIAL

Theo, what were the predominant religions on the continent of Atlantis?

The Law of One and the Sons of Belial were the predominant religions on the continent of Atlantis. They had a priest system that was very corrupt. They led the people and governed their lives so that the two major groups of people came to war with each other. It was greed on both sides that did them in.

When did the two prominent religions on Atlantis begin — before or after the First Destruction?

They began a little before. They were early concepts of beliefs. Before then, both were heart centered, but the Sons of Belial moved away from that to more earthly pursuits.

How many cultures existed on the continent?

Everyone is quite aware of the two major cultures — the Law of One and the Sons of Belial. There was also your group who practiced the Gentle Way. The people of Atlantis tended to split into the two major groups primarily for political reasons but also due to religious differences. There were a couple of minor cults, you could call them, as there can be in any society, but they had no influence. Your Gentle Way was the largest besides the Law of One and the Sons of Belial.

Bear in mind, each of the two major groups was controlled by men who were power hungry. The leaders were controlled just as is done today in the Middle East, as a prime example. Religion and state should never be mixed, as the state must be fair to all religions practiced in a country.

Who was Belial?

He was the leader of the movement that believed in materialistic comforts and looked down on the Law of One people.

What was the main dispute between the Sons of Belial and the people of the Law of One?

Greed — each wanted to rule the other and all the land. Each side wished to control the other. Greed and power corrupted them. It became a civil war, as they each wanted the power, and ultimate power corrupts, to use another of your sayings.

Did the people who followed the Law of One and the Sons of Belial live separately from each other?

Yes, of course, like the Jews and Arabs or the Sunnis and Shiites of today. They could not get along, although at one time they did. But as they sank into a quagmire of warring with each other, the families on each side lived separately from one another.

In reading other accounts about Atlantis, it seems the Law of One people were the good guys, but did both sides equally share the blame?¹

You could say the Law of One had more good people, but their leaders were as corrupt and power hungry as the leaders of the Sons of Belial.

Did the Law of One people generally believe that we are all related and should live by the golden rule whereas the Sons of Belial were materialistic and believed in satisfying their desires on all levels?

It was much more complex than that. Each side had their positive and negative points. One side was not all bad or all good. Don't forget that each side eventually destroyed the other. That should tell you neither side was perfect.

Were the Law of One people also known as the Sons of Light and the Sons of Belial known as the Sons of Darkness at some point?

You can imagine who came up with that description; the Law of One used it as a propaganda weapon. Naturally, the Sons of Belial did not view themselves that way.

Were there far right and left positions some people took regarding the Law of One or Sons of Belial?

There are always those who hold more extreme opinions than the mainstream, and they try to influence or convince people of their beliefs.

Theo, can you comment on the book by Jon Peniel,² given that he has transitioned?

---

1. An example of other accounts about the Law of One appears on http://lightworkers.org /channeling/165035/edgar-cayces-visions-atlantis-law-one-golden-age-atlantis. James Tyberonn channels information about the Law of One and Atlantis in this posting titled "Edgar Cayce's Visions of Atlantis: the Law of One & the Golden Age of Atlantis."
2. In *The Children of the Law of One & the Lost Teachings of Atlantis*, Jon Peniel wrote about his experiencers in a Buddhist monastery where he was given the teachings of the Atlantean Law of One during meditation.

Yes, he was able to receive in his meditations information about the teachings of the Law of One. Bear in mind that Atlantis was destroyed by greed on both sides. That does not mean that the information or the beliefs the people had were not good. So for those who wish to explore or revisit those beliefs, a few copies of his book are still available.

Did the Atlanteans have what we call churches or synagogues or temples as we do today?

They were similar but different. They are difficult to describe; it all depended on whether they were the Law of One or Sons of Belial. Each group had its own way of controlling the masses.

VARIANCES IN FAITH

Did they have what we call saints?

There were those who were admired more like diplomats rather than religious with the exception of the Law of One. But it was so ancient that it had little meaning for most of the Atlanteans. The leaders caused the wars.

Did the Atlanteans revere anyone as a savior?

No, not at all. They had their two main faiths: the Law of One and the Sons of Belial. They really had no one who stood out from the crowd, so to speak, and acted as a savior for either group.

Was the Law of One practiced both in Atlantis and Lemuria?

You are correct in thinking there was a connection, a similarity. Both societies had a religion that believed in one supreme being as compared to a number of beings.

Was there the equivalent of a Wiccan belief system during the time of Atlantis?

No, not the same as today's. They were a more scientific-oriented society. The Wiccan belief system known today grew out of the love of nature in Europe over the centuries.

Did the priests of Atlantis or the religious leaders of Lemuria live extraordinarily long lives — longer than, say, 200 years?

No, that was about the maximum they could extend their lives. It takes a lot of concentration, we'll call it, for this to occur. So please use this figure, as reports that they lived longer are erroneous. When you have people living normal lives of fifty to, let's say, seventy years at that time period, someone who lives three to four times longer would be held in awe. The priests that did that and held this information for just themselves had to balance these lives with quite short ones. Had they shared this information with the population, there would have been no balancing.

Were there spiritual advisors on both the Atlantean islands and the Lemurian continent who warned of the impending doom?

Some. Most were caught up in the hatred such that they encouraged the fighting for religious purposes, just as do some of your clergy in modern times. It was no different then. They realized too late what their actions had assisted in creating.

Did the concept of Poseidon originate on Atlantis or sometime later?

It originated in that period. Thus, Poseidia was named in his honor, you might say.

Did the Poseidon trident [see fig. 4.1] represent power, wisdom, and love — with love as the middle spike?

That's true. It was to remind everyone that all three are connected.

Were there different religions in Lemuria?

Yes, there were several, which was another reason for their demise. As you have seen in the past few hundred years how people interpret their connection with the Creator, so you can imagine how over 50,000 years there were all sorts of belief systems created — and their offshoots of offshoots.

Did their major religions believe in one god or multiple?

They believed in multiple gods.

Are there any religions in the world now that would resemble the religions then?

Their religious practices are difficult to compare to any today. Each country had its own religion, which naturally separated them from the other countries. Each had its own rituals. This has been consistent with the Adam man and woman from the beginning.

Did any compare to, say, the Hindu or Chinese religions of today?

Yes, the Shinto religion in Japan. It has evolved over the past 6,000 years or so to what it is today. However, over thousands of years, the religions evolved to a point where little would be recognizable.

Figure 4.1: The trident used by the Greek god Poseidon, brother of Zeus.

Did the Lemurians have some form of temples or churches?

This varied greatly from culture to culture. They were never so grandiose as these halls of worship are today. They were much more practical.

Were there one or more religions on Lemuria that worshipped the Earth, Moon, or Sun?

Most certainly, along with the stars, as there was a form of astrology. It was much easier to see the billions of stars at night with little lighting compared to today, so there was always the wonder of space, along with their ET contacts. Three of the countries had religions with similar beliefs. Some might have been Sun worshippers while the others were moon worshippers, and another would have been slightly similar to the Wiccan beliefs of worshipping the earth. Keep in mind that until they began warring, Lemuria was a very idealistic place to live in harmony. It took greedy leaders to lead them down a path of self-destruction.

Did the Lemurians meditate?

Most assuredly, they meditated.

On both the continents of Atlantis and Lemuria, after death were people generally cremated, or were they buried?

Almost 90 percent of the time they were cremated. The rituals were different on each continent and also varied according to religious beliefs.

Did both societies believe in ghosts?

Oh yes, these things were not different from modern times when some soul fragments would hang around. This was especially true during wartime.

Did they know about the Earth experiment?

Yes and no. Even then it was hard to explain to the average Atlantean or Lemurian, so only the religious leaders knew, and even those had differing opinions as to the concept and understanding. It was not something discussed around the dinner table.

What type of talismans did the Atlanteans and Lemurians have?

They were much different from today's talismans. They were based on the beliefs of those days and times and on the religions that were in place. Consequently, there were a wide variety of talismans, and some did not believe in talismans depending on the time. Some were based on the Sun and the Moon, on the deity they believed in, and so on.

Did the Atlanteans believe in reincarnation? What percentage would you say?

Yes, a number of them did. Again, there was a segment of the population that understood this but it was not the majority. The belief just did not fit into their belief systems at that time.

Many more people believed in reincarnation in the early days. They had much more contact with the ETs who explained to them how things are — over 80 percent. Then that percentage varied over thousands of years — higher in the formative years to much lower as they approached the time of wars and such.

What about the Lemurians?

Again, the same scenario; it is so much easier for people to think about going to a heaven or hell — those concepts were around even during those times — than to wrap their minds around multiple lives. But some understood. It has always been that way. In your lower earlier lives on Earth, you do not have the understanding and wisdom you gain through repeated journeys.

Did they all believe in life after death?

Some did.

Did the Atlanteans have similar psychic gifts as we do today?

Actually, they had about the same. They were more densely in the third dimension, so there was less than you see today. But there were people considered oracles who advised leaders and wealthy patrons at that time, just as it is done today. There were just fewer of them.

Was there a form of tarot?

Oh yes, there were cards that they used to help them read a person's future, not exactly the same but a similar style, if you will.

Did either the Atlantean or Lemurian societies interpret dreams?

Yes, much more so in the earlier years than as the final battles loomed on the horizon. They had people who were quite adept at interpreting dreams for others. There were those who could interpret their own dreams.

What tribes in Atlantis were connected with the crystal skulls, if any?

There was a connection even that far back, but most of them were carved and created later. Obviously, they were used in religious practices of the day.

Were there secret societies on Atlantis and Lemuria?

There were at times. They would come and go, as you might imagine, over thousands of years. People have always felt a need to be part of something, and a secret society would often fill the bill, we will say.

Do you think an understanding of soul contracts will bring everyone closer together?

Yes, absolutely. But this is pretty far in the future for the Explorer Race. Now you have too many younger souls in terms of Earth lives for this to happen overnight, you see.

Chapter 5

SCIENCE, TECHNOLOGY, AND HEALTH CARE

Gaia and Theo

Gaia, what did the Atlanteans mine besides crystals?

They had iron mines plus mines for a few other elements.

The Lemurians did not have crystal power, did they?

No, they utilized other energy sources, which did not include oil. That should give you a hint that they found another energy source.

What was orichalcum metal[1] composed of, its use, and its origin?

As was theorized by those who found the ingots in the sunken wreck, it is a mixture of gold and copper, forged in a manner not known today. This alloy, we will call it, had a number of uses in its day, and much study needs to be done on the ingots. It will take several years and many scientists, so I will not give away too much here. However, regarding its origin, it dates back to Atlantean times. They were more advanced than you are today in the forging of these alloys, as they found it almost indestructible. This knowledge was passed from father to son over many centuries before eventually being lost in time.

Was the orichalcum protection from the crystal death rays?

---

1. Orichalcum, or aurichalcum, is a metal mentioned in several ancient writings, including Plato's Critias dialogue, as being a precious metal from the days of Atlantis. Divers recently found some ingots of this mysterious metal on a sunken ship off the coast of Sicily. Sebastiano Tusa, Sicily's superintendent of the Sea Office, told *Discovery News* that nothing similar had ever been found. When analyzed, the ingots turned out to be an alloy made with 75–80 percent copper, 15–20 percent zinc, and small percentages of nickel, lead, and iron. (Rossella Lorenzi, "Atlantis' Legendary Metal Found in Shipwreck," *Discovery News*, Jan. 6, 2015, http://news.discovery.com/history/archaeology/atlantis-legendary-metal-found-in -shipwreck-150106.htm)

No, even this metal would melt if exposed to that energy. That should tell you how destructive those crystal rays were. So allow the scientists to study the chemical makeup of this alloy, as lasers or very high heat furnaces can break it down.

Did the Atlanteans have knowledge of the periodic tables?

Yes, but naturally they were not called that.

Did they have knowledge of calculus or sacred geometry?

Yes. They were much more advanced than you.

Quantum mathematics and quantum physics?

Here you have progressed further than their scientists.

Did the Atlantean scientists of any of the thousands of years of their existence have knowledge of quantum physics?

No. That is something that is a new development in modern times. Their studies were in a different direction.

Was their knowledge of subatomic particles superior to our knowledge today?

More on the same level.

Did the Atlanteans master antigravity?

No. They were able to fly but not really float in the air.

How fast were their aircraft?

Not nearly as fast as today's, closer to 200 to 300 mph.

What was the paper they used made from: trees, hemp, papyrus, or other plants?

Both used trees, as you do now, for their paper.

Did both the Lemurians and Atlanteans have ink pens?

They certainly had writing instruments, but not the same as yours today. They used different substances for their ink.

THE THINGS

Was it the Atlanteans who experimented with creating humanoids, other races, or extraterrestrials?

Ah, a nice question. These experiments dated back thousands of years, as the continents were just being populated. The extraterrestrial scientists experimented with different forms of life, and some experiments went better than others. They allowed these humanoids to live, and as mentioned earlier, the Nibiruans used them in mining. (This dates back much further than Atlantis.) The various humanoids were still around, and they were named Things by the Atlanteans, who used them for menial work. This went on for several thousand years before they developed enough to begin altering the genetic code of the humanoid creatures. Obviously some of the experiments just died out.

How was the continent of Atlantis originally populated?

As the rest of the continents were, by various alien worlds. The continent had its share of testing, so they coexisted with the Things.

• • •

Theo, did the ETs who conducted the body experiments know all the reasons behind what they were doing?

Yes, they did. Their spiritual advisors were under no restrictions, and the ET scientists who conducted the experiments were quite understanding of what they had to do. This work provided an opportunity to conduct what were for many of them first-time experiments on body creation, which is why you'll find a variety of skeletal remains. Of course, there was a lot of interference. Other less-high-minded people wanted to experiment too, which resulted in many different types of beings who did not last. Some of these experiments resulted in the Things spoken about by Mr. Cayce[2] — experiments gone wrong.

The ET scientists were not also creating animals, were they, including dinosaurs?

No, they were not. Creator loves variety, and the group souls for the animals were invited to provide animals for Earth, which they did.

Did the Atlanteans create clones, robots, or slaves from conquests to do all this work referenced in Edgar Cayce's writings?[3]

They were not clones or robots. They were humanoids but were the result of various experiments over a long period of time.

So the Things Edgar Cayce talked about were neither Cro-Magnons nor Neanderthals?

No, as I said before, they were the beings left over from countless genetic experiments left behind by those from the stars.

Were the Things in existence before the Adam man and woman were placed there?

Almost at the same time. There was much experimentation with body types then.

Did they only exist on the Atlantean continent?

There was experimentation with body types elsewhere on the planet, but not to the extreme found on Atlantis.

---

2.   Brad Steiger, *Atlantis Rising* (Dell Publishing, 1973) p. 63.
3.   Ibid.

Did any of the ET souls who conducted the experiments decide to take part in the Earth experiment, to be veiled, and so on?

Actually no, younger souls volunteered for the most part, knowing they would increase their vibrational level exponentially by taking part in the experiments.

As they experimented, they created what became known as the Things due to their mutant appearance, is that correct?

Quite so. They felt their job was to provide as many experimental subjects as possible, and that led to the Things.

They made them with quite limited brain capacity.

Yes, that's true. They wanted to study the bodies and gave them minimal brainpower.

You said previously that the Things were left over from previous experiments by ETs. Tyberonn channeled that the Aryans created them. Please explain.

Yes. That was incorrect yet correct. There were many experimental beings left over who lived on the continent of Atlantis for thousands of years. That's where the Aryans got the idea to create similar beings under controlled conditions to do their work. They created large numbers of those poor beings to do their dirty work — the menial tasks of that day and time — including the dangerous ones. It was slavery of the most heinous kind, and souls were trapped in these bodies with no feelings and no way to grow. The Aryans took on much karma for those actions. You can see where these ideas first originated that were later used again in Germany.

How long did this continue, hundreds or thousands of years?

This continued for thousands of years. They were quite entrenched in their usage of the Things.

Why didn't the ETs correct their mistakes instead of letting the Things suffer through thousands of years of abuse?

This was a sorry chapter of the experimentation that took place at that time. They were allowed to live, as those involved in that project thought they would not survive.

Did they become part of the Earth experiment?

Yes, they were allowed to become part of the experiment, as they needed to be balanced. There are many people alive today who had lives as Things in preparation for their first lives as humans.

Did the Things have a group soul, since I was told before that they were not ensouled until later?

They had no group soul, as they were the result of experiments.

Were they ensouled?

Eventually. The Atlanteans enslaved these subhumans. They had animal appendages and such, which is why they were not seen as humans. The images of beings with tails and nonhuman heads are correct.

Which were animal appendages — tails, horns, snouts, or what?

They had all those and more. You can also add multiple arms, legs, duplicate sets of organs, more than two eyes at times, extra ears, and multiple fingers and toes. Some of these humanoids were almost hideous in their appearances, which gave rise to the Atlanteans calling them Things. As they gained more scientific knowledge, they were able to start altering the genetic codes of these beings (after all, they were good test subjects) and slowly bring them to look like normal human beings. This took quite some time, and it was not completely accomplished when Atlantis sank to the bottom of the Atlantic Ocean.

How was it decided to ensoul them?

There was a number of souls who wanted to live on Earth, and it was decided that they could ensoul the Things to give them experiences and the people living here would feel compassionate enough to begin treatment of their mutations.

Wouldn't they carry over some deep-seated issues of being slaves and being disfigured?

Yes, but everyone must have lives as both the slave and the master. You must have one or more lives during which you are disfigured as part of your soul contract. Though they began with difficult lives, the experience also gave them great compassion for later lives. They tend to treat those who are different quite kindly, having been in their circumstances before, but on a conscious level, they don't remember.

Did the Atlanteans correct the genetic failures of the Things using DNA manipulations?

Yes. They were advanced enough by that time to correct these problems in that manner. They were still ahead of you in this department, but you are quickly catching up.

In those thousands of years before they felt compassion for the Things, did they assign personal names to them as we do to our pets?

Yes, the overall name used was Thing, and they also gave them individual names so that they could order them about.

Were the Things able to communicate and think for themselves? What were their IQs?

Yes, they were able to think, but their IQs were low, so that made it easy for the Adam man and woman to control them.

What was the life span of the Things?

Quite a number of years, which added to their misery.

Twice what our life span is today?

More than that. Three to four times your average life span today.

The Things were used for mining. What did they mine?

They were used for many jobs, and mining was one of them. They mined crystals, gold, and other precious metals as well as diamonds. Coal was not used at that time.

What did they feed the Things, and were they allowed to breed?

Keep in mind that they were slaves, and they were quite mistreated for thousands of years. The karma they built up was eventually balanced, as they had to have lives as slaves themselves. Some were allowed to breed, almost as you would have cattle or horses breed. It was procreation at its most basic level. It was a terrible situation.

The Things were never kept in zoos, were they?

No, but they were greatly mistreated and even kept in cages and similar confinement. At least the Atlanteans corrected this practice and helped the poor mutants later on through operations and such. This took place over a fairly long time, as there were many people who wished to keep them as slaves, but eventually this was forbidden.

Were the Things ever used as fighters or soldiers in any way?

They would have the things fight each other for their pleasure, just as humans have cockfighting and dog fighting today. This was a terrible time for the mutated creatures.

But they were never used as soldiers?

No, they were incapable of that. They were used as beasts of burden to carry equipment like pack animals.

Did the Things live everywhere, including farms, factories, and households?

Yes. There were thousands of the creatures.

Were they ever abandoned or left to fend for themselves?

Only if they were incapable of performing work. Most of the time, they were worked until they dropped dead.

EVERYDAY TECHNOLOGY

Did both the Atlanteans and Lemurians have a form of typewriter, or were there more computers?

Both had a form of typewriter, as these were the major forms of communication for the public. As I said before, computers were used mostly by the government and were not as sophisticated as today's models. You have come far in that area, which contributes self-empowerment. It helps you overcome cultural boundaries when you see how similar you are. So, yes, both societies used these as their major tool of communication.

Did both societies have concrete or cement?

Both societies had smooth roads. They both used a form of cement or concrete different from yours today.

Was the cement denser or sturdier than today's?

Yes, it was denser. Don't forget that the Atlanteans could use the crystal power as lasers to shape the stone blocks into any form and fit them together perfectly. The Lemurians were not quite so adept, but the uses were extensive even for them.

Did both societies have a form of rubber or plastic?

Yes, to both questions. Remember, these were old societies.

What did both societies use for paint?

Their paint was different, as they did not use oil in the same way. Here a discussion would get pretty technical, so let's leave this partially unanswered.

What about glass bottles?

Yes, both the Atlanteans and Lemurians had these since containers for liquid were a necessity for any civilization.

Did both societies use locks, and did they have safes?

Yes, both developed systems of locks, although the societies used different forms. As an example, the Atlantean lock system incorporated crystals. Both went long periods during which people did not use locks.

Did both the Atlanteans and Lemurians have a form of still cameras?

That's true, but they were powered quite differently from today's models. The Atlanteans used small crystals to power the cameras, and the Lemurians used different energy to power theirs.

Did everyone have clocks, or were sundials perhaps more in use?

Both used a form of clocks, just different from today's. And they got better and better as the years passed.

Did each society have refrigerators?

Yes, although not as fancy as is available today and they were powered differently.

Did both societies have something similar to the porcelain toilets of today?

Yes, but the designs varied widely, just as they do today. In Lemuria there were facilities where people would squat just as is prevalent in Asia today. The Atlanteans had more communal facilities since they had different beliefs about privacy.

But there were plumbing systems in place for both societies?

Oh yes, that is needed in every major developed society.

Were there dishwashers and clothes washers and dryers as we have today?

This varied widely in each society, as most things were done by hand back then. They had not developed these machines as far as you have today.

Did either the Atlanteans or Lemurians use a form of Morse code?

No, their development was such that they skipped that step. They had codes when they warred with each other, but that came later.

Was the air in both Atlantis and Lemuria clean, or was there pollution?

There was virtually no pollution, as the Atlanteans used crystal power and the Lemurians used another form of energy you have yet to discover. They did not burn coal and oil except in their very early years.

Was garbage handled about the same way it is today, or was there more recycling?

There was much less waste than you have now. They had landfills, but the people were not as wasteful as today.

I believe you mentioned before that the Atlanteans could control the weather. Could the Lemurians do the same?

Yes, both societies were well versed in controlling the weather, so it was not as violent as today. This was both good and bad, as there was no way Gaia could release all the negative energy that was building up. You will one day control the weather again, but by that time, the need for violent weather will have been greatly reduced, so the negativity will not build up. You are finding already that you can control the weather through benevolent verbal requests, as you practice, Tom. It's just that not enough people believe they can — to the point they doubt their own power.

LONGEVITY

Theo, how long was the average life span of the Atlanteans?

Well, they had the healing centers and people were not seduced into bad food choices as you are today.

Did they live 200 to 300 years?

No, that would have been more toward the beginning, not toward the latter part of Atlantean history. There was one exception to this: There was a portion of the priest class who had the ability to rejuvenate their bodies. This was both good and bad, as they stayed in power for longer periods. They lived to be much older on average; they could attain 200 to 300 years.

What was the average age men and women lived to in Atlantis?

They lived longer lives than you, as they did not have all the diseases you have today. Any medical problems were easily taken care of in their healing centers, which were more developed than any you have today, and they did not damage their bodies with foods that made them as overweight as your population does today. They ate much healthier foods at that time.

Therefore, the average age of men was around 90 years, and the average age of women was a little more. They had their 100 club, we will call it, but you are only now starting to have more people living longer lives.

What was the average age in Lemuria?

It was more in the same range as the Atlanteans but for different reasons. Life was much easier until the later stages than life today. There was less stress, but healing was different from the Atlanteans' techniques. They relied more on herbs. As war came to the Lemurians, their average lives declined as people were fighting and killing each other.

Were the left and right sides of the brain more connected for the Atlanteans than they are today for us?

Yes, at one time, they were, but this was modified over many thousands of years to where they were separated the same as your brains are today. This was by design from your souls, as it was seen as connecting you too much to your souls, and there had to be a disconnect for your learning. It was one of several adjustments to your body over many thousands of years.

MEDICAL TREATMENTS

Did they have doctors in Atlantis, or were there special types of healing centers?

They had both doctors and healing centers connected. Medical science is quite old. Only shamanism is older.

Did the healing centers use light — different colors — as I've been told or read?

Yes, exactly. The patient would go through a series of lights depending on what was wrong with the patient. These treatments could last for several hours, but the healing was very fast — much, much better than today's practice of drugs and operations. It was less intrusive then.

What source did the healing lights in Atlantis emanate from?

They emanated from the crystals, which intensified the light source into color spectrums, you see. Each spectrum has its own healing quality, which you will rediscover some day in the future.

Will scientists discover this, or will records be found about how to do this?

Actually both, as records will be found about Atlantis. But by then, much work will have been done in this field.

So the records will not be discovered soon?

Not soon — at least twenty to twenty-five years in the future.

How close to the Atlantean healing crystals are the ones who use the Vogel crystal healing unit?[4]

The Vogel healing unit is not very close. The crystals used during that time were enormous, and they have not been found. The Vogel unit does some good, but it is just not powerful enough to achieve the "almost instant" healing the original crystals achieved.

Was everyone treated in the healing centers, or were there people who were too poor to qualify?

No, you would call it a socialist form of government, as everyone could be treated in the healing centers.

Were the healing centers on Lemuria different from or similar to the Atlanteans'?

Quite different. They used a different energy but had similar results. I must point out again that you will rediscover these energies in the near future. And that includes free energy. You cannot imagine the great changes for your planet when a source of free energy is available, especially for those living in the most remote areas.

How did the Atlanteans and Lemurians handle eye problems?

They had glasses. The Atlanteans also had crystals that could be used as lasers, and the healing centers took care of many DNA problems. The Lemurians had their own healing centers, and they used different forms of correction.

Did the Atlanteans use birth control?

Yes, they had a sophisticated form of birth control you have not quite discovered yet. It did not involve the use of drugs, as is done today.

Did it involve the use of crystals?

---

4. Dr. Vogel (1917–1991) was a research scientist for IBM who received numerous patents for his inventions during the time he worked there. His study of quartz crystals led to the creation of a faceted crystal that is now known as the Vogel crystal and is used for light therapy.

That's correct. It was like a form of acupuncture but using crystals to shut off the ability of the female eggs to be fertilized.

Did both societies have pregnancy tests?

Yes, but different from today's. We'll let your scientists discover new ways to test for pregnancy.

I would think that our test would be the most modern and noninvasive.

Yes and no. Again, we hearken back to ancient times, but their advanced ways of determining pregnancy is still a little beyond what you are doing.

Back during the days of Atlantis, what else could be done besides healing with the crystals that is not seen today?

That would be quite a long list, as certainly their use of crystals is far beyond what they have discovered today. There was energy provided to run things by these crystals, and of course, there were healing centers you could go to that would heal sick people. They also had the ability to correct the Things' various imperfections and give them better lives. Crystals were also used in warfare; something that eventually became their downfall.

Did the Atlanteans and Lemurians experience depression and cancer, and if so, how was it treated?

As you know, these are two different subjects. Since they were typically human and not gods and goddesses, yes, they experienced depression for all sorts of reasons, just as people do today. But treatment was much better in the healing centers we have spoken about.

Cancer was almost unknown in these ancient worlds, as cancers in modern times are brought on by a combination of factors including diet, smoking, and so on. If it cropped up on occasion, it was treated in the healing centers. They are still ahead of you in terms of treatment of diseases. You must break free of Big Pharma, as you and others term it, and from doctors who run "pill mills."

What was the rate of suicides for both Lemuria and Atlantis?

It was much less, as they had the ability to completely change the mental health of an individual, so the percentile was quite low.

Was euthanasia allowed or even considered on either Atlantis or Lemuria?

As there was few diseases compared to today, euthanasia was almost unheard of on either continent. Yes, there were suicides, but that was a completely different condition. Both had their healing centers, so deaths were normal transitions.

Did anyone on Atlantis or Lemuria suffer addictions from any type of drugs?

There were a few — a small percentage of the population — not nearly the seemingly epidemic numbers addicted to drugs today.

Was there a percentage of the population of Atlantis and Lemuria who were alcoholics?

Yes, there were those who overindulged to the point of being incapacitated. The Atlanteans were able to treat these conditions using crystal power. The Lemurians used a different technique somewhat similar to what is used today to treat those with addictions.

Were there other addictions back in that time?

They discovered, over thousands of years during which each society was in existence, the types plants that would result in altered states if consumed.

This was for both societies?

That's true.

But it was a smaller percentage of the population?

That's so. Their addictions of choice were mostly alcohol-related.

Did people smoke in Atlantean and Lemurian times?

No, that is a modern addiction. Tobacco has other qualities not yet discovered, just as many other plants have undiscovered qualities and usages.

Were cocaine and heroin ever used on either continent?

Almost never. Those substances were considered highly addictive. They were products of continents not in the normal realm of either Atlantis or

Did they experience mental illnesses?

Oh yes. Those are soul contracts that can be fulfilled at any time on Earth as part of the bucket list, we will call it.

• • •

Gaia, did the Atlanteans use herbs, vitamins, medicines, or just various light therapies produced by crystals?

The Atlanteans definitely used a variety of herbs, as that was passed down from the early days. They were never very big on vitamins, though, preferring to obtain or maintain their health through herbs. They had a few medications, and their healing centers were designed for light therapy.

Were headbands used in Atlantis, and if so, when and for what use?

Yes, they were used for healing purposes. An electromagnetic headband aligned a person's magnetic field. Doing this allowed healing to take place, both mental and physical. You will have something similar in the coming years.

Were the doctors in Atlantis and Lemuria capable of handling accidents and times when they would have had to cut open someone's body?

Definitely, as these civilizations existed over thousands of years, so certainly both had doctors capable of handling any type of accident that might befall a patient. They had a form of emergency room different from yours today.

Were autopsies performed in both Atlantis and Lemuria?

Yes, they were. The cause of death was always of interest to the medical profession. They just used more advanced devices than today's. But you are moving in that direction.

Was energy medicine used in earlier times and is just now returning?

Yes, I know the term from its usage these days. Definitely there were herbs and supplements used much more extensively, let's say, on the continent of Lemuria at one time. This was actually carried on in Asia by those survivors who left Lemuria before the great destruction. Therefore, you have your Chinese, Japanese, and other medicines and herbs that have carried forth into modern times.

The West has just in the past few years begun to appreciate these methods. This surely includes the use of herbs to power the body. So there is a lineage there, although yours and their records do not show how old these practices are. Typically, the time listed for the use of any of these herbs or practices is the time someone thought to mention it in their writing. Even then, with all the local wars and such, records were destroyed.

Regarding Lemuria, it was a very loving environment for many thousands of years until the difference in beliefs between the countries caused division, and they were whipped up by the leaders who led them to warring and eventually destroying themselves. Their methods of dealing with crime were different from the Atlanteans', but still the number of people who had to be incarcerated was very low compared to modern times. People had more space; therefore they did not feel so hemmed in, shall we say. Food was plentiful, and drugs were not used as they are today. It was a much simpler time, almost idyllic compared to today until the leaders mucked it up.

How were dental problems handled in Atlantis and then Egypt after the migration?

They had some dental problems back then, just not the same as today, as their diets were healthier; therefore, they had fewer cavities. Don't forget that their society built themselves up over 50,000 years, so certainly they were ahead of you in some, if not a variety, of things, dental hygiene being one of them.

Therefore, in Atlantis, naturally their problems were similar to the ones in which people had teeth that grew crooked, so they were straightened in a variety of ways. Other dental problems were treated using crystals, as they had found any number of problems could be fixed using crystal power.

After you and your flock migrated to Egypt, you continued the dental hygiene and treatments to not only your people but to the Egyptian people you had found there when you migrated. The Egyptian people certainly needed assistance, so this kept you quite busy for a time treating a variety of medical and dental issues.

CRYSTAL POWER

Were crystals so plentiful on Atlantis that people started studying and using them in their early times?

Yes, you could say that, as there was much volcanic activity, along with a number of caverns where these crystals could be found in large numbers. The Atlanteans noticed early on there was great energy coming from the giant crystals, so natural curiosity led them to study this phenomenon, and eventually they came across using magnetics to generate power from them.

How long after the Adam man and woman were seeded on Atlantis did they begin using crystals?

Not immediately, but within a few hundred years. It was after they took care of their immediate needs of food, shelter, and clothing. Their ET uncles and aunts showed them the benefits of crystals and how they could use this free energy to heat their homes, give them light at night, and fend off the predators. The ETs never imagined them being used to war against each other thousands of years in the future. So the crystals were not used at the very beginning.

Were they all naturally occurring, or were any artificial or grown?

All were naturally occurring, as the crystals the Atlanteans used are millions of years old.

Did the Atlanteans pursue crystals the way we do oil exploration these days?

It was simpler during that time, as they had instruments that could identify locations of crystal deposits underground from quite a distance. Only in the early days did they need to be right on top of the crystals.

Were the crystals used on the continent of Atlantis found there or elsewhere, and were they similar to those found in Arkansas or Brazil?

Yes, first they were found on Atlantis, as they had huge deposits of these crystals and eventually large mines to carefully remove these large clusters from the ground. Then they became of a quality closer to those in Arkansas than those of Brazil. The Brazilian crystals, as you have noticed, do not have the energy of those found in Arkansas, simply due to the minerals present in their

Figure 5.1: Gypsum crystals in Naica Cave (Cave of the Crystals) in Chihuahua, Mexico. Note person for scale. Photo by Alexander Van Driessche.

formation. It takes a special type of crystal, so it will have the energy needed to be the energy source for thousands of vehicles of all types.

Were all the crystals used by the Atlanteans quartz?

Yes, that is quite correct. All were quartz, and many were mined in what is now the state of Arkansas, as they found huge deposits of crystals there. There are still large numbers of quartz crystals located there, even some extremely large ones well below the surface.

What was the size of the largest crystals used on Atlantis — perhaps twenty feet?

Yes, around that size, and some were even larger. Just look at the images of the crystal cave in Mexico to get an idea [see fig. 5.1].

Was their height at least twenty-five feet?

Quite so, even higher and thicker. The largest were thirty to forty feet high.

So a man could not put his arms around these crystals at their base and touch his hands?

No, it would be impossible, as these crystals were not thin.

Then were their giant crystals possibly as tall as fifty feet?

No, none were that huge. Stick with the figure of around twenty-five to thirty feet on average.

What was the size of the smallest crystals used?

Some of them — actually a large number — would fit in the palm of your hand.

Did the Atlanteans cut the crystals into certain geometric shapes to enhance their functions?

Yes. This was done more often with the smaller crystals, as they had to fit into certain instruments.

So the final shapes of these crystals varied quite a bit?

Yes, they did.

Are the Atlantean crystals still active in the Atlantic?

To a certain degree but not like they were during the Atlantean times. Most were shut down by brave souls who had the chance to escape but knew they had a duty to reduce their crystals or deactivate them.

Are there any still active in the Bermuda Triangle?

Yes, they are the cause of abnormalities in that area, leftovers from Atlantis.

Was there a protective bubble of energy over the continent of Atlantis?

No, what might be perceived that way was the bubble of energy formed by the giant crystals that everyone was able to tap into with various devices to run everything. It was not a protective bubble of energy per se.

Was the artificial moon simply used as a reflector, or did it actually have its own power supply, which gave the crystal power more coverage? Or did it simply aid in lengthening the effectiveness of the crystals?

It had its own power supply, we will call it, of crystal energy — the same energy the crystals beamed. But the crystals were aimed at the moon and bounced off it to lengthen the area of coverage. Again, we return to the crystals' limitations. It was a cheap energy source but limited in distance. The same could be said for electricity today, which is limited in its ability to send a current out over a long distance, much less across an ocean to another continent. Therefore, using crystals for power had many advantages. Today you shy away from exploring the use of crystals, as many people had previous lives in Atlantis and remember, on a soul level, the destruction caused by its use as a weapon.

Were the crystals in Atlantis automatically powered?

Not automatically, as they discovered a process in which they could raise the vibrational level of the crystals to the point that they ramped up.

Did they use some form of magnetics?

Exactly. By putting these crystals in a magnetic field, they were able to bring the power of the crystal to the point they would not need the boost from the magnetic field.

Then they were able to transfer this energy from one crystal to another?

They could direct this through magnetics anywhere, including other crystals so that the smaller crystals could receive this energy at a certain wavelength. For me to go further, you would need more scientific knowledge than you possess in this life.

Was the magnetic energy used to power the crystals natural or human-made?

The magnetic energy was human-made. I'm not allowed to go further than that in explanation to you.

Once the crystal had been powered up, was it sustained, or did it need to be recharged?

It needed to remain in the magnetic field, but it really was like free energy. It's difficult to explain, and we don't want to give away too much here. The larger the crystal, the longer it could stay powered, but certainly the magnetic fields kept them powered constantly, so there was no up and down. The smaller crystals had to be repowered more frequently.

Were the Atlanteans' crystals that were used for power clear or colored?

The main crystals used to power their cities and such were enormous with clear to somewhat opaque colors. Colored crystals were used in such places as their healing centers and as weapons. To go further would get us into territory where scientists need to experiment with the crystals and stones to see what powers they can generate. Crystals will never again be used as weapons, so scientists need to get past this deep-seated fear from their past lives as scientists on Atlantis.

Did the Atlanteans have to use line of sight to transmit their power from the crystals, or did the energy bend to the curvature of Earth?

Line of sight, except for the largest ones that had to boost across the ocean. They bent a little, and there was a limit on the strength of signal or beam of energy. There were limitations, which is why there were crystal stations, we will call them, in both Europe and North America. Again, we are getting into the scientific realm here, and this is something for your scientists to figure out.

How far apart were the crystal booster stations needed to power their flying machines and other transportation?

On the Atlantean continent, they were every twenty miles or so and sometimes closer than that. Larger booster stations were needed for travel, let's say, to what is now Europe and North Africa (Oz). When the Atlanteans left, they abandoned some of these booster stations all over the Mediterranean if it was too difficult to bring them back with them. They knew they could not be used by the locals. There are still a few in existence but buried under the sands of time.

Were they just set up singly or in groups?

For the most massive effect, they were set up in groups, and they were set up singly too. But in groups, their power was massive. The Atlanteans, through thousands of years, knew how to generate this crystal energy and to transmit it to wherever it was needed.

Were the energy beams emitted from the crystals visible or invisible, and could these energy beams be measured?

They were not visible, as you can imagine it would look like hundreds if not thousands of flashlights lighting the sky at night. It was more like a radio wave that could be tuned into, just as your radios are able to tune into radio station towers these days. It is the same concept — with the exception of when the beams were narrowed to use as lasers. That beam can be seen with the naked eye and can be measured.

Is it similar to the energy beam emitting from the Bosnian Pyramid of the Sun today, or is it different?

It was on a different wavelength. It was not shaped but broadcast, you might say, by the pyramid. Crystals set in a magnetic field, from very small ones to larger varieties, could receive the energy transmission.

You described the energy as being like a radio wave set to a certain frequency?

Yes, it was much more on the order of a radio wave and therein lie their limits. It was like a radio tower today broadcasting at a certain frequency. But there was a limit on the distance it could be received, just as there is a limit on radio stations today, because of the curvature of Earth.

Where does the electromagnetic energy in a crystal fall on the electromagnetic spectrum?

Here we get into science you have little knowledge of, and even if you did, we want scientists to learn this and have one of those "aha!" moments of discovery.

Was their knowledge of subatomic particles and waves superior to our knowledge today?

Yes, certainly in regard to crystals, but this question could be answered with a yes or no, depending on the actual subject. Again, this is a question for your scientists to mull over.

Did the Atlanteans have the equivalent of quantum physics we have today?

No, you are past them in that field.

Did the Sons of Belial and the Law of One both have priests and scientists?

Yes, both had people with a working knowledge of the crystals.

Did they use a form of phones to communicate with each other, and if so, was it powered by crystals?

Yes, they communicated using crystals, as the energy has many bandwidths. Therefore, their telephone system was similar, but as you guessed, it was powered by crystal power. Theirs was more of the over-the-air type system as compared to having a lot of wires strung from location to location as you do today. Their system was much more efficient than yours, although you've been making advances in this area and will continue to do so until you reach that same level and surpass it one day.

Then the Atlanteans used a triangulated power grid system called posers?

Yes, that was the name, and these grid systems were triangulated to hold and harness the power of the crystals.

What about ground and air vehicles? Did they have the equivalent of our cars and trucks in their modern era?

Definitely, and with different power trains than you have now, as they used crystals to power them. And of course, they were more involved in magnetics than you are today. It was a combination. There were ground vehicles for both public transport and private transport, but certainly not as many as you have today.

How early did the airships come into use in Atlantis?

It was very early, definitely 50,000 to 60,000 years ago. After all, you developed flying within the past 2,000 years, so it's not too large a stretch to understand that these people did the same.

What about the size of the aircraft?

They were similar in size to the ones you have today. But they were different shapes, of course. Their capacities were about the same.

Were the power supplies for the airships and vehicles in Atlantis internal or external?

They were external, receiving their power from central sources as if they were locked in on a signal. It's very hard to explain in the terms you use today, but these rays of energy were sent out and the ships tapped into them.

How far from the continent of Atlantis could the airships travel with this external power source?

They could fly over a thousand miles but certainly not around the world. It was like a tether that would hold them as they reached the farthest these ships could lock onto the power source.

You had said before that the Atlanteans were limited in their range of flying due to the crystals. I assume they never explored Asia?

No, they did not. It was too difficult, and the Atlanteans considered it just a vast land with tribal people.

Were the crystals utilized on the North American continent?

They had them on all three continents; however, there were larger ones in Atlantis and North America. Still they had auxiliary power sources in the Mediterranean too.

ANCIENT INFRASTRUCTURE AND FREE POWER

How were the homes, apartments, other buildings, and elevators powered — crystal power?

Of course, it was their source of power.

Was this free energy, or did the people have to pay for its use?

No, it was free. Each home had receptors of a sort, which brought in the crystal power generated by the huge crystals.

Then there were no cables or lines of any sort to each house or dwelling?

No, you would call it wireless power.

After the power was received in the dwelling, how was it used for cooking and to light the family room and so forth?

Devices were made very different from today's. Each device had a mini-receptor to power it.

Was the Atlanteans' trash disintegrated by crystal power?

Yes, it was simple to take the collected garbage to giant furnaces powered by crystals and disposed of there.

Did they have a similar infrastructure of water and sewage pipes as we have today?

The infrastructure was quite similar to today's.

I would think they had sewage disposal plants powered by crystal power?

For a fact, crystal power was used. Some things never change, and one of them is the need to dispose of waste.

Was their system of waste disposal better than the one we use today?

Not really, as crystal power was the only difference in the way the sewage disposal plants were operated.

You had previously stated that computers were mostly for governments. Was that because the average person felt they could access all of what they needed through crystals?

That's a correct assumption. The crystals would be considered almost as supercomputers today. They retained information from thousands of years.

WEATHER MANIPULATION

Gaia, did the Atlanteans know how to control the weather at that time, or is it only in recent times that we are starting to learn how weather can be controlled?

No, the Atlanteans were much more proficient than you are today in regard to weather control. They were able to use crystal power to knock down dangerous storms, which flowed across North America just as they do in present times. So they were able to have the beneficial rains and snows without the tornadic winds or hurricanes. Keep in mind they had thousands of years to work on controlling the weather.

You didn't need the tornadic winds to dissipate the negative energy being generated by the conflicts between the two groups?

Yes, I did, and that was another in a long list of reasons why Atlantis was destroyed. The negative energy built up over time as the conflicts grew worse and worse.

They still had weather, just not as violent?

That's quite correct. They were able to lessen the wind strength, and stop the rotation associated with tornadoes and hurricanes.

Were there survivors from both the First and Second Destructions who knew how to generate energy from the crystals, or did they have to be reintroduced each time?

No, there were plenty of people who understood their function, as it is fairly simple after they saw them in action one time. It was just that locating the crystals was a little difficult, especially when the Second Destruction occurred and much of the continent was lost. Still there were a few, and they discovered or searched out more large crystals. Don't forget they had the ability to locate the crystals and each of the islands had crystals of one size or another. There were enough to go around, you could say, and then there were the crystals from the Arkansas mines.

CONFLICT AND REGULATION

Could someone be imprisoned in a crystal?

No, not imprisoned per se, but they could be incapacitated very easily by a crystal. The crystals were used as sort of a stun gun at times. There are many uses of crystals, as they were studied quite heavily, and many experiments were tried to see what all a crystal could do. They were not like light sabers from *Star Wars*. These crystals had a lot of energy, though, that could be directed at people to incapacitate them. But no one was ever imprisoned inside one like the Superman movie you saw of the three criminals.

Were criminals imprisoned as they are today?

That's correct, but their prisons were perhaps much more humane than yours, as they had healing crystals to alter their mind patterns so that they could return to society and be useful citizens. Needless to say, they required many fewer prisons than you do today, as the population never swelled, except in war.

Wasn't there much violence between the two factions?

There was, but not too many committing this violence went to jail or prison.

Were there ever wars over who controlled the crystals, or were they so plentiful it did not matter?

That was one of the main contentions — who owned the crystals — and it came to war.

Did the crystal healing centers remain after both the First and Second Destructions and last until the end?

Yes, this was very important to them, so they were reestablished quickly. Also keep in mind there was not much left of a person who had been struck by one of the ray guns. Few lived.

How were the crystals in Atlantis deactivated before the Final Destruction?

At that time, much more was known about crystals and how they worked and the energy they emanated. Therefore, it was not that difficult to activate or deactivate a crystal. It was no hocus-pocus; it was the science of crystals. You as a human race have been avoiding exploring crystals, as deep down you fear using these again and destroying your civilization. I can assure you this will not ever happen again.

Did the Lemurians use crystals as the Atlanteans did?

No, they did not. They had a form of atomic power — not the same but similar. It was very destructive. Yes, that image I'm sending you now was a giant explosion. It tore the continent apart, although it wasn't supposed to.

As the Lemurians did not have atomic power, what type of energy did they have, since you also said they did not use crystals as the Atlanteans did?

Yes, they did use a form of magnetism. That's the best description I can give you, as you're not a scientist. Your scientists are not aware yet of the possibilities of using magnetics. This knowledge and the crystal knowledge have been kept from you until it was felt you would not use it to destroy yourselves again. Soon this knowledge will be allowed to be used.

CRYSTAL POWER THROUGHOUT THE UNIVERSE

How many pyramids existed in Atlantis, let's say, before the Second Destruction?

Yes, that would have been when the pyramids reached their maximum numbers. There were several thousand spread all over the continent, of all different sizes as this was a fairly large continent and the pyramids were of use not only by the religious sects but also to help beam the energy of the crystals.

Are there other societies in the universe that utilize crystal power?

Yes, a few societies do. Naturally, it all depends on whether there are crystals on the planets. Studies of other planets will take up many centuries of time. There are many planets that do not have crystals, but those that do, if the society is quite advanced, either use them now or have used them at some stage in their development in the past.

Why didn't the Atlanteans wish to travel in space?

Because they had their friends the ETs to offer assistance, and they did not want the expense involved to develop it with just crystal power. That power was cheap to produce while the other would tax their resources.

Did the Atlanteans settle Arkansas in order to mine the crystals, and are there giant crystals beneath the surface of Arkansas that are now being activated? If so, for what purpose?

Let's begin with the settlement. The Atlanteans had a presence there mining crystals, as you know they are quite plentiful, and yes, there were some giant crystals mined there. The Atlanteans had ways of detecting these crystals buried deep within the earth to pinpoint their location.

When the islands of Atlantis appeared to be about to sink, some of the crystals were reburied in Arkansas, and those are the ones being activated again to assist you in bridging over to the fifth focus. They are carefully controlled by your ET friends so as not to have the same results as last time. You can still use their beneficial vibrational level to raise your level up to the fifth focus.

What is the different "flavor" of the Arkansas crystals, and what could they do that the crystals mined on the Atlantean continent not do?

Here we get into an area where your scientists will one day discover and experiment with what these crystals can do and not do. Therefore, I can only give you a little information and remind you of conversations we've had before about crystals. The Arkansas crystals are good record keepers, as we have stated before. But you have yet to discover their capabilities, so this is where a scientist should experiment to see whether they can hold light or be put into a magnetic field to see what occurs.

Naturally, the larger the crystal, the more dramatic the results. There are scientists on Earth right now who worked with these crystals in Atlantean times, so if they can overcome a deep-seated fear of what occurred before when their power was misused, then you will unlock the secrets of the crystals.

Are the Arkansas crystals I presently have in my house large enough or the right type to power anything?

No, not really — perhaps a very small device of some sort. The crystals used at that time were monstrous in width and height. The crystals you have are mostly used as record keepers. They will someday be used to look at your work.

For what can the average person use these Arkansas crystals?

You surely notice the energy they are emanating. People can run their hands lightly above these crystals to feel the energy, just as you can feel the energy emanating from the red rocks of Sedona. You can touch them and receive energy. Large crystals can be put outside on your property. I would also recommend trips to the Arkansas commercial mines where they can see large crystals on display. People can find their own crystals.

Are there one or more crystals in Arkansas that were just activated?

Yes, that is a correct story. These were giant Atlantean crystals moved there, as was reported at the end of Atlantis. They were just activated to assist in your ascension to the next focus.

What about the huge ruby crystal reported in Brazil?

Again, it is used in activation.

Where is the ruby-red crystal located in Brazil?

It's located deep in the earth and not accessible to humans at this time. It was deemed prudent to keep it out of sight by humans, also on a soul level. It's the same with the crystals underground in Arkansas and Mount Shasta, plus a couple of other places.

Were rubies used as crystals in Atlantis?

Yes, they were, in conjunction with the giant crystals.

Is there a giant ruby crystal in the Bermuda Triangle?

No, that information is incorrect.

Is there any benefit in wearing rubies today?

There are some benefits. There are books, as we have mentioned before, describing the benefits of each stone.

Edgar Cayce, in his channeling of information about Atlantis, talked several times about the "night side of life." Was he referring to atomic power or to some other energy?[5]

Ah, that was a reference to the energy that was being generated by the use of the crystals. It was not atomic power — but just as destructive in the end,

---

5.   A.R.E. website, Reading 2896-1, http://are-cayce.org/ecreadings/Default.aspx.

as it broke up cellular structures and basically disintegrated the molecules and such in both living organisms and even the ground they walked on. That's why even today there is a great inborn fear felt of all those souls who lived during those times when you could destroy yourselves the same way. This is why you have stayed away from understanding the power of crystals.

Will we regain knowledge of crystal power to be used in a benevolent manner?

Yes, this knowledge will be slowly filtered down, but there will be other energies, which will be even better for your purposes. But certainly you are recovering your knowledge of how crystals served you in the past.

*   *   *

TUNNELS

Theo, did the Atlanteans have giant tunnels beneath the earth?

Yes, that is correct.

How deep were the tunnels under Atlantis that were used to travel to other continents?

Quite deep, about two to three miles. They had to be below normal earth movements but not so deep as to make it impractical to get to the starting point of these tunnels.

How did the Atlanteans construct the tunnels they used, and what form of transportation was used in the tunnels?

Again, crystal power was used in the construction of the tunnels.

How many miles did they run?

Typically ten miles or more, the longest connecting to Europe and North America. They were not welcomed in Oz, so any tunnels found there would have been destroyed.

So over 1,000 miles?

Far and wide, thousands of miles. They used the crystalline energy to power the construction, and they took advantage of the huge chasms beneath the earth's surface, which made it easier to establish their power sources.

Were the tunnels used as much as air travel?

Actually, a little bit more, as it was quite easy, and they could go farther than the aircraft, which were tethered to their energy source on the ground. Under the ground, crystals could be moved along the routes and act as energy stations for the continued movement of underground vehicles.

Who dug the miles-long tunnels in Central and South America?

North America too, as there are tunnels there. Obviously, these are ancient tunnels constructed with the knowledge that they would be used in the future for safe travel between many locations, as it was known they would be needed in the future. That should tell you some things just by my statements. First, they were constructed thousands of years ago. Who had that kind of knowledge and ability to see the future? It was your friendly ETs, of course.

We have discussed how quickly tunnels can be constructed by liquefying the earth. You could use the phrase "slicing through soft butter." The devices used to make the tunnels were beyond human knowledge at that time. Several miles of tunnels could be constructed in just one day, as there are hundreds of miles of tunnels yet to be found, much less the many tunnels yet to be explored.

Are the tunnels over 10,000 years old?

Yes, double that figure and even add more to it. These were done early on knowing they would be needed to protect the people indigenous to the area from such interlopers as the Atlanteans. They were not made by the Atlanteans but rather because of them.

Then would they be 30,000 or more years old?

No, about 20,000 to 25,000 years in age.

Did the Lemurians have tunnels too?

Yes, a few. But not nearly to the extent the Atlanteans did. Their source of free energy required much more complex machinery than the Atlanteans with their crystal power in order to create the tunnels. So they were much shorter in length. They did not have tunnels to, for example, what is now Japan or the coast of what is now Asia.

Were there tunnels on the other continents, such as Asia, Europe, Australia, and Oz? Were they constructed by ETs?

Yes, there are some extensive tunnels still in existence in the interior of all those continents and also in South America. They were constructed so that the ETs could travel long distances without being seen by humans. This certainly became a necessity after the Earth Directive came about. They wanted to be able to keep an eye out and to do readings and such on humans from hidden locations.

Were these tunnels large enough for scout craft to fly through, or did they use some other mode of transportation in the tunnels themselves?

They were constructed just wide enough for the smaller scout craft. If the craft was a little too large for the tunnel, they could temporarily enlarge the size of the tunnels for passage, closing them up behind them as they passed. This is easy work for societies as advanced technologically as these ETs were with millions — and in some cases billions — of years of existence.

Did the locals use the tunnels at times, such as the Aborigines in Australia?

Yes, they felt responsible to guard the entrances and would use them if their lives were threatened. They have those stories in their verbal history.

Chapter 6

THE GOVERNMENT AND THE MILITARY

Theo and Gaia

Theo, were the citizens of both continents very patriotic?

That's true. This is still a lesson many people are learning today: how their governments and the opposition twist facts and invent stories to disparage their opponents and create hatred in the citizens. Then it's easy enough to have them kill each other.

This is a lesson that needs to be learned by people in modern times. For example, just go back to any of the wars the United States engaged in to see how the press was manipulated so that men and women would volunteer for military service in order to have them fight for some made-up purpose. In reality, the reasons were simply that their leaders were power hungry, or the people who controlled them wished to profit from the wars.

Were there some sort of national flags in both Lemuria and Atlantis?

Oh yes, banners, flags, and other forms of identification, as that is part of separating people.

Did the citizens of both continents have some form of passports or identification documents?

They did, depending on the time. As both continents existed for thousands of years, their governments used various forms of identification.

Did either the Atlanteans or Lemurians have the high-tech capability to use nano chips for identification instead of papers and passports?

No, this is an invention of modern times. As stated before, they had papers, seals, and stamps to identify their citizens.

Did both the Atlanteans and Lemurians have police forces?

Yes, these were necessary, but the police had much fewer crimes to investigate. As we mentioned before, there were family fights to break up, just as there are today. Humans are humans, and they had the capacity for violence just as there is today. They were less stressed, so there was much less violence.

Did the police carry the equivalent of guns?

They did have devices on both continents that could stun someone. These were lower-power devices and were not meant to kill. This changed as each society had more and more conflicts.

Did the police have cars, or was it mostly foot patrols and perhaps bicycles?

All three were used, but there were many more foot patrols. The more rural districts needed transportation to cover wider areas.

What was the crime rate like?

Here we return to times that existed for thousands of year. The crime rates naturally increased toward the end. It was much less during many thousands of years. Bear in mind that there were periods when the Second Destruction occurred that people were simply surviving after all the coastal towns and cities all over the world were wiped out. The people were terrified not knowing what had happened, and many worried when it might occur again. There was migration away from the coasts for those who survived. Gradually, over several generations, the memory faded to a simple story, and people returned to the coasts for commerce and fishing.

Were there courts of law — justice?

Yes, there has always been a need to handle disputes between people. As you have seen in your history, sometimes justice was meted out by a king, an appointed governor of some sort, and at other times by people appointed to judge. There were forms of juries ranging all the way from, let's say, three people to over a dozen. So many forms of justice appeared during thousands of years. Some were quite good and some were very bad, depending on the time period.

Was there a wide difference in court systems between Atlantis and Lemuria?

Yes, and there were wide differences between countries or factions. Some were single judges, some were three or more judges, some had a jury system, and others were ruled by monarchies. Then there were also courts ruled by the military of the time. Any form of court system in existence today, or in your history, was used at one time or another on both continents.

Was the system more male-oriented?

Almost exclusively, as women in both societies were expected to do chores at home and not have an active work life, except as the equivalent of secretaries, food servers, and such.

For murderers on both continents, what was the punishment?

They did not believe in the death penalty until the very end of their conflicts. They could change the DNA to rid the people of any thoughts of doing harm to others.

How different were prisons compared to now?

The differences were almost night and day. They were much more interested in rehabilitation, including treatments for antisocial behavior, compared to today when humans are caged like animals. They would alter their DNA so that they could be returned to society. You still have a long way to go in this area. As wars became more numerous, spies and other war criminals were sent to prison when they were caught.

Were the prisons in the various Lemurian countries similar to the Atlantean prisons?

Yes and no. Yes, for a period of time, but there were developments to change the personalities of the criminals, so few prisons were in operation at the time they destroyed themselves. You will learn in the not-too-distant future how to alter the personalities and traits of people who are a menace to society. It is coming and not too far in the future. First there will be drugs and then complete alteration of the DNA.

Did the Atlanteans and Lemurians have embassies in each other's countries?

No, the Atlanteans were the closest to being able to do that, but the crystal power did not allow them to venture too far without booster stations being built. There was just a little contact by those who would meet as ships sailed, but always keep in mind even the Atlantean ships were limited by their use of crystal power. So to answer the question, no, there was almost no contact.

Were there kings and queens in either or both Atlantis and Lemuria?

Of course, Atlantis, during its 60,000-year history, went through a time when there were kings and queens, but they slowly disappeared over time. Lemuria had several countries on that continent. So, yes, there were those who were considered royalty at one point. That practice died out and was replaced with antagonistic rulers.

Were the officials in government appointed or elected?

They used both. There was a wide variety of election processes. Remember, these societies began 60,000 years ago and lasted 50,000 years. Your records today only go back 6,000 to 8,000 years with the early records being quite inaccurate. So you could say they had in excess of 40,000 more years of history than your modern civilization today. That is one of the most difficult things to wrap your mind around. It's hard for you to imagine a civilization that lasted that long with virtually no records of its existence.

Were women allowed to vote during the democratic times?

This really varied over thousands of years. Just look at the many changes that have occurred in your modern history, and you will have some idea how difficult it is when you multiply the modern-time years by a factor of five, let's say. So to partially answer your question, they were allowed to vote at times but were subjected to the will of whoever was in charge. There is not a simple answer, as life ebbed and flowed over the ages.

Could it be said that, on average, the people of the United States were on one side of the Atlantean conflict and the people of Russia on the other side?

An interesting premise, but no. There was a mixture of both sides in each country. Generally, people who had lives on Atlantis had more than one life, which means they would have balanced by having lives on both sides.

Did the Atlanteans or Lemurians have death penalties?

In the later stages of the conflict between the two sides, there were death penalties for spying, but not for violence caused by a DNA trait. Those were still treated in the healing centers. The Lemurians used other methods. Both had death sentences for spies.

Is there any truth to the story of President Obama having been a leader during the days of Atlantis?

Yes, there is some truth to that, as those were lives in preparation for this one.

Was he a leader for the Law of One, the Sons of Belial, or both?

He was a leader for both, as he needed to see both sides of a conflict. It gave his soul perspective.

THE MILITARY

Theo, did Atlantis have a military — an Army, Navy, and Air Force? If so, how did it vary over 57,000 years?

Yes, it had its military, which grew, then contracted, slightly similar to militaries of this day and age according to whether they were expanding their empire. They subjugated much of the Mediterranean area and tried to subjugate Oz, but the attempt proved too costly in lives, as the tribesmen were fierce fighters even though they did not have the weapons the Atlanteans had. You see, this played out in modern times when such nationalities as, say, the Vietnamese waged a guerrilla war that went on for years until first the French and then the United States withdrew. That was the case in Oz.

The Mediterranean was different. The Atlanteans were fairly successful in expanding into this area. It lasted hundreds of years before they had to withdraw, as the political factions were at each other's throats.

Then there was an Army, Navy, and Air Force?

Yes, somewhat similar to today's, but with much different weaponry, as they did not use gunpowder as is used in modern times. They naturally had crystal power, which as their history shows, was much more dangerous and destructive than gunpowder.

Would you say their military developed and peaked at the First Destruction or sometime before the Second Destruction?

More the latter, as the First Destruction definitely reduced the number of military due to the tsunamis and the rising ocean levels, which wiped out many coastal towns, villages, and cities. Of course, this was worldwide. It took many years to recover from that, but over several hundreds of years, they did.

How many men and women were in the Atlantean military before the Second Destruction, and how many were in the military before the Third Destruction?

About 10 percent of the population was in the military before the Second Destruction, and then before the Third Destruction, it was over 50 percent, as they were at each other's throats. The population was much lower in the remaining islands after the Second Destruction, so the numbers were not greater, just the percentage.

After the Second Destruction, did both the Law of One and Sons of Belial have their own separate Army, Navy, and Air Force?

That's correct. Many eventually died from these conflicts, culminating with everyone left on the islands going down with the ship. It was as bad as you can possibly imagine — each side at the other's throat.

How long did the Law of One and the Sons of Belial war? Was it for the full 18,000 years between the Second and Third Destructions?

No, people were in survival mode for quite a long time. Then slowly but surely their beliefs collided. Their warring only became truly destructive after those crystal ray guns were invented.

How many years did they war — 1,000, 5,000, or over 10,000 years?

It did not become seriously nasty and destructive until the last 1,000 years.

Look at the Sunnis and Shiites today. Their hatred goes back several thousand years. It was the same with the two Atlantean warring factions. They despised each other for several thousand years, but the clashes were small compared to the end.

Did their soldiers suffer PTSD after returning from wars?

Yes, much more toward the end for both conflicts as the fighting ratcheted up and men were on the front lines for months. The Atlanteans handled it with their healing centers, and so did the Lemurians — but differently. One of your accomplishments as a human race in the future will be to learn how to treat mental breakdowns and other diseases associated with great stress.

Did the soldiers' wives receive pensions for those who died in war?

Yes, but not as much as today. They were forced to quickly remarry or move in with their relatives.

Did distinct military units wear differently colored uniforms?

Yes, there was a differentiation to make the various services unique in the case of Atlantis. Lemuria had different countries, so they used a variety of colors too.

Did both have camouflage to mask themselves?

Yes, they did.

THE ARMED FORCES OF ATLANTIS AND LEMURIA

Did they have a volunteer military, or was it mandatory?

Over 57,000 years it varied according to the risk to their nation and whether the military was used to widen their influence or were pulled back. During most of their history, they had sufficient volunteers, but there were times when they made military service mandatory.

Did the Atlanteans have the equivalent of military academies?

Yes, of course. They had to train their officers just as you do in modern times.

How many people were in uniform? Was it over 5 million?

No, but close to that number, counting all the services. This was a good percentage of the total population.

Were women included in the military?

Yes, but not in combat roles. It was similar to what it has been up until recently.

What was the percentage of women in uniform?

Approximately 15 to 18 percent. These included the military nurses, drivers, cooks, secretaries, and so on, very similar to today's armed forces.

Were the mutant Things used in the military?

No, they were for simple duties, not complex ones. Don't forget, they were eventually helped and either allowed to die out with no reproduction or received medical treatment to correct their mutations. These acts were performed to balance past lives during which they mistreated the mutants.

At the height of their power, how many military aircraft did the Atlanteans have?

More than half a million, which included all types of aircraft, from military transports to the equivalent of your fighter jets today.

Did the Atlantean Army also use the equivalent of ray guns?

In a way, yes they did. They would recharge them. If they were out in the field and there were no normal rechargers available, they would have backup portable crystal generators. Normally, that was not necessary. But as you noted, their weapons were not like the combustible guns of today. They were of a completely different design.

I assume their larger weapons were of a similar nature?

That's correct. They could destroy what would be the equivalent of a tank today.

Did the Atlanteans have shields to protect them against the ray guns?

It was almost impossible to protect someone from one of their ray guns.

Did the Atlanteans have any sort of bombs or missiles?

Yes, quite a few, but they were different from those you have today, as they did not use gunpowder. Still, they were quite lethal.

Did they use some sort of magnetics too?

That's correct. You might say a reverse charge.

What about the Atlantean Air Force?

Yes, again their weaponry was crystal-based and required recharging after each mission. It brought terror to those they used it against. Your *War of the Worlds*[1] movie was based more on those aircraft than the aliens, as those who created the movie had previous lives in which they saw the craft in action.

Were the Atlanteans often visited by extraterrestrials?

They were visited many times. That was the major reason the Atlanteans

---

1. H. G. Wells and Barré Lyndon, *War of the Worlds*, directed by Bryon Haskin (Los Angeles, CA: Paramount Pictures, 1953).

adopted the saucer shape for their aircraft. They were copying what they had seen in the skies. They were able to carry a fairly large number of people inside the craft, depending on use.

Did the Atlanteans ever achieve space travel themselves?

No, not in the way you mean — more like suborbital, as they had to rely on those external power sources, which had their limits.

Is it true that some or all of the Atlantean aircraft were powered by "personal vril" (a controllable form of energy)?

That is not correct. We have covered recently that you are now moving toward being able to control such things as a camera with your mind, and people with disabilities are learning how to use their minds to perform certain functions. This is what the people of Atlantis learned over several thousand years. But to say they actually powered the vehicle is a misnomer. It was only the controls.

I'm sure these vehicles had different appearances over the years. Could you give me an idea of what they looked like at the beginning and then later on? Did they have the appearance of a dirigible and then later a saucer-type craft?

No, from the beginning, they tried to imitate the ET craft that, as you recall, had full license to come and go as they wished until the Earth Directive was instituted. Therefore, they had round shapes overall.

Did any of them have the appearance of the alien spaceships in the War of the Worlds movie you referred to above?

No, not exactly, as these spaceships in the movie were curved downward and the Atlantean aircraft were more round.

Did any of the Atlantean ships look like saucers as we see in photos these days?

Yes, a few, but not many.

Were the ships made out of metal, wood, or some type of plastic?

They were metal in construction.

None of them had wings?

Only those that were similar to the gliders you have today as, after all, they, like you, noticed how birds fly. But it's as if they skipped a step thanks to the intervention of the ETs. You, in modern times, are approaching the time when you will use saucer-shaped craft.

How many crewmembers were on the Atlantean fighter craft?

They only needed two. One was the pilot, and the other controlled the weapons, similar to today in which the copilots are in charge of weapons.

Were the laser guns contained in the interior of the craft or on the exterior?

They were located in the interior. They had thousands of years to perfect their placement.

Did the Atlanteans have parachutes?

Quite so. They wished to survive if one of their craft was in trouble. They did not use them for sport.

Did all the countries on the Lemurian continent have an Army, a Navy, and an Air Force?

Yes, they did. It was necessary with so much conflict between them.

Was military service in Lemuria on a volunteer basis or required?

Both — throughout the 50,000 years of their existence. Remember that Lemurians were kind and gentle people for centuries before they sank into war and conflict. That changed drastically in the years leading up to the final battle. It started slowly and then became worse and worse. Many of the gentle people were led to abandon Lemuria and move to quieter surroundings on the mainland and even Japan.

More people on the mainland survived, but if they lived on the coast, they perished too. They could not avoid the impending disaster even though they believed they were safe. They had no idea that the whole continent would sink into the ocean.

Were women in the military in Lemuria?

Yes, especially toward the end when a large percentage of the countries were conscripted to manage the front lines — their borders with the other countries. But the percentage of women remained low, no more than 20 percent. Again, they were almost exclusively in noncombat roles.

WEAPONRY

What sort of weapons did their armies use?

There were not ray guns or rifles as there are in modern times. You could almost describe them as bolts of lightning, as they had that appearance. But these weapons used a different energy. They are difficult to describe, as you have not rediscovered them yet in this time. It will soon become available to you again, however, this time for peaceful purposes.

Did their guns somehow use magnetics?

A close approximation of how the energy was generated. Let's leave it at that, as we could get into scientific areas in which someone will reinvent this energy or learn how to harness it in the near future. Yes, these guns, we will call them, were quite mobile.

Were the aircraft on Lemuria saucer-shaped or some other shape?

The same as Atlantis, as they copied what they saw in the skies in their earlier days when being constantly visited by the ETs.

Did both the Atlanteans and Lemurians have a form of radar and sonar?

Yes, but differently powered.

Did both have tanks and submarines?

Yes, both developed these over time, nothing new there.

Was a wide array of warships used?

Not as much as today. Both had their warships, and both tried to utilize them as time passed.

Were their naval ships mostly the same or quite different from today's ships?

The sizes of the ships ranged from the tiny to as large as today's naval vessels. After all, the creators of today's naval ships, at least a number of them, created warships during Atlantean times.

Were the submersible vessels for war or just explorations or tourists?

That's an interesting question. They had a variety of uses, but the major reason for them was war. They did not have contact with any undersea races or dwellers. Those were at depths that they could not achieve. That was a built-in safety factor for those who would be considered water beings.

What was the fastest speed of boats back then?

There were limits due to the use of the two different energies. Therefore, most boats were limited to 30 miles per hour, give or take a few miles. Things were slower paced compared to today.

How large were the crews of the warships of Atlantis?

No more than, say, one hundred for the very largest ships.

How large were they for the different countries of Lemuria?

More on the same order, but a little less, a maximum of, let's say, eighty-five.

Were all countries on Lemuria at war with each other?

Naturally, there were alliances, so there were combinations of the countries that sided with each other.

When both the Atlanteans and Lemurians were at war, were there war correspondents and journalists who reported from the front lines?

Yes, but they were controlled by whatever government saw fit to allow them access.

Was Atlantis ever at war with the Lemurian people?

No, actually they were not. They had internal civil wars between the two groups. Their relations with other peoples of the world were fairly quiet. They got along with others better than among themselves.

HAPPENINGS OUTSIDE OF ATLANTIS AND LEMURIA

How did they influence the civilizations they came in contact with? Did they establish any trade agreements, or were they just in a conquering mode of operation?

Most of the civilizations they contacted were far behind them in development, so they treated them, or attempted to treat them, like the Europeans did when they started settling North America and encountered the Native Americans. They met resistance at times, and there were battles. Sometimes they would trade basic goods for what they needed. The people of Oz were fierce warriors and made up for their lack of firepower with ferociousness. The Atlanteans learned the hard way and backed off. Other groups in the Mediterranean area fought guerrilla campaigns, which eventually pushed the Atlanteans back. There was the Mediterranean Sea at that time, just at a lower level than today.

So during the height of the Atlantean civilization, as well as Lemuria, were other societies on Earth as technologically advanced?

For the most part, they were agricultural and they hunted, but several countries had cities, so there was some sophistication there. No one had the crystal power, and gunpowder had not been invented yet, so they were "easy pickings" to be conquered, even though some had sophisticated societies and scholars.

How old are the paintings (purported to be the oldest in the world) discovered in the Spanish cave?[2]

They date back as far as the scientists presume or have calculated — over 40,000 years. Your comment that there were simple folk populating this region is correct. When the Atlanteans came, it was as if they were dealing with African tribesmen but of a different color and race. They left them alone for the most part. They simply explored the area.

Did the Atlanteans settle the island of Crete, and if so, were their descendants Minoans?

No, they did not settle this area. Those from the North settled it.

---

2. The Cueva de El Castillo, or the Cave of the Castle, is an archaeological site in the complex of the Caves of Monte Castillo located in Puente Viesgo in Cantabria, Spain. The oldest of the paintings is a red sphere from a cave called El Castillo. There are over 150 figures already catalogued.

Did the Atlanteans extend their empire as far as the Eastern shores of the Mediterranean?

Yes, they did, and even then it was sparsely populated and much more tribal in nature. They saw little to cause them to establish more than an outpost in the region. It was a little more verdant than today but not something to write home about.

What about Greece and that region?

The Atlanteans were a little more forceful with the Greeks. Yet the Greeks were more resistant than some of the other societies in the Mediterranean. They could not win direct battles (they found out the hard way), so they would use sneak attacks — guerrilla style, you might say — which proved to be the most successful for them. And it was the same in Italy where they also had to combat the steep terrain.

What were the reasons the Atlanteans warred with the people who lived in Greece and Italy at that time?

The Atlanteans wanted certain locations as satellite cities, and there was resistance by those who inhabited the area.

Were these simple peasant folk? Were they able to organize, or did they have weapons to fight the Atlanteans?

They were not sophisticated but clever. You would call them guerrilla fighters today.

What actions did the Atlanteans take along what is now called the French Riviera? How populated was it at that time?

It was sparsely populated with fishing villages and farms along the coast. There was little resistance to the Atlanteans with their superior firepower, so they did not resist as much as the Italian and Greek populations.

So Sainte Marguerite Island near Cannes, which I've visited, and its neighboring island Saint Honorat were once connected to the mainland?

You're correct. They made up the coastline, you see. That is a major reason why old ruins can be found there.

The Atlanteans could be found up to Scandinavia. What were the results there?

There was reason for the Atlanteans to adopt the name Aryan as the name of their island later. It was because the Scandinavian people were fierce fighters, and woe is the Atlantean who encountered one of the large men without his ray gun! It was better to run the other direction, given the chance.

How populated was the Scandinavian area at that time?

Their population had swelled to 40,000 before the Second Destruction. Only those who lived in the interior survived.

More than 40,000?

Yes, more than 40,000 but less than 50,000.

One more question about the world population. You said millions were killed in the Second Destruction, yet places like Scandinavia had populations of less than 50,000 people. Am I not receiving this correctly? Where were these millions located?

It would seem that there were limits, but when you consider the hundreds of thousands of miles of shoreline around the world, you can perhaps understand how many people gravitated to the shores of all the oceans. It all added up, I assure you.

• • •

THE OZ WARRIORS

Gaia, were the Atlanteans ever at war with a race of Amazon women in Libya, and is there any truth to the story about the race of women emigrating from there through Egypt to the Black Sea?

No, that story is not true. When the Atlanteans attacked and conquered the towns and cities in the Mediterranean area, there definitely were women who fought alongside the men, but they were no match for the Atlantean weapons, as they did not have the huge numbers of warriors like the areas farther to the South. That's how the Atlanteans were defeated in the other areas where there were thousands of warriors who overcame them. This was not the case on the coast of the Mediterranean, which as you know was a much smaller sea then. Therefore to summarize, there was not a race of Amazonian women living in what is now Libya.

Speaking of the whole continent of Oz, was there any commerce with them at one time, or were there always hostilities between the two because the Atlanteans wished to subjugate them?

There was some commerce for such things as fruits and vegetables. There was a port, which is no longer in existence due to the ocean rising. Atlantean ships would come to port and purchase these commodities.

What did they use for payment?

As you guessed, mostly gold and silver. They did not give them crystals, as even then they knew their power, and their government prevented them from offering crystals as payment.

Did crystals power the ships, or were they sailing ships?

They were mostly sailing ships. The distance back to their homeport was short, and they did not want the Oz inhabitants to become too curious as to what they used to power their ships. This all occurred before the First Destruction and before the Atlanteans decided that they wanted to conquer Oz. Relations went south when the Atlanteans showed up with warships and several thousand soldiers. They thought they would be pushovers like the Mediterranean towns and villages, but then there was the counterattack by thousands of Oz warriors, wiping out the invading force even though they had ray guns. They were no match for the massive numbers of Oz warriors that threw themselves at them wave after wave.

Hundreds of thousands of people, as we have discussed before, had lives during those several hundred years, and there were plenty of people who met their ends in fierce fighting with the warriors of Oz. Even though they had superior weapons — those crystal-powered ray guns — they were still no match for the hundreds of Oz warriors who swarmed their armies and took no prisoners. This went on for several centuries as first one ruler and then the next would think they had a way to defeat these warriors. Eventually they decided it was not worth the effort and left them alone.

Was I killed in a battle with the Oz warriors in one or more of my Atlantean lives?

Oh yes, more than once. This war or attempt to conquer went on for several hundred years.

How many Atlanteans were killed in a typical battle with the warriors of Oz, and why couldn't they use their aircraft?

They had their aircraft, but they were not as sophisticated as today's and were limited to daytime operations. The Oz warriors took advantage of this and attacked. A typical battle would involve over 1,000 Atlanteans, as they thought those numbers large enough, but the Oz warriors would just double or triple that number and overpower the Atlantean soldiers even though they had those ray guns.

• • •

ATLANTEAN COLONIZATION

Theo, what's the origin of the Basques?[3]

These are a very ancient people who have been around since before Atlantis sank into the sea. They were simple folk at one time until the Atlanteans began to explore that area. They were a mixture of simple local tribes before the Atlanteans came and started to civilize them.

It just developed from there, although they remained a close-knit people. Even the Atlanteans' efforts were not enough to change their basic makeup.

---

3. The Basques are one of the original seedings of the Adam man and woman model in the western Pyreenes between Spain and France.

Naturally, they were there when thousands of people streamed through the area migrating away from the collapse (or rather the impending collapse) of Atlantis.

Were the Basques a people who had been put there originally by one of the planetary groups?

Yes, that's correct. They wanted to see how people would adapt to a mountainous area. They were settled about the same time as the Atlanteans by their own ET society. As I mentioned before, they did not mix well with the Atlanteans, nor did the Atlanteans with the inhabitants of Oz. They were able to subjugate the Basques for a while but not very long when you consider how long the Atlanteans were in existence. The Basques were quite resilient and used the mountains to their benefit. This took place over several hundred years.

Was this before or after the Second Destruction, or both?

After the Second Destruction, as the Atlanteans faced growing turmoil back home and needed their troops there.

Did they withdraw all their forces from the Mediterranean, or did they leave some?

Just a few smaller, well-guarded settlements until it became obvious they could no longer be sustained.

Were they more successful at one point in subjugating the Mediterranean area than they were with the Basques?

Only partly, as their conquests lasted a few hundred years, which is not so long when you take into account how long the Atlanteans existed.

Did the Atlanteans have any identification papers — or what we call passports these days — to identify themselves as they traveled over the Mediterranean?

Certainly they had a form of identification, but it was not as sophisticated as today's. They used a form of seals and such.

Did the Atlanteans settle Ireland?

Yes, they actually did. They were the first to move to that island as Atlantis was beginning to destroy itself. So you have their influence in Ireland and Scotland, as these people settled there and mixed with a few peoples who preceded them.

Is Ireland actually a derivative of the term Aryan and that of Aryans — the people in northern Europe? Your comments, please.

Yes, that is entirely true. The earliest settlers were those of Aryan blood. But they were small in number. When the Atlanteans arrived, they were so much more advanced, including their weapons, that they subjugated these people fairly easily when they gave them any trouble. But the Atlanteans, to give them their due, tried to assimilate as best they could, and over time, they blended completely with the Aryans, whose genes were dominant.

Atlantis had outposts, as you call them, or colonies or settlements in Europe, and there was a great influence over these peoples. The Atlanteans were seen as almost gods, as they came in modern aircraft or vessels far beyond what the average farmer or villager of that time had achieved.

Did Aryan — the Atlantean island — control the islands of Og and Eyre?

Yes, that is accurate. They controlled not only their own island but the other two as well.

Is that how Ireland to this day is known as Eyre?

That's correct. That name is a carryover of the Atlantean island's name.

But was Ireland the original island of Eyre?

No, it was not. They just brought the name with them, just as you see today many places named for European cities, towns, and even countries. It was a reminder of their beloved island that sank into the Atlantic.

Did the Atlanteans have colonies in North America?

Yes, as we touched on before, their colonies were mostly up and down the East Coast. There were a few small ones farther inland, but they had restrictions due to the crystals' power limits.

I would assume they would have done the same as they did in the Mediterranean and had some booster stations?

Yes, but not to the extent of the Mediterranean where there were more people they could conquer in their heyday.

Was one of the interior colonies located in what is now Arkansas where they mined the crystals?

Yes, it was. There are mines running deep within the area there, and a few have been discovered, but kept quiet by the locals who do not wish "outsiders" to interfere with their simple farming lives.

How large was this colony?

Oh, just a few hundred people. There are few traces of them, as this was over 12,000 years ago, and any traces of their existence are mostly limited to the mines.

Was this where the large crystals came from?

Yes and no. The continent of Atlantis had its own crystals, but the ones in what is now Arkansas had a different flavor. They were used for different purposes. You can see the difference even today if you examine the crystals found there and in Brazil. There is a great difference in mineral content, and yes, the energy of the ones in Arkansas is quite distinctive.

So back to the colonies on the North American East Coast, were these large towns or more like small villages?

A combination of both, but when the Second Destruction occurred, all of these coastal villages and towns were just wiped off the face of the Earth by tsunamis, along with the rising levels of the oceans. Even if you were to excavate underwater, little would be found compared to the great effort it would take to even find a location that might be promising. The ocean floor has built up over these many thousands of years, just as the land was built up by thousands of years of woods and grass growing and then dying, adding to the level inch by inch over hundreds and then thousands of years.

• • •

Gaia, was there a group of Atlanteans who migrated to southern Colorado and, if so, how did they get there — land, air, or tunnel?

The Atlanteans explored beyond the crystal mines of Arkansas; that's a given. Here it becomes a little murky. Atlanteans explored as far as Colorado, but there was never a permanent settlement there. There was no mass migration of a group of Atlanteans to Southern Colorado. Those people were part of the migration of the Anasazi people who came from the Northwest.

The Atlanteans were not very comfortable going too much past their safety net of the crystal power. So, on one hand, the crystals gave them great power, but on the other hand, they were tethered to it. So they had limitations. Definitely there were explorers, just as there are those today who do not mind the inconveniences of not having power, but this was a small part of the population as a whole. The rest were too attached to the good life.

Chapter 7
MIGRATION TO EGYPT
Theo, Antura, and Gaia

Theo, in our communications over the years, you said that I was either the first or one of the first to request most benevolent outcomes (MBOs). Did a person teach me this, did it come to me by inspiration, or did I receive it in a channeling?

That's a good question. You were taught this through inspiration. You did not channel this. You were inspired; rather, I whispered in your ear that you could do this.

What were the circumstances and how long ago?

Oh, quite a few thousand years. Yes, this dates all the way back to your days in Atlantis when you had a group of followers. You were given a way to show them this gentle way of living. You were not caught up in the dramas of that time. You led fairly peaceful lives. So the requests for MBOs are from a long, long time ago.

How many people practiced the Gentle Way back then?

Actually, there were over 1 million people. It was quite popular with the average person, not the scientists and priests of that day.

MBOs are only necessary on Earth, aren't they?

Yes, you are the only veiled people in the universe, so using this special spiritual tool is wonderful. It was a great inspiration when you originally received the information in Atlantis.

When I utilized or was inspired to show others the Gentle Way, did I also communicate with you as I am doing now in meditation?

Yes, you meditated then as you do now and were able to advise your flock of the need to move when the time was right. This was a very important life for you, as you were able to have some breakthroughs on several different levels.

In my flock, did we address each other as Beloved Brother and Beloved Sister?

That's correct. It may sound quaint now, but your flock truly had love for one another, as your lives were so much better than all the hatred being spewed by the two warring sides. You can see it not only in the writings of the people who send you their stories of simple MBO requests but also those who report amazing results when their lives were in danger or other highly important occurrences in their lives. The Eagles' song lyrics "peaceful, easy feeling" apply here.

What percentage of my newsletter readers were with me in Atlantis during the first benevolent outcome life, if any?

A number of your readers were with you during that life on Atlantis. Let's see if you can pick up the percentage — yes, 48 percent of your readers, which is a nice percentage. This means you're attracting people who have raised their vibrations enough to align with your work of requesting benevolent outcomes.

How old was I when I was inspired to create the Gentle Way back in Atlantis?

You were in your thirties at the time.

What type of employment did I have before I started the movement?

You were a writer and were inspired, as we have said before.

Was I already some sort of preacher or just a common man?

You were what would be considered today a clergyman. So when you were inspired to create the Gentle Way, you already had a congregation to introduce the concept to. Then it grew from there. You were a proponent of peace at a time when the majority of the population was on one side or the other.

Was my Gentle Way group my sole occupation, or did I have a day job?

No, you were supported by contributions, similar to how clergies are supported today.

Did I give talks about it? Did I have a form of church or gathering place?

Certainly, you gave many talks about it. You traveled extensively and were supported by donations of a sort so that you were able to spread the word.

How did I spread the word?

It was as it is now, done by word of mouth that this was something everyone could use in his or her daily life. There was less resistance compared to today, as churches seem to have much control over their parishioners. So it spread much faster — to hundreds, then thousands, and eventually to approximately 1 million people, living a gentler life, and as we have said before, not caught up in the politics and warring of the day. Therefore, yes, it took a few years, but again there were not as many obstacles as there are today.

How long did it take to spread the word?

It was over a period of twenty-five years. It spread quickly by word of mouth with many testimonies similar to today but without the hindrance of so many different religions. There were only two to choose from, and many people were quite unhappy with the choices. Yours was like a breath of fresh air; your peaceful alternative appealed to a large number of people, and they could continue to worship as the Law of One or Sons of Belial, should they wish.

Did the priests of those religious sects take exception to people living the Gentle Way?

Yes, they did, as they saw they were losing control over a portion of the people, but by the time they recognized the threat, they had more urgent problems at hand. So you were looked at as an aberration that would someday go away. You were not looked at as a threat to them, just some people running around requesting benevolent outcomes. You weren't trying to unseat those in power, so they allowed it to continue.

Were there people following the Gentle Way on the Sons of Belial–controlled islands?

Yes, a few had learned about it through friends and neighbors. They had to practice it at a lower key so as not to incur the wrath of the radicals.

Did the Lemurians on the continent of Mu practice the Gentle Way?

No, they were unaware of you or the Gentle Way, as there was not a lot of contact between the two. But they were ahead of you Atlanteans in living peaceful lives for a very long time until the leaders got greedy and wanted war.

Did I establish a school for meditation?

That was one of the developments, you could say. Meditation was already in existence, but you encouraged it.

How did Antura and I first meet?

Antura was attracted to the Gentle Way just as others were. He was very passionate about the method, you became good friends, and he became a member of your staff. Keep in mind that you had an instant connection, as both of you were from the same soul cluster. It was natural for him to assist you when it became apparent that the Atlantean days were numbered. He did not just appear and volunteer. He was a trusted member of your flock and staff.

PRELUDE TO LEAVING ATLANTIS

How old was I when I migrated with my flock to Egypt?

You were in your mid-fifties.

Did I ever return to Atlantis after we migrated?

No, you completely cut ties with everything there, but you prayed for them every chance you had.

Was there a way for the people who went with me to communicate with their loved ones left behind in Atlantis?

Yes, the crystal devices of that time allowed for communication. This helped bring more people to Egypt as conditions continued to worsen.

Did I have a family, and did they all go with me?

Yes, you had a family, and they all migrated with you, except for a few remote relations. But you had no immediate family, as your work kept you very focused in that life, but you had distant family — cousins and such that accompanied you to Egypt.

In the migration life, did we live on Poseidia or Aryan or another island?

It was Poseidia. That would have been too difficult with everyone whipped up to a war frenzy. Even on Aryan and those surrounding islands, there were people who practiced the Gentle Way, just as there are people in many locations starting to live the Gentle Way now. Most were not able to escape before the final battle.

DECISION TO LEAVE ATLANTIS

Did I have a life at the end of Atlantis, and if so, did I perish or leave?

You left some time before the end of Atlantis with your flock.

Why did I decide to leave Atlantis? Was it quite evident that the destruction was coming, or was I directed to do so?

It was quite evident — as plain as the nose on your face, to use your idiom. You were told that time was becoming short and that you should move during your meditations. So you hurried up the process and sent people out ahead of the group to arrange transportation, food, and such for a large number of people.

That sounds like the beginning of my travel agent/tour days, Theo.

Yes, exactly. Becoming a travel agent and handling large groups of people in this life came natural for you, as you had done this for your flock of followers in that life. That is good recognition as to how one life can be affected by another. The knowledge you gain from one life can carry over into another. A child who begins playing the piano at an early age is another example of this.

Describe the time 200 years before the last islands of the Atlantean continent sank.

Chaotic would be the best description. The Law of One and Sons of Belial were at each other's throats. There were also a number of earthquakes rumbling things.

Were there Earth tremors all the time, say, similar to what Japan and New Zealand experience now?

Yes, and even worse. There were constant movements. It was a daily occurrence that everyone just learned to live with, but Gaia was giving ample warning that the continent was not safe, as parts of it had already sunk into the ocean, so the residents understood what could happen at any time. Yet they continued fighting and warring with each other right up until the end.

What route did I take?

Through Spain to Egypt, as that was a very fertile place then. Later it would change to a very dry country.

Then Egypt was a tropical environment when we arrived?

Yes, it was. It gradually became desert over a period of several thousand years.

Why did we choose Egypt and not one of the other closer regions such as what is now France or Italy or Spain?

You were guided to bring your flock to Egypt for a number of reasons. First, the climate at that time made it easy to feed everyone. Then there were other people in those regions you mentioned. There would have been conflicts; you were absolutely tired of any conflicts and wanted a peaceful existence after all the warring you saw on Atlantis. I guided you through your soul to move to that location for a peaceful life and to set up the future for the Egyptian priesthood and the many Egyptian kings and queens to come. This very complex migration had a great impact on the future of that part of the world.

When did the migration from Atlantis begin, how long did it last, and how many people migrated?

That's a fine question. It began over the last few hundred years of Atlantis's existence, as many people could not take the constant warring and the breaking up of the continent that was well under way. Many people migrated; several million souls left the continent, but there were hard liners who fought to the very end and went down with the ship, so to speak. Therefore, the period of the migration was spread out over a number of generations. This was not an overnight occurrence.

There must have been chaos during that time.

Absolutely. Chaos reigned supreme as the Sons of Belial and the Law of One warred.

How many people were left?

Several million remained, but these numbers dwindled considerably toward the end, as it became quite clear it was hopeless.

So I understand that I had decided to leave due to all this turmoil. Was I actually aware that the islands' days were numbered, or did I just wish to escape all the fighting?

You could see the direction events were going. You were told in your meditations and dreams that Atlantis's days were numbered, and you began a search for the best place to resettle. What is now Portugal and France were considered, but it was already populated, which would have created conflicts over the land. Then you turned your attention to a much less-settled and very verdant area — the African coast. There were smaller villages and towns in that area, but there seemed to be plenty of room. Then Adama showed up to take you there for a scouting trip, and that's when you made your decision. After that, it was a matter of logistics. Antura assisted.

Did Antura travel with me when Adama took me on the scouting trip?

Yes, he was a close confidant and was by your side, as you wished to have his input.

EGYPT OR BUST

Was I able to communicate with you by this time?

Yes, in a way. We would give you messages in your meditation.

Did I leave with my flock just before the Third Destruction?

It was really a significant time — 200 years before the Final Destruction. That would seem close in comparison, but it was certainly long before that when you were able to make the crossing to Spain and on to Egypt in an orderly fashion, as compared to those who waited longer when many died trying to flee at the last possible moment.

How many months or years did it take to plan the move, inform everyone of my plans, and give a deadline on making the decision to leave or not?

It took a couple of years. After all, you had to notify about a million people of your plans, and they had to decide whether to join you or not. For many, it was a difficult decision because their families did not share the same beliefs they did. People were all wrapped up supporting one side or the other.

How did I relay this information to my Gentle Way flock (to use your expression)?

You got in touch with them in myriad ways, as communication was quite advanced at that time. So you used the equivalent of telephones, word of mouth, and your speaking engagements. It also made the news of the day, and many said, "Good riddance."

So those who were not followers publicly knew this?

Yes, and there was some animosity, as you can imagine, since they felt you were abandoning the fight. On the other hand, there were many who bid good riddance so that they could take over the houses and dwellings and anything else left behind. There were what are called fire sales in modern times.

• • •

Antura, how much were we able to take with us?

It was not as if you had a bunch of moving vans to transport all your possessions. Everyone was limited to what could easily be carried by hand and small, wheeled carriers slightly similar to those wheeled racks to carry luggage. So you all moved with virtually the clothes on your backs, to use a popular phrase.

How many people migrated with us from Atlantis to Egypt — a few hundred or a few thousand?

Twenty-five thousand migrated with you. Certainly much less than 10 percent of the people who practiced requesting benevolent outcomes in their lives. Some of your flock had already migrated before you decided to pull up stakes, and many could not leave their families, so they stayed behind. They lived out their lives on Atlantis before it actually sank into the sea. Some would send their children to join you, so there was a continuous trickle until it was too late. A few hundred more came later. Then, at the last minute, a few hundred more came, but it was a mixture of people of the two beliefs, or factions.

Their grandchildren's children were not so fortunate. Yes, it was down the line, as we moved some 200 years before it finally sank. Therefore, the flock that migrated was much smaller than the number of people who practiced the Gentle Way, and it took a couple of years to move everyone. But of course you were living the Gentle Way, and things would seemingly magically happen to assist you in moving this large group of people out of harm's way. That was a life of high achievement — good karma, we shall say.

• • •

THE ROUTE TO EGYPT

Theo, how many Atlanteans eventually resettled in Egypt?

Over 100,000 Atlanteans eventually migrated to Egypt. It was not very populated, so it easily absorbed the people who did not arrive all at once but rather in waves. Your group was one of the first to resettle, and it was fairly large. There were other groups who came later as things continued to worsen.

Why did we travel through Spain and not fly or go directly to Egypt?

It was because there was a limit to the range those flying machines could travel due to their need to be locked onto the external power sources. Spain was at the outer boundaries of their range, so some of you first flew to Spain and then went overland and by ships to the coast. It was quite a long procession if you can imagine a wave of people traveling together down to the coast. They had to be fed, and various types of transportation were used in this migration. You had people who went out ahead to arrange such things.

[On another day, I received a slightly different answer]: When my flock and I left Atlantis, did we travel by boat, air, or tunnel?

Most of you actually traveled by tunnel to what is now Portugal, as that was a busy highway. From there, you went overland, crossing Spain, and then on to Africa.

[Then I asked for clarification]: Theo, you have said that we went by air and by tunnel and possibly by ground to Egypt. Explain exactly how we got there.

You had to use a variety of transportation. First, you used the tunnel, as that was a very fast and easy way to reach Portugal and then Spain. Here is where it will be a little difficult for you: The flock split up. Some went overland, some went by air, and some went by ground. It depended on your flock's interests. You allowed them complete free will. You did not dictate to them how they had to travel. Some wanted to explore that area a little more. You had made the recommendation as to what you felt was the best place to begin again, but you always allowed for a difference of opinion.

They came to Egypt over a period of time, which made it somewhat easier to start building houses, or rather apartment-type buildings, and of course they — your flock, I mean — certainly had the capability to do a lot of work themselves. There was great sadness at having to move away from their beloved Atlantis, but people knew it was just a matter of time. There were frequent earthquakes, and of course, the governments were quite unstable too. Therefore, they moved by almost any and all means possible, as there were too many for just one mode of transportation; the capacity of these systems was not large enough to handle such a large group. Yes, it was sort of like your saying: by land, by air, and by sea.

Was the Egyptian migration the same as if we moved to a Third World country?

It was quite similar. The Egyptians had a very fertile but not too densely populated land, so many Atlanteans could settle there. However, they were not nearly as far along in their scientific development. They were a simple people until the Atlanteans arrived. Of course, you must remember that there were many other settlements from what is now Portugal all the way through Spain into France and so on. That whole area was available, for the most part, so someday even more ancient settlements will be found in these areas — some under modern-day cities and towns.

* * *

THE SIRIANS' ASSISTANCE

Antura, were the Sirians described in Lois J. Wetzel's book Akashic Records[1] *as half-man from the waist up and half-fish from the waist down from your planet or another in your star system?*

No, they were some of our ancestors.

But their appearance was described as looking like men from the waist up and fish from the waist down.

Yes, they took on that appearance for various reasons. But I can assure you the description of what my counterparts and I look like is very close to what you have already asked.

[Note: in my book *First Contact*, Antura described himself as an amphibian, somewhat similar to the Abe Sapien character in the *Hellboy* movies.]

Why were they there at that time?

They were there to assist the many refugees from Atlantis, along with the folk who were the original inhabitants of Egypt. Then the Earth Directive came down, and they had to abandon their small colony. They were already causing problems in which people from another country were trying to infiltrate the caretakers so that they could either undermine our efforts or use whatever information was being passed on for their own advantage.

When we arrived in Egypt from Atlantis, were the Sirian water people mentioned in Lois J. Wetzel's book there already, or did they not arrive until later?

Yes, they had recently arrived, knowing you and I would be arriving too. So there was an immediate connection.

Then it was not you and I who returned to Egypt after our Atlantean/Egyptian lives?

You're quite correct. These were Sirian beings who were contact people, not too far different from what I do, but they were more a contact people for governments.

* * *

THE PRINCESS ASSISTANCE IN EGYPT

Theo, what significant lives have I had with my wife?

1. Lois J. Wetzel, *Akashic Records: Case Studies of Past Lives* (Hot Pink Lotus Press: 2011) p. 92.

There are, of course, other lives more significant, such as back in Egyptian times when she was a princess and you were newly arrived from Atlantis. You were impressed with her authority and how she handled situations. She was able to assist you in some of your endeavors. Through her meditations, she understood who you were and your significance when you brought your flock of people with you to resettle. She was pleased that you were nonviolent people and welcomed you to their lands. This was a very significant life together.

Can you tell me about other lives we had together first on a linear basis and then whether any were later in time but before that Egyptian time?

Yes, let's take them in linear order first. This dates back quite a large number of years when you had your first lives together. This goes back well over 60,000 years ago but not millions. Certainly, you were there, having had a few lives already, when she had her first life on Earth. On a soul level, you knew you would have a number of lives together; therefore, you were there at her beginning. This was a very simple life she lived, and it was not significant for either one of you. You were a simple shaman in that life.

Since her first life, you have run into her in quite a number of lives — yes, including a few out of your 180-plus that you lived in Atlantis. You had some similar interests, and she had a number of very different lives, as she needed to gain knowledge that would not only assist you in this life but also would complement your knowledge in future lives. This knowledge will be quite useful to you both when you meet again in AD 3400 and fly off to explore the stars.

You could say that you have been friends, lovers, family members, and even enemies in past lives, as you both needed a round education, and you acted as an enemy out of love for her growth and understanding. You all must have balancing lives, which we keep stressing. You can't be goody two-shoes in every life.

Will Dena's next life in Egypt be part of a priest class or monarchy, and how long after the life she lived when she met me will that life be?

It will again be in ancient Egypt and not too many years after the one in which she assisted you in settling in that area. She will be part of the new priest class, which you established. But she will be a man, a very important figure in that priest class. She, or he, will not be part of the monarchy but will be the power behind the throne. This will be a significant life for her (him). He will be a good guide for his people.

In Egypt, was I aware of the group that migrated to the Yucatán?

Yes, the new refugees told you of their departure, but you had no reason to contact them.

After I migrated to Egypt from Poseidia, did I live in what is now Cairo or perhaps Alexandria or some other place in Egypt now covered by the sands of time?

You lived not far from the mouth of the Nile River in a very verdant zone, even much more so than today. Because the country was lightly populated, there was space for the several thousand people who migrated there to live simply and peacefully with their neighbors. You needed to be near the seat of power at that time to work with the Egyptian people's leaders as their representative. The healing bowls and other instruments you brought, gave you power, and you never abused it. You never denied healing to the Egyptian people who came to you.

How many years after we settled in Egypt, after we migrated from Atlantis, did the desert take over the verdant land where we settled?

It would be several thousand years, as this process was quite slow. You can see this in modern times as a desert slowly encroaches over villages. But where you settled endured for many generations.

•   •   •

Gaia, does the area still exist where my flock and I settled after migrating from Atlantis to Egypt, or is it covered by either sand or water?

You settled in a fertile part near the coast, not far from the Nile River, because you needed to be close to the seat of power in order to represent your people. They did not all stay in that area but rather moved miles farther along the coast, claiming fertile, untilled land. The sand eventually gobbled those lands up. The land closest to the coast was covered by water when the islands of Atlantis sank approximately 200 years later.

•   •   •

Theo, was Edgar Cayce correct in stating that the Egyptian pyramids dated back from 10,390 to 10,490 BC?[2]

Yes, Mr. Cayce was correct in his dating of the pyramids, at least the major ones.

[Referring to the time when I immigrated with my followers from Atlantis to Egypt 200 years before the final destruction.] Then these pyramids were built a long time after we migrated from Atlantis to Egypt?

Yes, you had been gone for quite a long time when they were built. But of course they were built with assistance from your friendly ETs, who were allowed to be more involved due to the importance of the project.

---

2.   A.R.E. website, Text of Reading 5748-6, http://are-cayce.org/ecreadings/Default.aspx.

So they were allowed even with the Earth Directive in place?

Yes, it was considered of major importance for many reasons, as you will discover in the not-too-distant future.

Was the Library of Alexandria in existence before or after we immigrated to Egypt?

No, it was created long after you had left the scene. There were records contained in them about your immigration and that of others from Atlantis. In fact, the whole history of Atlantis was contained there.

Why was it allowed to be destroyed?

There were a number of reasons, including that it was decided you needed to have mysteries to solve. Having that library in existence answered too many questions about the world history and about the involvement of ETs. It was felt you needed to start anew with few records of your existence prior to the forming of the great religions of the world — again, all part of the soul's learning, the quest to know.

The Things were long gone by that time, were they not?

They were gone for literally thousands of years. It is hard for people in this time, when you only have records going back about 6,000 years, to understand that the Atlantean people existed and flourished for over 50,000 years before they destroyed themselves. That is a long time. As I have mentioned before, you have not yet achieved some scientific developments even though you have already surpassed others.

There seems to be a contradiction in information. Edgar Cayce said there were healing temples in Egypt, which were used to heal people and the Things.[3] That would mean they still existed after the Third Destruction. Please explain.

Mr. Cayce was incorrect with that part of his reception. You were a healer when you came to Egypt, having smuggled out a healing bowl with you. Eventually, the priest system was established, and there were places the people could go to receive healings. You and your flock had initially taught the priests how to heal, and it became something only the priest class knew how to do, as it could be dangerous for people to try to heal not knowing the proper techniques. Much was eventually lost over thousands of years.

Were the healing bowls we used back in Atlantean times similar to those used today in Tibet — the brass ones?

No, only the shape. The bowls used back then had true mystical properties, which were elevated through verbal chants and mental concentration. The bowls could be rotated, so we are speaking of some really unique bowls.

---

3. A.R.E. website, Reading 254-42, http://are-cayce.org/ecreadings/Default.aspx.

THE SPINNING BALL AND PYRAMID BOOK IN ANCIENT EGYPT

What can you tell me about a spinning ball above a shallow bowl that one of my readers (Bruce) saw in meditation being operated by an Egyptian priest? He said that it came from Atlantis. Why would I have been familiar with it?

Yes, you were quite familiar with these, as you were the one who brought them out of Atlantis to Egypt. They were not supposed to have left Atlantis, but you brought this with you when you and your flock immigrated to Egypt before Atlantis sunk below the surface of the Atlantic Ocean. You used the ball and bowl for healing purposes, and they were passed down through your sons, who were considered priests, as they had powers left over from the Atlantis days. You helped create the priest class of Egypt.

What is the meaning of a glowing, golden pyramid book in another of Bruce's visions?

Ah, this is a good vision. The book is quite special and had to do with the early priesthood in Egypt. You used it extensively, as there were many chants and other rituals you have not discovered in this life you were able to use back then to assist your flock and those who came to you for help. Its very shape (pyramid) gave it great energy.

Where did it come from?

It was given to you by a friendly ET who saw your work and dedication.

Is it still in existence?

Yes, but well-guarded, as the people who have it know of its power but are not able to interpret it sufficiently to use the rituals correctly in a benevolent manner. Anyone who touches it can feel its energy, even more so than, say, a large crystal.

Where was the friendly ET from who gave me the pyramid book?

He was from your Sirius B system. They wanted to assist you as had been decided before your birth. Naturally, in that life, they needed to disguise themselves a little in order not to frighten you, but as you were veiled, you were thrilled to receive such help and assistance.

Why was Bruce so involved in this?

He was your understudy and worked closely with you throughout your life there in Egypt. You two had a very good relationship, as you both wished the best for your people and the Egyptians as well. You were both gentle people.

Is the book in a museum, or is it still guarded by some sort of priest class?

It is still guarded by a priest class in Egypt. They just don't know how it works, but they recognize its importance.

Will I regain access to any of the chants or rituals in this life?

No, your work will be much more like it is now but better, and you will assist people without the need for chants and rituals, as was needed in those lower-level vibrational times.

So I take it that it will not be used again?

That is correct.

RA-TA AND THOTH

Edgar Cayce received the information that he had a life as Ra-Ta, an Egyptian priest[4] banished but brought back to deal with the Atlanteans. Did the priest Ra-Ta live before, during, or after our arrival? As you had previously said, I became the first priest due to the healing objects I brought with me and used to treat many.

Yes, this is a little confusing; he was there during the time you lived in Egypt. His position was as a ruling class priest. You had dealings with him, as you needed to assure him you had no plans to take over as a ruler. You simply offered your services to assist your people and the local Egyptian people as well. They were concerned about losing their power, as they saw you as a possible threat.

So he lived during that same time?

That's correct. He had been banished and then brought back, as he had dealt with Atlanteans before. Keep in mind, Atlanteans were not very trusted since there were memories of times when the Atlanteans were strong and subjugated many of the Mediterranean people. So there was a healthy mistrust and fear of Atlanteans. Atlantis was far advanced compared to Egypt, which was mostly populated by younger souls.

Did I have the ability to extend my life?

You lived long but had an average life, not 200 or more years. You had completed your work, seeding the Atlanteans with the Egyptians. And you were the first person to be considered a priest, as you helped heal the sick and wounded with your Atlantean tools, we will call them.

How long could the priests of the Law of One or Sons of Belial extend their lives?

It was longer than the average population, but no longer than, say, a life of 200 years. Thoth learned this as part of the priest class on Poseidia. He was a mid-level priest, and he had gained that knowledge through his studies. Thoth had the ability to extend his life, and he lived for quite a long time. And Ra-Ta lived a long life — but not as long as Thoth. And Thoth came after Ra-Ta.

---

4. A.R.E. website, Report of Readings 2062-1 and 294-153, http://are-cayce.org/ecreadings /Default.aspx.

Edgar Cayce said Ra-Ta lived between 10,000 and 10,500 BC.

Yes, but that was what Mr. Cayce received. It was a general statement and not the exact years, I can assure you.

Can you narrow the number of years Ra-Ta was alive?

We have already covered that he was alive when you and your flock of Atlanteans arrived 200 years before its final destruction. He was about the same age as you — middle-aged, we can say. You had many discussions with him, as he was eager to learn more about the Atlantean advanced society. You withheld much information, as you did not want another Atlantis, which would eventually destroy itself. You were able to claim that the instruments needed to do many of the advancements were left in Atlantis, which was quite true. And you hid some of the instruments you possessed, as you did not want them to fall into the wrong hands.

What years did Thoth live?

There is not an easy explanation. It was after you had transitioned in Egypt. He had the knowledge to live longer than the average person.

Did he live at the same time as Ra-Ta?

Not exactly, as he came later.

Did Ra-Ta live longer than the average person?

Yes, they had been learning how to do this, and he did live longer.

Was it hundreds of years?

No, longer. But that was not the length of time Thoth lived.

THE LIVES OF THOTH

Was Thoth alive when my flock and I arrived in Egypt?

No, he was gone from the scene at the time you arrived.

I'm confused on this timing. Did we arrive before or after Thoth?

It was before. That is the correct timing.

Was Thoth in Egypt before or after we immigrated?

He lived both before and then again after you immigrated. He returned to a new life after you passed from the scene.

Why did he wish to come there from Atlantis in the first place?

He recognized the potential there, as he — like you — was able to see that the islands of Atlantis were headed to destruction and oblivion. Then he fell in love with the country as it appeared at that time and found it easy to manipulate the locals.

Figure 7.1: An example of Thoth depicted in Egyptian art.

What was the longest Thoth lived in either of his two lives?

The second would be his longest life. It was approximately 200 years, much longer than the average life span at that time.

Then it was not about 400 to 500 years?

No, not nearly that long. Still, he was revered as a god, you see, and can be found in a number of depictions in Egyptian art, as seen in fig. 3.1.

How many years before my flock and I arrived in Egypt had Thoth been alive and transitioned?

It was not a long time. We shall say, for your purposes, less than fifty years.

Then how long after I (and I assume most if not all the original members of my flock had transitioned) did he arrive again?

He arrived less than fifty years after you transitioned.

When he returned, was he born there or did he arrive from Atlantis?

He needed the training and devices in existence in the Atlantean islands. He had some balancing to do in future lives in order to return a second time with virtually the same personality and memories of the first life. His plan was very different from yours. He was interested in power, and you were not. Your group tried to keep a low profile, as it were, so as not to scare the Egyptians, since there were so many of you who immigrated there within a two-year period. Thoth came alone with just a few assistants. He had to dazzle them with his knowledge.

Was Thoth's name the same in each life or just the second one?

He used the same name in each life; he was able to manipulate the second life to remember his first. Even his appearance was quite close in the second life to the first, but by then, everyone who had known him in the first life had all transitioned. Still the memory was good enough to impress the ruling class at that time, and he had enough tricks up his sleeve to convince them he had returned with full powers.

There seems to be a contradiction in what you have told me. Previously you said I originated the priest system in Egypt, but you also said the same of Thoth. Which is correct?

You did in a more humble way, as you did not organize it the way Thoth did. Thoth took what you had begun not as a priest system but a process out of your love for humanity and created a technique — a vertical structure with levels of attainment. This is something humans are good at. You need structure — a hierarchy — and Thoth recognized this, creating a hierarchy.

But because he came to Egypt before me, wasn't it already in place?

Yes, there is some confusion here. Thoth came earlier and was gone by the time you arrived. He set up the priest system as a ruling class. When you came along, you set up a priest system of healers. Therein lies the difference. Eventually, it appeared that they combined but not really. The healers would have been viewed more as doctors, you could say. So the confusion comes from both the rulers and the healers being called priests. Language was much more limited in those times, as the Egyptian people were a simple people.

Why did he reincarnate to the same place again? What's his story?

He tried to manipulate his lives. This can be accomplished, but the act creates some karma along the way, which, I might add, he's balancing today.

Thoth was an Atlantean in both lives?

Yes, he was. That report is accurate.

Was he the high priest of the Law of One, the Sons of Belial, or a lower priest in one of the two?

He was a mid-level priest in the Law of One. He was in such a position that he was able to know the secrets of the priest class, so when he migrated to Egypt, he seemed like a god to them.

Did he introduce writing or hieroglyphics to them?

Yes, quite so. He did not use Atlantean letters, as he felt that the average Egyptian would have trouble learning their complicated way of writing. Instead he invented symbols so that an Egyptian of average intelligence could decipher the meanings. After all, someone had to invent the use of these symbols.

So the hieroglyphics that he invented were in use at that time?

Indeed, you and the rest of your flock quickly learned the symbols in order to communicate with the Egyptian people.

What other things did he accomplish — both good and bad?

His main gift to the people was writing. He also set up the priest system in Egypt, as they had none before. He contributed knowledge about the universe and many other things that they kept secret in Egypt from the average Egyptians; again, this was a control factor, as you like to call it. He also contributed to the health of the Egyptians through his knowledge of remedies. As you can see, he did a lot of good, but creating a priest system, as we know, had its drawbacks.

So he arrived in Egypt before the Final Destruction, correct?

Long before the Final Destruction, that is true. But he could see the handwriting on the wall, as you say, and migrated to a place he would be treated as a king.

Did he pass on this information to his followers in Egypt?

Part of it. He did not want to lose his power, so he kept much of the information to himself.

Was Thoth still alive when the Atlantean islands sank, and if so, how did he handle the survivors who made their way to Egypt?

He was still alive and very much in charge. The survivors who made it there with barely the clothes on their backs were in no position to usurp Thoth's authority, whether they were the Law of One or Sons of Belial. They recognized what a disastrous series of events had occurred, and all they wanted was to find a safe haven. They simply blended into the population. They had no special tools (as you did) to set them apart. By the next generation, they only had the stories that their parents told them of the war and how terrible it was.

Were Osiris[5] and Amenra[6] imposters?

No, they were not. The question pertains to the lineage, and you would have to read more about this so that we could discuss it more fully.

Was Thoth associated with Maat,[7] the youngest daughter of Ra and Nete?

Yes, eventually he was, as he prolonged his life.

Did Thoth have any connection with Amun[8] or Amenra?

Yes, in a way he did. He was their consul, you see. They learned from him when he came to Egypt. As I said before, he created the priest class in Egypt, and they were part of that class system.

---

5. Osiris was the brother of Isis according to ancient Egyptian lore. Learn more about Osiris at http://www.egyptianmyths.net/osiris.htm.
6. Amenra is the god in whom Amun and Ra were combined: the god of the universe and the supreme Egyptian god during the period of Theban political supremacy.
7. Amun was one of the most powerful gods in ancient Egypt, at his peak known as the King of the Gods. When Amun combined with the sun god Ra, he was even more powerful (www.ancientegypt.co.uk/gods/explore/amun.html).
8. Maat, or Ma'at, was a goddess who regulated the stars, the seasons, and the actions of both mortals and the deities. She set the order of the universe from chaos at the moment of creation (https://en.wikipedia.org/wiki/Maat).

Did the Christian word "amen" at the end of a prayer originate with or from the name Amun or Amen or Amenra in Egypt?

Yes, of course it did. This very ancient word was said all over Egypt for thousands of years, so it was only natural for the Jews in Egypt to adopt this word when they prayed to their God. It was as if they were saying, "Okay, I'm praying to one god, but I'm not taking any chances." So they would say, "Amen," at the end. These were very basic people back then and were subject to superstitions.

Did Thoth have a third life as Hermes?[9]

Yes, he returned for one more life.

Then was this one more manipulation?

In a way, yes.

Hermes is thought to be mythical, so when did he live, and how did the story that he was the son of Zeus originate?

Yes, he was a real man — a human being. He was born and lived in ancient Greece, as you may have guessed. It was so long ago that legends regarding real people were passed down and embellished until they became mythical. Therefore, this dates back only less than 1,000 years after Atlantis and the islands sank into the sea.

Hermes was able to tap into his past lives to a certain extent and use this to his advantage. He was more of a rogue in that life — you might say the rebellious teenager who never quite matured — and the son of a king. In some ways, it was a balancing life for him. These mythological stories derived from that time. Many legends began as true stories, and as you can imagine, over thousands of years of being passed down from generation to generation, each time they are embellished just a little more. There are many other instances of this happening when people who cannot write try their best to repeat a story, but it changes just a bit from generation to generation.

You said that Thoth is balancing his karma today. Did you mean that literally or figuratively?

I meant that literally. He is incarnated now and is leading a life in which he is balancing those times.

Is he a politician or a clergyman of some type?

He is a clergyman, as you say. He will be the next pope.

Am I getting this correctly, Theo? He will be the next pope?

9. Hermes was an Olympian god in Greek mythology, son of Zeus and the Pleiad Maia. He is known as a god of transitions and boundaries, working as the emissary and messenger of the gods (https://en.wikipedia.org/wiki/Hermes).

Figure 7.2:
Emerald Tablets
of Thoth.

Yes, that is correct. He has vowed to have no secrets this time around, and he will be the one to open the Vatican Archives.

Is he aware that in a past life he was Thoth?

No, he's not. He's veiled. He will open up the Vatican Archives through inspiration; as he prays, he will receive guidance that he must do this.

What are the Emerald Tablets of Thoth [see fig. 7.2]?

These tablets date back to his time in Egypt. They are now kept by priests under lock and key. More will be learned about them in the near future.

How accurate are the translations of the Emerald Tablets?

The tablet translations are not very accurate. You found inconsistencies even in the first chapter regarding dates, just as one example.

Was there a place under the surface known as the Halls of Amenti[10] as was reported in the translation?

No, there were and still are places under the earth where ETs are able to work without those on the surface knowing of their existence but not as described in the verbose fashion as in the tablets.

• • •

10. It has been theorized that the Halls of Amenti became the underworld (http://buildreps
    .hubpages.com/hub/Where-or-What-Are-The-Halls-of-Amenti).

Gaia, why did the Atlantean calendar not go to Egypt? Did it go to the Maya in the Yucatán?

Well, it did — at least a version of it. But like any vibrant society, it evolved over thousands of years to the point where it was not recognizable. Keep in mind that although the Egyptians were fairly simple folk at the time you arrived, when Thoth arrived he started shaking things up a bit. There were many advances, including the calendar, which didn't change much in Central and South America. Also, there are findings about which the Egyptian government kept quiet if they did not agree with the official story. More will come out in the future.

THE GIZA PYRAMIDS

What time period were the Giza pyramids built, as we have already established that the Bosnian pyramids were built some 26,000 years ago and are the oldest of them all, am I correct?

Yes, they are the oldest. The Giza pyramids came much later — thousands of years later. They were built after Atlantis sank, partly to replace the Atlantean pyramids. You might notice they are on a grid line that would have intersected those previously constructed in Atlantis.

There were pyramids on Atlantis?

That's correct. Pyramids had been used since the early days of Atlantis.

Did ETs build any pyramids?

No, they simply suggested where the pyramids should be built for maximum energy. Your scientists still have not yet discovered their use, so we will leave it for them to learn through deduction with little hints along the way, such as the beam of energy coming out of the Bosnian Pyramid of the Sun.

But I thought the Earth Directive would have been in force then?

Yes, but they were allowed to assist the Egyptians in creating those pyramids for several reasons: Their energy was needed, and it was understood that millions of people would be intrigued by the mystery of their construction. There were a variety of pyramids, including some that were constructed without any assistance. So, to answer the question, it was around 10,000 years ago, earlier than archaeologists have estimated, as they have had no way to carbon date the pyramids as is being done in Bosnia.

Was it possible to move the blocks of stone, which were used to build the Giza pyramids, using tones and sounds produced by their throats?

No. However, your verbal sounds can be more powerful said in unison than you can imagine at this time. Other devices, we will call them, were used to move and then liquefy the edges so that they fit perfectly together. Although the stonemasons were good, they were not *that* good.

Were the Atlanteans connected to the Bosnian pyramid system since it dates back almost 26,000 years?

No, this was another people, and they were assisted by a group of ETs.

Was Egypt known as Khent in ancient times?

Yes, it was known this way long ago — thousands of years ago. The name Egypt was adopted long after the Atlantean Islands sank into the sea.

Did the Atlanteans build any of the pyramids in Egypt?

No, this was done long after the Atlantean Islands sank into the sea.

Did the Atlanteans build the Sphinx?

No, they did not build it. This is a mystery that will one day be solved.

Did the Giza pyramids exist when my group arrived from Atlantis, or was it well after my life there?

The pyramids were built well after you passed.

Did I have anything to do with the Giza pyramids?

Yes, you in fact did have something to do with their construction — many thousands of years ago. You were involved in their planning but not their implementation. You knew where they needed to be built and the angles they would need to do their energy work.

Then it was not the life I had when I took my flock, as you called them to Egypt from Atlantis?

No, it was another life, one we have not discussed before. You had several lives there.

Was I a priest of some sort or simply some sort of architect?

You were a priest with the ability to receive these concepts and put them on paper. You guided the architects, we'll say, for clarity.

What years were involved?

It was over 10,000 years ago.

• • •

ANCIENT EGYPTIAN MYSTERIES

Theo, is the Egyptian Book of the Dead[11] significant, and has all of it been discovered, or are there parts still left undiscovered?

It is significant to scholars and archaeologists, and there is still more to be revealed, as some discoveries have yet to be announced.

Is the book older than they estimate?

---

11. The Egyptian Book of the Dead is an ancient funerary text (https://en.wikipedia.org/wiki/Book_of_the_Dead).

The information in it is much older. Those records are still buried in the sands of the Sahara desert.

Does the information date back all the way to the time I was there or arrived there with my flock (approximately 12,700 years ago)?

No, it came much later — several thousand years, as knowledge gave way to superstition and belief in, or the imagination of, what lay ahead for those who transitioned.

When will more of it be revealed?

Not for some time, as the carbon dating would put it back well before the time when Earth was created according to the Muslim religion.

What, if anything, did Dr. Shaheen[12] of Cairo University discover in or beneath the Giza pyramids?

He made some excellent discoveries that must be kept quiet until there is acceptance by the general population that Earth was created and people inhabited Earth for millions of years instead of thousands as their Muslim religion states. Many of these finds will be amazing to see, and this will occur sooner rather than later.

Was the discovery alien or extraterrestrial in nature?

No, far older than the estimated ages.

Are Egyptian officials hiding any recent findings on the Giza plateau?

Yes, there are a few that would cause riots in the streets by those fundamentalists who do not wish to accept the idea that people have existed for hundreds of thousands of years more than their holy book says. When the Quran was originally written, and this goes for your Bible too, it was much simpler times, and it was inconceivable that people had existed on Earth for millions of years. Even now in the twenty-first century, as finds are made further and further back, you revise your history almost every year.

Egypt was easily inhabited 500,000 years ago, but the officials, as I have said before, would be in danger of losing their lives to point out or publish their findings of civilizations being discovered beyond recorded history. This will greatly change in the future after the arrival of the Pleiadians. So, yes, there are finds made all the time that have to be kept under wraps, you see.

When and who built the many miles of underground tunnels in Egypt between the pyramids?

This is one of the great mysteries for those who know about them.

Were they built long after my flock and I had transitioned?

---

12.   Dr. Alaeddin Abdul Mohsen Shaheen is head of Egyptian antiquities for Cairo University.

They were constructed quite long after. Many generations had passed.

So it was not Thoth's doing?

He had a hand in the initial tunnels, but they grew over thousands of years. The priests and pharaohs wanted to be able to move undetected under the surface from one place to another.

Were they built by normal digging, or did people have the ability to move the dirt through some sort of chants and rituals?

Exactly, you still have not yet learned in modern times the power of the spoken voice. This dates back to your early days in Egypt, but your chants and such were intended to heal people. This sounds strange today that it will be hard for people to accept. But how else would miles and miles of tunnels exist with no great piles of earth sitting above ground? Where did this earth go? It was moved aside and not removed.

Had they used slaves to dig these tunnels, there would have been some sort of records kept, such as shelter and so forth. There are none, so one must ask: "How were they created?" It was not done by any sort of digging machines or lasers.

You can find these same sorts of tunnels in the Bosnian pyramid complex too, as you have read.[13] The Bosnians post their findings about the tunnels, whereas the Egyptians do not. The Egyptians have chosen to keep these secret as long as possible, but the day will come in the future when they will be revealed, sparking great discussions and theories as to how they were built. Yes, your *National Geographic* magazine will have a field day.

How could King Tut's DNA be 99.5 percent Western European?

Because they will find that over millions of years there were migrations in which people came down and settled in Egypt, along with migrations from the east. Then there was the commingling with the Atlanteans who also commingled with the Europeans. This all happened before much of their recorded history, so it is very perplexing to them, as their religious texts only cover so far back. It was inconceivable to people living at that time that they could have ancestors from over several million years ago. Even now, you are just slowly discovering your lineage, which goes further and further back as your archaeologists find other settlements.

Your archaeologists still have not discovered some of the other major

---

13. Recent Bosnian pyramid discoveries are posted on their website, http://piramidasunca .ba/eng/.

settlements along the coast, as the sands covered them. The Egyptians of King Tut's time are predominant in the DNA from these cultures who had migrated to fertile lands as they explored.

How was Tutankhamen as a king during his reign in Egypt?

He was average — pretty well in the middle of the road, so he was not despised.

Did he have any contact with ETs?

No, this was after the Earth Directive, so he had no contacts.

How did he die?

It was not a violent death. He had internal problems that the priests were unable to treat.

Why did he disappear from history until his tomb was discovered?

Because he was not a vicious ruler nor did he have great accomplishments to be written about.

Chapter 8
THE FALL OF ATLANTIS
Gaia and Theo

Gaia, how many times have humans destroyed themselves? Can you list them for me?

Atlantis and Lemuria were four, that much you know. Before those destructions, there were two others. One was alluded to before. It was the time when humans inhabited Antarctica and did not heed my warnings to move, and they died when I changed the poles. Even the Atlanteans and Lemurians had no records of that destruction or an even earlier destruction of a smaller population with the same circumstances. Those are alluded to in the stories of gods who lived and fought each other.

Did Edgar Cayce accurately receive the descriptions of the three major Atlantis continent destructions?[1]

Yes, he did. Edgar Cayce was quite accurate. Remember, he was an Egyptian priest in a previous life, so he had access to all the records that were available about the continent of Atlantis before it sank into the ocean and before the library at Alexandria was destroyed.

According to the book Edgar Cayce wrote on Atlantis,[2] there were three major points, or times, of destruction of the Atlantean continent: 50,000 BC, 28,000 BC, and 10,000 BC. Are those fairly accurate dates?

Yes, they are close to the actual dates for the breakup of the continent.

The islands, including Poseidia and Aryan, were formed after the Second Destruction?

That's correct.

---

1. Brad Steiger, *Atlantis Rising* (Dell Publishing: New York City, 1973) pp. 60–62.
2. Edgar Evans Cayce, *Edgar Cayce in Atlantis: The Edgar Cayce Series* (Grand Central Publishing, 1988).

Were two of the islands named Daitya and Ruta?

Yes.

But there were no destructions before 52,000 years ago?

There were none that affected humans. This continent was uninhabited. That does not mean that humans had not visited it, but they did not stay permanently.

Then to return to my question about the Second Destruction, was it less than or more than 30,000 years ago?

That figure is very close for the Second Destruction. You can use that figure.

But not 35,000 years ago?

No, it was not that much more.

What about the northernmost portion of the Atlantean continent? Did it disappear in the First, Second, or Third Destruction?

The Second Destruction, which was the time I was shifting poles. Humans caused the Third Destruction.

Is it true that the ocean levels are 300 to 400 feet higher than they were in the past, and if so, how much did the Second and Third Destructions of Atlantis and then the sinking of Lemuria contribute to the rise in these levels?

Those estimates are fairly correct, about 375 feet, so as you can see, the scientists have done their studies well. Regarding the Second and Third Destructions of Atlantis, the Second Destruction, as you can imagine, was the largest jump of a little under 160 feet, and the Third Destruction (of just the islands) was between 40 and 41 feet. Then when the whole continent of Lemuria sank, there was an additional 150 to 175 feet. So it was fairly well split between the two, as both continents were around the same size, just different shapes.

How far did the shoreline of North America extend before the ocean rose?

Obviously this question has a number of different answers depending on what part of the North American shoreline we are discussing, but the farthest it extended was several miles, where the continental shelf was shallow and less so where there was a steep drop off. Is it any wonder that there are no signs of prior life when the ocean levels were so much higher?

Just imagine what a small rise in the ocean levels of just two feet will have on the world today, forcing those living in low-lying areas to relocate, and eventually washing away their homes as if no one had lived there. Multiply this by many times, as each settlement was obliterated by first the sinking of most of the Atlantean continent, then by the islands sinking, and then by Lemuria sinking. Between those times, the ocean levels were fairly stable, and they did not rise 1.5 feet per hundred years as scientists have hypothesized.

Did Atlantis and Lemuria have to be destroyed?

In a way, yes, as your souls needed to understand the great consequences of your actions. By destroying these continents on a soul level, you never want to have that happen again, and you will do everything in your power to make sure it does not happen in the future. Remember, you reached a vibrational level in 1987 that you term the Harmonic Convergence, in which you will never destroy yourselves again. Had you not crossed that threshold, you would have continued down a path of utter destruction again, and we would have started over with the remnants of civilizations, as has happened in the past. There was a great celebration on this side of the veil when you crossed that line, I can assure you.

Was there a matriarchal society at any time on the Atlantean continent?

No, had there been, they would not have destroyed themselves. All the leaders during that time were male. In your future, there will be more and more women leaders, and you will find that wars will become a thing of the past.

Did the sinking of Atlantis cause the great biblical flood?

Definitely. There were great tidal waves that swept across most of the coastlines more than once as chunks or great portions of Atlantis sank into the sea. There were several tsunamis connected to these events. But the reported forty days and nights of rain did not occur during the first Atlantean periods; it occurred much later.

How many people lost their lives worldwide from the ensuing tsunamis and rapid rise in ocean levels?

You can easily say about 60 million, as there were many coastal towns and villages during that time. There is no other time in the history of the Explorer Race when so many transitioned at one time.

Didn't the destruction of the continent of Lemuria several thousand years later result in similar numbers of deaths?

No, more people were able to escape compared to the Second Destruction. Also, the continent of Lemuria was not as heavily populated as Atlantis had been. There were a number of people who migrated away from Lemuria who did not wish to join in the fighting.

I would think that it would take a long time for those who survived the sinking and tsunamis and rise in ocean levels to get over this.

Yes, people were terribly frightened, and it took several generations to rebuild not only the cities and towns but also their lives. These were great catastrophes, although certainly these were the soul contracts of all those affected.

ATLANTIS: THE FIRST DESTRUCTION

Atlantis became inhabited about 57,000 years ago. Then came the first of the three destructions around 50,000 BC. It had been inhabited for 5,000 years and grown to a population of approximately 1 million people.

Gaia, what caused the First Destruction of Atlantis? Was it a natural disaster or human-made?

The first one was a natural disaster.

Was it a shift of the poles?

Exactly.

Did Earth experience a shift in poles, a pole reversal, or did the axis shift, causing an enormous wind, perhaps?

Yes, I understand it is confusing, since you are not a geologist who has studied these events. Again, we are speaking of the First Destruction. There was a shift in poles, which was dramatic, as it occurred in one movement and not gradually as is happening now. I needed that shift in poles immediately to clear off a lot of what was called the civilized world at that time.

But it was not a shift in the axis; the actual movement of the poles caused frigid temperatures and winds and such to move to areas that had not experienced this. So Earth itself did not wobble and suddenly tilt. The axis remains pretty much where it was before the shifting of the poles.

How populated was Atlantis at the time of the First Destruction?

The colonies seeded on the continent had all thrived and, by that time, melded together, even through the typical wars for territory. The number was slightly under 1 million, not a huge population yet.

I would have thought the population would have been higher, as they had over 5,000 years of growth before this happened.

Yes, they did, life was hard for many, many years, and life spans were short due to the harsh conditions. It took quite some time before their numbers could increase, so the 1 million figure is correct.

Had Atlantis discovered crystal power yet?

Quite so, and that allowed them to jump-start their growth and influence.

Don't forget that your ET uncles and aunts, who had shown them this free energy source, were also aiding them. Little did the ETs know it would be turned into such a destructive power in the future.

Was the continent of Lemuria inhabited at that time?

Very few Adam and Eve model humans existed there. They came later.

When you shifted the poles in the First Destruction of Atlantis, did any part of the continent experience an ice age, and did any of the 1 million inhabitants perish in the shift?

The continent did not experience an ice age, as it was located a little to the south of the freezing line, and the ocean currents circled the continent, which became somewhat distorted when I shifted the poles. So, no, there was no ice age for them. They experienced some very turbulent weather, which lasted several years.

Regarding whether anyone perished on this continent when I shifted the poles — yes, there were deaths on the coasts as the water surged. A few thousand people died at that time and then more in the violent storms that followed. The numbers lost were nowhere near the numbers that other parts of the world experienced when suddenly the temperature dropped below zero. They were not able to find shelter quickly enough to survive.

Were there dinosaurs and other similar beasts alive on Earth before the First Destruction of Atlantis and after Atlantis settled and had progressed scientifically?

They were a major problem at that time all over the world. The dinosaurs were still alive, but they were not on the Atlantean continent. The only reason your scientists have not discovered this is they were alive where the oceans have covered their remnants.

It was because of the dinosaurs they had the big council, or meeting, in Atlantis in which leaders from all over that world were picked up by the Atlanteans and brought there to discuss how to get rid of the beasts, which were a great danger to the humans. Of course, the poles shifted before anything major could be accomplished, and for the most part, they disappeared, along with millions of people.

Which societies took part in the meeting about the dinosaur problem?

The Atlanteans were limited in how far they could reach, being tethered as they were to the crystal power. Therefore, amend the statement about contacting other societies of humans to just those in Europe and along the Mediterranean shores. They left most of the continent of Oz alone, as those people were tribesmen and not worth the trouble it was thought to include. Those tribesmen looked at the red-skinned Atlanteans as invaders, so the Atlanteans made a hasty retreat. This animosity continued for thousands of years, as the Atlanteans tried numerous times to conquer Oz, and each attempt was met with failure.

Did Earth's population shrink drastically at that time?

Yes, to much less than half — even almost a fourth of what it had been. Atlantis lost people on the coastal cities, as we said, but much of its interior was not affected, except by storms that were caused by the changes.

WHY THE POLES SHIFTED

Why didn't the ETs assist the Atlanteans in the First Destruction when the poles shifted? Or did they?

Yes, they assisted the Atlanteans as best they could, without altering their soul contracts, as (keep in mind) everyone has soul contracts to experience all Earth has to offer.

How far did the poles shift — several hundred miles or thousands of miles?

For your purposes, use the figure of a few thousand miles. It was a major shift. The poles shifted to where they are today.

So the poles did not turn upside down?

No, but the tilt of Earth shifted.

Regarding the shift of the poles, was this a shift of the poles or a shift of the axis? That's confusing.

In this case, the poles shifted several thousand miles. That caused me to have new North and South Poles, from almost 0° to the present 23°. You can imagine, or possibly you and the readers cannot even imagine, the destruction that occurred as a whole continent was suddenly at –50°F. The seas slopped over the coasts, inundating the surrounding areas. It was a mess.

Why was this needed?

In order to prepare Earth as it is now, as there was great farsightedness as to which continents would have what conditions. It was needed for the Earth experiment; I needed to cover parts of the earth where there had been ancient societies well before Atlantis and Lemuria. As I mentioned before, there are no records of these societies, and I needed to finish covering them.

Did all continents experience this great shaking as Earth tilted on its axis?

Exactly. This was why there was the First Destruction of Atlantis. Yet all the continents experienced the same thing, some much worse, such as Antarctica, than others.

So this showed the small probabilities for the Atlanteans to make it to the Harmonic Convergence level? Can I conclude that their vibrational levels would not make it, or was it too early at that time to tell?

No, there were indications that even with thousands of more lives, the population would not raise their vibrational levels sufficiently. But it was decided to take it as far as it would go since there were many experiences the souls could have that would help in later lives. You were one of those examples, Tom, as you had many lives there and were able to experience much that all souls must experience. So bear in mind that time is an illusion and all those lives you lived in Atlantis are still taking place. It is extremely complicated to understand when you must think in a linear fashion.

So there will be no more shifts of your poles or axis or both?

As you already know, my North Pole and, for that matter, the South Pole are both moving but at a slow rate. They will not shift overnight as has happened in the past. It will give you humans plenty of time to shift your activities.

Why is there no proof of a climate change 50,000 years ago?

Because there was not one. There was severe destruction, and all the coastal towns and cities were wiped out around the world by tsunamis and the rise of ocean levels.

Did the original people who settled or migrated to Greenland perish when you shifted the poles during the First Destruction?

That's correct. That whole area was green and had about the same climate as northern Europe today. When I shifted the poles, all but the coasts froze over, and the people who had migrated there perished. I suggest your readers look at a map to see how close Greenland is to the North Pole [see fig. 8.1]. The population was not large, but they settled there.

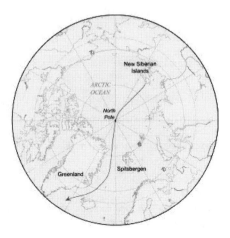

Figure 8.1: This view of Earth's Northern Hemisphere shows just how close Greenland is to the North Pole.

One of my readers recalls dying in a past life when cold suddenly came to her land. Their clothing was made from animal hides. Was this Antarctica or somewhere else?

No, she was not in Antarctica but another land when I switched the poles. The people in Antarctica were not part of the Earth experiment and actually were well developed past the time for wearing hides, as this lady mentioned. Where she had lived had a climate similar to, say, Europe's today, but then it turned too cold for them to survive.

Would this have been closer to the North Pole?

Yes, it was. Had they been farther south, they would have adjusted just like other groups did.

ATLANTIS: THE SECOND DESTRUCTION

A little over 30,000 years ago, almost the entire continent of Atlantis sank into the sea, caused by great earthquakes and volcanic eruptions, as the continent sat on the middle of the Atlantic ridge. Millions of people lost their lives not only on the Atlantean continent but also all over the world.

Did the Second Destruction happen 30,000 BC, 28,000 BC, or more?

Use the figure of 28,000 BC. That would put the Second Destruction at about 30,000 years ago.

Was the Second Destruction caused by the continent splitting up where it sat on the Mid-Atlantic Ridge?

Entirely — you could say it was split asunder.

Where the Mid-Atlantic Ridge is today, was there a chain of volcanoes that existed down the center of the Atlantean continent?

Precisely. There was great seismic activity and earthquakes along this line, just as there is today along the Ring of Fire, as you term it. Eventually, this pressure became too much and caused the destruction of the continent. Again, this was a natural disaster as you term it today.

Did the giant crystals the Atlanteans developed contribute to the breakup of the Atlantean continent?

They did not. This continent was very unstable because of its location on the Mid-Atlantic Ridge. I sank it with the souls' permission.

I am a little surprised that the crystals were not involved in making the ground more unstable, Gaia.

No, the instability was caused by the two continental shelves colliding.

You mentioned before there was a chain of volcanoes running along the fault line too. Were any as tall as, say, Mount Vesuvius [Southern Italy] or the volcano on Hawaii [Kilauea]?

Absolutely, and there were several more of similar size. If you can imagine what happened to Mount St. Helens [1980, Washington, United States] when it blew apart, then you might be able to partially understand the pressure that was exerted when the volcanoes erupted in unison. The water rushed in, and the continent broke apart.

Did the Atlantean scientists have the knowledge to track earthquakes as we do today?

They were not quite as far along as you are today, but they had instruments to record earthquakes.

Did the southernmost part of Atlantis remain until the Third Destruction, or did it disappear in the Second Destruction?

It disappeared before the Final Destruction — most of it anyway, with some parts remaining until the Final Destruction. Most of it had disappeared before that final confrontation. Don't forget that this whole area was very unstable for many years; there were many earthquakes. There were constant movements. The islands kept shrinking in size until the end. It was not something that happened overnight in the southernmost portion of the Atlantean continent.

You said the oceans rose approximately 160 feet. After the Second Destruction was there a mud shoal left, and if so, for how long was it impassable?

Yes, there was a massive debris field of mud and buildings. Bodies intertwined in the wreckage, and this lasted for many years. It was impassable for some time. The Atlanteans could only move about by air. Boats and ships were almost impossible to use.

It remained impassable for nearly ten years; afterward, there remained a flotsam of rubbish. Those traveling by boat from the Mediterranean and northern Europe who either went to investigate or were on business were forced to turn back. Eventually, the flotsam disappeared into the depths of the ocean or washed up on seashores where it slowly disintegrated.

THE ISLAND OF POSEIDIA

After the Second Destruction, Poseidia was one of the islands that remained?

That's correct. It was considered the main island.

How large was the island of Poseidia during Atlantean times before it sank into the sea? What could we compare it to today? Was it, say, larger than Jamaica?

Yes, considerably larger than Jamaica. It was about the size of Cuba [42,426 sq mi] — perhaps a little larger than that.

What about the other islands? Were they all fairly close together or were they scattered?

They were fairly scattered. Poseidia was a northern island.

How large was the island where the Sons of Belial lived?

Not as large as Poseidia, perhaps one-half to two-thirds as large. The Sons of Belial occupied several islands, so you might say things equaled out. Those islands were located in the south.

Were any of the other islands named Gadeiros, Amperes, Eriamon, or Antokhton?

Yes, these were names of several of the islands, which related to the legends Plato had read and heard about.

Where did Plato obtain his information?

He had old manuscripts, you see, which he never revealed.

Did the Second Destruction cause a worldwide freeze?

Most assuredly. Weather systems were disrupted, which caused severe weather.

Were the Atlantean islands in a sort of cluster after the Second Destruction or in a chain ranging down to the south?

Somewhat of a cluster. Three of the islands were far to the south, so they were not really inhabited, as don't forget, it took many years to recover when the continent broke apart. Had they been farther apart, there might have been a chance for them to continue without attacking each other, but as you can imagine, nothing happens by coincidence. The islands were meant to be within close enough proximity to have to adjust to each other's beliefs. They found it impossible, leading to their destruction.

You will not make that same mistake again. You will learn to live together. This might seem impossible to you today, but I can assure you that it will happen.

Did the Lemurians know when Atlantis sank?

Yes, it was quite easy to know, due to the tsunamis that traveled around the world. However, by the time the tsunamis reached them, there was much less energy. This was accompanied by the ocean level quickly rising — not like how I plan and do an inch at a time now in modern times.

Was this because of the ocean levels, small tsunamis, or did they have the capability, such as we would, to hear about something happening from our news broadcasts?

All of the above. They had the capability at that time of communication, and suddenly there was none. Then came the ocean, and even though they were half a planet away, they felt the effects as the waves crashed about.

As quite a bit of the Atlantean continent sank in the Second Destruction, I would think that the major increase in ocean levels came at that time.

You're correct, but what was left by then was a very large island and several smaller ones. When they all sank, it displaced a great amount of water, so the combination of the rise in ocean levels (by several feet) plus the tsunamis created by the sinking affected the whole world, including Lemuria.

How far south of Poseidia were the islands occupied by the Sons of Belial, including Aryan?

Not a huge distance — several hundred miles. It was within the range of the aircraft of that time. That is why the remaining islands were not as occupied, as they were far to the south away from all the others.

How close to Spain was the island of Poseidia — 1,000 miles, 1,500 miles, or more?

It was a little more. The Atlantic Ocean is fairly wide, and Poseidia was not located in the exact center but slightly to the west. Even though it was a large island, it was diminutive in relation to the ocean. If you transposed Cuba, let's say, and rounded the shape, that would give you an idea of its size.

Speaking of islands, Gaia, I wish to verify information previously received. Are the Canary Islands and Bermuda remnants of the Atlantean continent?

That is correct.

So were they part of the islands that made up those occupied after the Second Destruction?

Yes and no. The Canary Islands were not occupied at that time, with the exception of what you would determine as outposts and crystal-boosting stations. Bermuda was different. It was at least a partial remnant of one of the islands remaining after the Second Destruction. But between the warring and rise in ocean levels, along with the tsunamis, all the people living there perished. Archaeologists would have to dig deep in order to find any remains of civilization there.

Were the Azores or the Bahamas considered one of the three?

Yes, a portion of the Azores (as don't forget the ocean level was 200 feet lower than it is now) plus one of what were the Bahama Islands today. It is hard to visualize when you see maps today, as between the islands you see ocean and not land. Even England was connected to Europe until Lemuria sank.

Are the ruins off the west coast of Cuba part of Atlantis or another society?

No, these were part of the Atlantean Empire, we will call it.

Did it sink before all the other islands in the Third Destruction?

Yes, before. This can be dated to around the Second Destruction.

Why wouldn't the ruins be on the east side of Cuba instead of the west?

Because the Cuba you know was not fully connected to the Atlantean Continent, but it was close by. There are many artifacts and ruins yet to be discovered under the sea that were part of the Atlantean Empire.

Did the tsunamis created by the destruction of Atlantis submerge the land known as Dog-gerland³ off the coast of Britain and Scotland, and if so, was it the First, Second, or Third Destruction?

Of course, this land was too close to Atlantis not to have been affected by tsunamis and the increase in ocean levels caused by the land displacement. The ocean simply covered this lower-lying land, making Britain and Ireland islands instead of the original European continent.

This happened mostly during the Second Destruction, but it was also affected by the Third Destruction and the sinking of Lemuria as well.

How many people inhabited this area?

Tens of thousands of people inhabited Doggerland — many more people than your scientists have been able to deduce so far. But these cataclysms decimated populations.

• • •

ATLANTIS: THE THIRD DESTRUCTION

Theo, was the third destruction caused by the warring factions?

Absolutely. They used the crystals to destroy each other.

Did Atlantis finish destroying itself by fire or simply the sinking of the islands?

The crystal-powered ray guns had great bursts of energy and therefore burned thousands and, yes, millions as it destabilized the very molecular structure of not only the people but also the islands they lived on. Many people saw firsthand the awful power of the ray machines.

How many islands were there before the final destruction?

Besides Poseidia, there were eight, of which five contained the majority of the Sons of Belial. The others were small islands at the bottom of the chain by what is now the Bahamas.

Did they sink all at once?

No, they tried to destroy Poseidia, but they met great resistance and weapons. It was a horrific time, as the rays killed thousands and the islands were structurally disintegrated. You can imagine why it would be ingrained in so many people to never use ray guns again after that experience.

THE FINAL BATTLE

How many days did the final battle between the two antagonists last?

---

3. Around 6500 or 6200 BC, Doggerland, which once connected Great Britain to mainland Europe during and after the last ice age, gradually flooded and now lies beneath the southern North Sea (http://en.wikipedia.org/wiki/Doggerland).

A little less than two weeks. By then, the islands completely broke apart. People tried to flee; however, there were few survivors. Most were either killed by the ray guns or fell into the ocean when their part of the island collapsed.

Did the Sons of Belial attack Poseidia first?

The Sons of Belial attacked first. Much planning went into the attack, as they wanted to serve a knockout blow and destroy their enemies, thinking they would not be able to retaliate.

Was this similar to the Pearl Harbor attack during which a large number of aircraft attacked all at once?

Yes, and with even more aircraft than took part in the Pearl Harbor attack.

Would that number be over 200 aircraft?

Yes, more than 325. That was almost exactly the number of aircraft that attacked Poseidia.

I assume they attacked not only the Golden Gate city but also their military installations, including their airfields?

Yes, they thought they knew all of them, but some of the bases were hidden from view.

How many people were slain in the first attack?

Approximately 1.5 million, as Poseidia began counterattacking. Then millions more died in the days that followed.

Yes, it had to be millions based on the populations at that time.

Quite correct. It was a bloodbath, to use your term. They would have kept on killing, but they needed to regenerate their crystal power on board.

Why couldn't they tap into the crystal grid of Poseidia?

The Poseidia military was sophisticated enough to shut down the grid, forcing the attacking aircraft to retreat. The planners had not considered that.

How many aircraft were lost in the first attack?

Well over one hundred were lost, as there were batteries of ray guns that shot down many before being disabled.

I assume the aircraft attack was planned for the surprise factor and did not include any naval vessels?

That's correct. But they also honed in on the warships at port and destroyed most of them. And just like in the Pearl Harbor attack, there were warships not in port, which were ordered to retaliate against the Sons of Belial people. That included aircraft on board the warships, along with aircraft hidden from view on Poseidia.

Did the Poseidians respond the first day, or did it take a second day?

There was an immediate response; however, it was not as massive as they endured at the hands of the Sons of Belial.

How many times did each side attack?

Over and over again, as besides Aryan, there were the other four smaller islands. It was a terrible conflict, as millions of people died in this war. No other war in the history of the Explorer Race, including modern times, saw so many killed — incinerated — at one time.

Then we can safely say that well over 3 million people were incinerated before the islands sank?

You can double that number. Then pieces of the islands started collapsing into the sea. Few escaped.

So Poseidia did not sink all at once but rather in pieces or chunks of land?

That's true. And the same can be said regarding Aryan and the four other islands in the cluster.

Surely the leaders of the Sons of Belial knew they would destroy Poseidia with their attacks?

They did not care. They hated their enemy so much that they wanted to literally wipe them off the map. They just had not taken into consideration that they would suffer the same fate too.

You previously said that each side's leaders were equally at fault. What had the leaders of Poseidia done that made the Sons of Belial want to wipe them off the face of Earth?

They were in conflict before the sneak attack with all the aircraft. They had already had battles at sea and among their aircraft, so this was an active war. However, it had not escalated to a point of attacking each other's homelands.

The Sons of Belial were steadily losing men and ships, and they felt there would come a time when they would not be able to respond. They believed that a massive attack would make Poseidia incapable of responding. But just as was demonstrated in your WWII attack of Pearl Harbor, there was an immediate response.

Was our Pearl Harbor somehow connected to either the Atlantean or Lemurian wars?

Yes, you keep coming back to learn lessons, and WWII was the big lesson. There have been conflicts since that time, but they have not been worldwide in scope. Nuclear weapons have never been used again.

Did any of the planners of Pearl Harbor or WWII generals and admirals have prior lives in Atlantis or Lemuria during which they performed similar duties?

Yes, some did. These were soul contracts, you understand, as they were quite good at commanding and planning. So they had lives on both sides of the World War II conflict. There are some souls whose main interest is being a soldier, and they live lives from the equivalent of privates all the way up to generals and admirals.

Did either side use their armies to invade?

No, this war was fought with ray guns from the sky and from naval vessels. Each side tried its best to obliterate the other and in so doing sealed its own fate.

But you have said the leaders of Poseidia were no better than those on Aryan?

That's true. They ordered attacks much smaller in scale before the large attack. There was a steady drain on the military as the attacks by both sides escalated. This was not something that happened to a peaceful society. What was horrific was the scale of the attack and the millions of people who lost their lives. Civilians were caught up, just as occurs today when bombs and armies kill women and children as part of the strategy to thwart the supposed enemies.

Were the weapons on aircraft attacking from the sky, or how did they transmit the rays, since I assume it had to be line of sight?

The saucer-like aircraft delivered the killer rays. Warships also delivered some, but the majority came from attacks from the air. That's why the movie *War of the Worlds* was so scary at the time. Many of the people in the audience had memories of that life on a subconscious level. As you recall, the aliens in that movie used death rays, but on a much smaller scale than did the Atlanteans.

• • •

Gaia, were the Atlantean islands totally disintegrated or just destabilized to the point that they sank? And was the destruction accomplished by heat, sound, magnetic destruction, or what?

There was not total destruction by these giant ray devices, but the land turned liquid on the surface, causing destabilization of the land surface as the molecules were torn apart. This is the best way I can describe it at your stage of development.

But was this heat, sound, or magnetism in some form?

It was a combination of heat and magnetism. That's as close as I wish to describe it for you.

• • •

Theo, how many people were able to escape the final sinking of the Atlantean islands, and did those islands sink all at once or over a period of time?

Bear in mind that the warring factions had the giant crystals and were able to use them as giant weapons of destruction. They used them on each other, so the islands sank within a fairly short time of each other. The wars, and the severe earthquakes that resulted, weakened their underground structures. To answer your question, those who stayed perished. There were a few thousand who were able to leave, but that was very few compared to the original size of the population.

I assume many of these airships and such were lost as they tried to escape at the very end?

Oh, quite a few crashed as they lost their power source. Those people waited too long and paid the price, so to speak. But of course their contracts were over.

What a horrific war when you get into the dirty details.

Yes, it was — the worst in the history of the planet.

Was Florida underwater at the time of the Atlantis destructions?

Yes, it was at times during those 50,000 years. It was a low-lying area of land and was washed over by the destructions.

When did it become dry land?

After the third, and final, destruction.

How high did the waters rise after the Third Destruction?

About forty feet. These were islands that sank, not whole continents, but still the displacement of six islands sinking in the ocean would be as if a large island, such as Japan, sank.

• • •

ANCIENT MAYA

Gaia, what percentage of understanding and knowing the history of the Mayan civilization have archaeologists uncovered so far?

Ah, an interesting question. Obviously, from the constant discovery of Mayan ruins deep in the jungles of the Yucatán and down to Central America, there is much more to find and learn about, about 30 percent. The Mayan civilization is much older than previously thought, and archaeologists are just scratching the surface of their older settlements. The grand pyramids and cities came much later.

There will be many discoveries that are more significant in the next ten years, and even more for years to come as more ruins of early settlements are found. Then there was the influence of the Atlanteans who resettled there as the islands of the continent began warring.

Did the Maya come from Atlantis?

There were a number of Atlanteans who resettled in that part of the world. They melded fairly well with the local populace, as they were far above them in technical skills. Over time, this was lost to future generations. But to answer the question, there were already people living there, which the Atlanteans eventually commingled with and added their DNA to.

How many Atlanteans migrated to Mexico and Central America before it sank? Was it over 100,000? Was it over 500,000?

It was more than that number — about 600,000 to 700,000, but over a period of 200 to 300 years, so they were absorbed fairly easily into a large amount of territory.

Did the Mayan calendar originate in Atlantis?

That's correct. The Atlanteans taught them about the stars and planets and cycles, as the Atlanteans had been around for 50,000 years. Again, I point out how much you have accomplished as Earth societies in just the past 6,000 years. They had almost ten times as much time to build on. Plus they had a lot of contact with your ET friends until it was decided they were on a path to complete destruction.

There must have also been some migration to Oz toward the end of Atlantis.

Not much, as the people were not very friendly toward each other, so they tended to migrate in other directions.

Were there some areas that retained some spiritual purity in Atlantis toward the end?

Yes, there were still people who practiced the Gentle Way all the way to the end of Atlantis, as I might remind your readers that they could not all follow you to Egypt due to family obligations. That would certainly be the largest group of people who were not caught up in the hatred and greed spawned by the two groups.

Didn't I have a life during which I went down or drowned in the final collapse of the Atlantean islands?

Yes, you did. That was one of those lives you lived to balance, or atone, for your misdeeds that caused the continent of Mu to disappear — you, along with several other leaders. It was not your act alone.

Was I a child, or had I reached adulthood yet?

You were a child, and this was simply one of your balancing lives after your life on Lemuria.

How did the sinking of the Atlantean islands affect the ocean currents?

Actually, not as much as when the continent broke apart, you see. Before then, the ocean current from the south ran along both the North American and Atlantean coasts, as they were fairly parallel to each other, and warmed both. So that coast had milder weather than the coast facing Europe, as the current went around the northern coast of Atlantis and curved down again. After the main part of the continent broke apart, there was a period where the currents were fairly erratic as the islands split the currents. After the islands sank, the currents slowly formed to what they are today.

Did the sinking cause the Ice Age?

Yes, in a way. The warm air did not block the arctic blasts; therefore, snow and ice built up — but not to the extent it had many thousands of years before.

Did either the Law of One or Sons of Belial have settlements on the North American continent before the final battle?

Each definitely had settlements, but they kept completely separate. As you were told before, when these islands destroyed themselves, most settlements were wiped out by tsunamis. Those who were living farther inland rebounded for a time until the continent of Lemuria sank, and they were wiped out when the waters rose over 170 feet all over the world. People migrating from Asia over several thousands of years eventually repopulated the coasts.

Were the Vikings descendants of the Atlanteans, or were they plopped there by an ET society?

It was much more the latter. They were a nomadic people who existed before the Final Destruction of Atlantis, and they were almost wiped out by the tsunamis generated when the Atlantean islands disappeared. Only those who were on higher ground survived.

So you're saying the tsunamis reached all the way past Europe to Scandinavia?

Yes, of course. Massive waves were born from the sinking, and these tsunamis circled the globe. Obviously the farther away from the Atlantic, the less damage was caused, as the tsunamis lost their energy. But Scandinavia was not that far away if you look at in on a map. Certainly, the lands closest to the Atlantean islands took the brunt, and millions of coastal people died.

Chapter 9
LEMURIA
Gaia, Theo, and Antura

Gaia, were the Lemurians and Atlanteans always separate, or were they once together?

They were always separate. They were seeded at slightly different times and by different off-worlders. Their makeup and mindset were different from the Atlanteans. They were much more spiritually in tune with nature compared to the Atlanteans, who were of a much more scientific bent. The Lemurians allowed and accepted the Atlanteans as they were, but because of their differences, they generally went their own ways, having just diplomatic ties rather than a great mixing of cultures. The Atlanteans looked at the Lemurians as rather quaint and strange people. They sort of looked down their noses at them.

Mu and Lemuria are one and the same?

Yes, the continent is Mu and the people who live there are Lemurians. It's as if you said the "Murians," you see.

Are the names "Mu" and "Lemuria" interchangeable?

That's correct. Lemuria is the more formal name.

Was Mu located in the Pacific Ocean?

Yes, it was surrounded by the Pacific Ocean.

Was there more than one country on the continent?

Yes, actually several, which was part of the problem, you see.

Were there more than five countries on the Mu continent?

No, that number was just enough to cause conflict and the desire to subjugate and to add on and expand their borders.

Were any of the countries on Lemuria landlocked?

No, all had their own coastline. As this was a smaller continent, the coastal area built up first, similar to your Australia today, and slowly expanded into the interior. Unlike Australia, it had few dry places, as they received much more rain than Australia does today. I use Australia as a comparison, as we have previously said Lemuria was slightly larger than the Australian continent of today.

Was Lemuria a female-dominated country? Was it mostly rural?

I can answer yes to both questions; however, the rural slowly gave way to cities over an extended time, and the female gave over to the male.

As they eventually destroyed themselves, was there a height of their existence when they were a loving people before they deteriorated into warring with each other?

Yes, just a few thousand years before their decline. The decline happened slowly, as these were normal people with karma that built up over many lifetimes, because there had to be balancing — just as was the case for Atlantis.

Were there several forms of government — kings and queens, dictators, democracies?

Yes, yes, and yes. There were all those and a parliament-type government too. They had quite a variety on that continent because of the number of different countries.

Did the people speak different languages in each country?

Yes, of course. This was one of the problems they had: the inability to accept each other's cultures and traditions. Each country thought its ways were the best.

Were there multiple religions?

Yes, another difference that was part of the problem — which you had to readdress in your times in order to solve the problem of multiple beliefs. You were not able to solve that problem back then.

Did any Lemurians lead ethereal lives?

Yes, but only at the start.

• • •

MU'S RELATIONS

Theo, in the past you have told me that Lemuria was inhabited several million years ago, but then you used the figure of 50,000 years of inhabitation. Why the great disparity?

There were a number of early experiments done on that continent, but they were later abandoned. Then a second wave, if you will, of inhabitants were installed approximately 50,000 years ago, about 13,000 years after Atlantis was seeded. The land of Mu lasted about 5,000 years after Atlantis sank into the sea.

Was the continent of Mu connected to Japan before it sank?

It was much earlier. But when the main portion of the Atlantean continent sank, the ocean rose 160 feet, and when the islands destroyed themselves, it rose another 40 feet. Therefore it was no longer connected.

Was Korea connected to Japan?

Quite so. Again, the connection was lost at the same time as was the Japan-Mu one.

Did any Mu country subjugate Japan or Korea?

There were forays into both lands, but it was more for trade with the local people. Bear in mind that for thousands of years, the Mu were gentle and loving people. "Live and let live" was their motto, you could say. Then it turned nasty in those last few hundred years. Their attention was turned toward each other and not to those lands. So there were people who migrated there to escape the wars and animosity.

Did Mu sink 7,000 years ago?

Closer to 7,500 years. Using the figure given to you before of it sinking 5,000 years after the Atlantean islands sank is a good approximate figure.

Was the continent of Mu ever below sea level except for mountains surrounding it at any time?

No, that was a misconception. Before the continent of Atlantis sank, its shores, just like those all over the world, were 150 feet above the sea. When the Atlantean continent sank, it lost all of its shoreline below that line. Then when the Atlantean islands sank, it lost another 40 feet of shoreline. They lost several million people, just as the rest of the world did, and they had to rebuild towns and cities.

There was not a specific event, as the Atlanteans experienced, before their wars?

No, the Lemurians lead an idyllic existence for several thousand years before the slow but sure decline took place. It was just seemingly small things that divided the people into countries. You could compare it to parts of Asia or Africa or even Europe, where countries were created according to their beliefs. The people all had a similar appearance, so race was not an issue. Beliefs and governments and greed cast a shadow over the continent and eventually caused their demise.

In chapter 2, you stated that the Lemurians visited Hawaii, as that was a peaceful place away from the hatred growing between the two factions. Were there beach resorts on the island, and if so, how did they keep the two sides apart?

It was quite simple; the beach resorts were limited to one or the other.

There was absolutely no mixing of the two factions. There religious beliefs were too strong, including what they would wear to the beach. The people were well aware of where the other faction's resorts were located, and people were forbidden to contact them.

When Atlantis's Second Destruction occurred, these beach resorts were wiped off the map as the ocean rose over 150 feet. Then there was no time for vacations, as centuries passed with the people having to recover from losing all the continent's coastal towns and villages, along with the loss of millions of people.

I would have thought that the resorts were at such an early stage that the animosity would not have been so great?

It was much less later, so it was more that they were of different beliefs. There was a simmering cultural difference mostly kept in control. It was just felt that because of these differences the beach resorts would be kept separate. This was long before the animosity grew to hatred and war.

Did people see the end coming in Mu as I did in Atlantis and migrate away?

Yes, they did. That's how Asia and Japan became populated. Small groups migrated there and integrated with those who already existed. But this was different from Atlantis in a way; most of the population stayed, not knowing that their leaders would trigger their doomsday bombs. But to return to your original question, yes, a few thousand years before their demise it was an idyllic, almost utopian existence. They just were not able to sustain it.

Speaking of the population, did Lemuria have a larger population than Atlantis?

Yes, before that continent's destruction, the number of people swelled to over 40 million, and the population of Atlantis was just over 25 million before the Second Destruction. The population of Atlantis was greatly reduced before slowly building up again, but it never rebounded completely. Lemuria did not have the same problem that the Atlanteans had living on a very unstable landmass on top of the Mid-Atlantic Ridge.

Then the Atlantean population was over 25 million but nowhere near the 40 million living on Lemuria?

Not even close. As I pointed out before, families had fewer children on both continents. Large families will be a thing of the past one day here in modern times.

What was the average size of the families?

Four to six was the average size. It partially depended on religion, just as it does today.

THE LEMURIAN WAY OF LIFE

What was the Lemurians skin tone like?

They were, for the most part, a lighter skin tone, not red-skinned like the Atlanteans. They were browner in color. To answer your next question, they did not have multiple races, only one.

Were they Asian in appearance or Caucasian?

More Asian.

Was the average height of the Mu people the same as the Atlanteans?

Yes, perhaps a slight difference but not too much.

Did the Elven¹ race originate on the continent of Mu?

No, it did not. This race of beings was more centered in Europe, but their colonies were scattered all over the world — of course in a different focus. The Creator, may I remind you, loves variety and felt that humans needed to interact at times with these people.

Did one or more societies in Lemuria use tones for their names?

Yes, there was a particular sect that chose tones or musical notes for their names. This was not widespread, but a particular group of people explored sounds.

Do the Lemurian crystals, as they are called, have ties to Lemuria?

They is a type of crystal that resonates at a certain pitch or level. Therefore, this vibrational level is connected in a way to modern society.

*   *   *

Gaia, how many crystal skulls have been discovered so far — more than five?

No, the number is less. There are skulls that are modern copies. So keep the number down at three to four.

Was the crime rate in Lemuria the same as today's?

The crime rate was much lower, even in the end. The people lead pretty normal lives, with the exception of the leaders who whipped up their citizens' passions and hatred of the other countries, just as is done today.

How advanced were the people? Did they have air travel, as an example?

Yes, but not the same as the Atlanteans. They were fairly well progressed but different. They were powered by energy different from today's. Their aircraft was fairly close in speed to the Atlanteans' — about 200 to 300 miles per hour.

---

1. Elven, or Elves, are supernatural beings in Germanic and Norse mythology and folklore.

. . .

Theo, in chapter 5 you stated that the Lemurians used a power source different from the Atlanteans. Was it a power source we have discovered and used or another?

It is another one. Again, due to the longevity of these two societies, there are energies you have not yet discovered, just as it took those two societies time to discover it during their 50,000 years of existence.

Then it was not atomic power, was it?

Correct. It used magnetics, but not in the same way as the Atlanteans did to power up their crystals. It is a power source you will soon discover.

How many people could their aircraft hold?

They carried very few. They were mostly used by the military, so certainly most of the craft carried fewer than ten people.

How did they travel during the days of Mu? Did they transport by portals?

No, it was much more conventional. They had trains and other forms of public transport for the typical family to use.

How fast did their trains travel?

The trains were fairly fast, but not as fast as the Japanese, or French Train à Grande Vitesse (TGV), of today's travel. Sixty to seventy miles per hour is about the top end — sufficient for a smaller continent, especially when the countries started closing their borders and people were prevented from traveling to each other's countries.

How large were the cities?

The largest city had several million people — higher than you might have thought, I believe.

How tall were the buildings in the cities?

They, like the Atlanteans, tended to keep their buildings under twelve stories, as they had space. They were not as densely populated as you are now.

Did they live in houses or apartments or both?

They lived in both. It depended on whether they lived inside or outside the cities, you see. The houses certainly were not as grand as those today — simpler cottages, you would call them.

Did the inhabitants of Mu have what we consider bathrooms in their buildings and houses?

Yes, of course, although there were areas on the continent that were definitely more rural in nature. But Lemurians had sanitary systems. They were quite advanced with over 50,000 years of inhabitation, just as the Atlanteans had. But greed, corruption, and power did them in, just as it did the Atlanteans. They could not live together, so that's why you — meaning society as a whole — have these same challenges today, which you are slowly but surely solving. You will not destroy yourselves this time, I can assure you.

Did they have public or private baths?

They had both, partially depending on their religious persuasions or beliefs, just as you do now.

Did they eat meat or were they vegetarians?

Religions came into play here too regarding what they ate, just as it is today.

Did they have a form of TV?

Yes, toward the end they did. The societies become more advanced, but again this was one of the causes of their demise. They developed a form of rocketry, not the same as you have today but slightly similar.

Did they have books, newspapers, and magazines?

Yes, but not to the extent you have today. Most were state-run newspapers to control the information given to the people. There was much propaganda in these publications.

Did the Lemurians have schools similar to today's?

Yes and no. They had schools that taught the basics, but some were of a religious nature.

So I assume they had math, geography, language, and so on?

Precisely. These were more sophisticated people who had been living on this continent for 50,000 years, so they had progressed in most areas. But as we have discussed, they could not live together, and again, that's why you are working on this in modern times, as you did not solve it in either the Lemurian or Atlantean times.

•   •   •

Antura, did we ever have a life together on the continent of Lemuria?

No, the number of lives we had together had to be quite limited due to the similarity of our energies. The same can be said for the rest of our soul cluster. Keep in mind that our souls wish for us to have as many different experiences as possible in these Earth lives, and living together in any form diminishes the varied experiences. That's the way most clusters operate, shall we say. There are always exceptions, but that's the general rule.

• • •

THE SINKING OF MU

Theo, I've never asked you whether I had any lives on the continent of Mu or Lemuria.

Yes, certainly you had a number of lives there before it disappeared from the face of the earth. You were quite instrumental in causing its demise.

I was one of the bad guys, then?

That's quite correct, my friend. It took you many lives to correct, or balance, the scales. Remember, you have to be both for your soul's knowledge.

I thought on the continent of Mu everyone was very peaceful and the continent sort of just disappeared into another focus.

That's not a true story. They had their conflicts just as the Atlanteans did. In the Lemurian lives, you were both good and bad.

Weren't the people of Lemuria much less oriented toward inventions and such than the Atlanteans?

That's true, but they were human. They were not just some blissful people who went around in a state of bliss or ecstasy. They had problems and conflicts too.

If I was a bad guy during the days of Lemuria, didn't I incarnate to be a bad guy, and if so, why did I have to spend several lives balancing?

Good question. Yes, you incarnated to be a bad guy to balance the good lives, but you went overboard in what you did and therefore contributed to the demise of the land of Mu, as it was called then. Your position of power made you even greedier than you were supposed to be, and you took actions that contributed to the deaths of many people.

What was my position back then? Was I a political leader or some sort of religious leader?

In this case, you were a corrupt religious leader.

Where was my country located — in the southern, northern, eastern, or western part of Mu?

Your country was in the western part.

How many lives did I live on the continent of Mu?

You had several but not as many as on Atlantis — about sixty-five.

How many lives did it take for me to balance the bad life on Mu?

It was quite a few, about eighty-four. It took you quite some time to balance that life, as you can imagine, with all the destruction you were responsible for causing.

What sort of lives did I lead to balance the Mu life?

Obviously there were many tragic lives when you died in wars. You also had to witness others being murdered in war and to be part of their families to feel that heartache. You lived lives as religious leaders during which you accomplished much to bring love to those around you. Those lives of attrition are finished now, and you can look forward and not dwell so much on what you consider your worst life on Earth.

Was there a conflict between groups in Lemuria as there was between the two groups in Atlantis?

Yes, there was great conflict.

Did religious conflict sink Mu?

Yes, partially, as well as cultures and most especially the leaders who wanted more territory for themselves and wanted to subjugate their neighbors.

Was one of my balancing lives after that the benevolent life in Atlantis?

Yes, that was a great balancing life for you, but you had to have others — many others — in order to completely balance.

Did the continent exist before, at the same time, or after Atlantis?

It existed both before and at the same time. Its demise occurred several thousand years after the demise of Atlantis.

Then I had to go back in time for the benevolent life on Atlantis?

That's true.

Regarding my soul contract, you said I had balanced the life in Mu. Was that true, or am I still trying to balance it?

In a way, you are still trying to balance it, as it hung heavy on your soul for quite a long time. But you are balanced. It is just ingrained in your persona to try to assist people.

How long ago was Mu populated?

Actually several million years ago was the first time it was populated with humans. Almost as far back as you can imagine.

• • •

Gaia, on the continent of Mu, how large was the population before its destruction — 60 million?

No, not quite that much. It only reached about 40 to 42 million.

Then was this just before the continent exploded or imploded or sank?

Yes, that was one of the reasons. Density of the population and, as we discussed before, greed. There was a period when things were quite idyllic, but that disintegrated over time as the population grew and the countries started warring with each other. All the souls learned valuable lessons and many were able to cross off events they had to have on their bucket lists, as you like to call them.

Did many people leave Lemuria before it sank?

Not as many as did Atlantis. Don't forget, Atlantis broke up into islands first; many people perished. Some people started to migrate away after the first catastrophe. But Lemuria had a slower migration; therefore, many more people perished when the warring countries blew themselves up.

Are the underwater ruins near Yonaguni-Jima, Japan,[2] part of what was Mu?

Yes, they are. Researchers should do further studies in that area.

Were the ruins at Yonaguni part of a city, or were they some sort of religious structure?

No, they were part of a city — fortifications, if you will. Again, I will say that much work should be done on these ruins, as many ancient artifacts will be discovered beneath the sands. It is a treasure trove of findings for archaeologists. You will see some of that come to light in the next few years, as more scientists will be attracted to these ruins to either prove or disprove when they were constructed.

When was it constructed?

It was constructed during the last few hundred years of the continent's existence. These were massive fortifications, and they were not constructed overnight. It took much work.

How far below the sand does it go?

Not too much further, but surely well over 100 to 200 feet more.

Did the author of The Art of War [Sun Tzu] have any lives on Mu or Atlantis?

Yes, that was his soul interest. He was a great tactician who needed lives in both continents before writing his well-known book.

Did Mu have siege battles for the coastal cities? Is that the reason for the fortifications?

Yes, there were threats and they most certainly made the necessary preparations. There were some attacks on coastal cities during that time period as well.

How long before the end did the wars heat up — 1,000, 500, or closer to the end?

It was a little over 500 years. Before that, there were conflicts but not to the extent of those fought during its last 500 years. You can see this even in today's

---

2. To learn more about the ruins discovered by divers in 1987, see http://news
.nationalgeographic.com/news/2007/09/070919-sunken-city.html.

times when wars will suddenly break out between different countries and different belief systems. It was the same then — a growing animosity between the people living in those five countries.

Were the wars on Mu between the countries mostly on the ground up until the end battle?

Largely. There were some dog fights, we will term them, if any aircraft ventured into the other country's airspace, but it was mostly light infantry with some armored vehicles and what we'll call artillery — but not the same as today.

Were any missiles used?

No, those were restricted, as they were quite powerful.

Was there any use of biological or chemical weapons?

No, that was truly verboten. Those have only been used in modern times.

Did all the Mu countries have an infantry, a navy, an armory, and an air force, plus I assume some form of air defense?

Yes, they had all these in the later stages before the final battle.

THE FINAL BATTLE FOR LEMURIA

What events led up to the last battle for the Lemurians?

It was slightly similar to the Atlantean debacle, as all the countries were connected with no water in between, save rivers and mountains. These were natural boundaries, and they served to keep the warring factions apart.

There were constant skirmishes and smaller battles going on in those last days. Diplomacy was tried by all sides but to no avail. They could barely agree on what day it was, similar to negotiations today in which each side is rigid in their beliefs. Each wanted the others to disappear. This resulted in much hatred between the countries, and there was no end in sight.

How large were the bombs, or was there just one fired by my country at the other? And were they as large as the atom bombs dropped on Hiroshima and Nagasaki?

They were even larger. Bear in mind, these people used a different form of energy than you do today.

How were the bombs delivered — aircraft or missiles or in some other way?

It was quite standard. They just dropped them on the targets.

How many did we send?

Two, which you believed they would have no capability of defending. You were right on that score, but the other countries sent a massive retaliation, and then you retaliated again. By this time, many of the cities in each country were destroyed, and with the use of the superbombs (we will call them) came the destabilization of the continent. Great pieces of the continent began falling into the sea. They were more powerful than anything you've seen in modern times. Today, you cannot imagine how terrible this conflict was. It was even worse than the final battle of Poseidia.

How many people died in the first attack — the two bombs in Lemuria?

Yes, just like what had occurred 5,000 years earlier on the Atlantean islands, well over 1 million people perished.

Did they drop the two bombs on one country or two?

On two that were aligned with each other.

You had previously said there were five countries that made up the Mu continent; is that correct?

That's correct.

Did they all retaliate against the first country, or was one or more aligned with the people who dropped the bombs?

No, there were no countries aligned directly with the first perpetrator. One or two of the countries had tried to remain neutral, but when the first country attacked, they were sucked into the war. The war quickly caused the breaking up of the continent with these massive bombs cracking Earth's crust. You might say the whole continent shook and shuddered with a dying gasp. Then the waters rushed in, as you can imagine.

How long did it take for the continent to split apart?

Not long, just a few days. The continent could not sustain its stability, as the bombs were so much larger than those used against Japan at the end of World War II. There were huge earthquakes — much larger than any seen in modern times — and the continent began to split up with first one section then another and another dropping into the sea. Enormous tsunamis were created that washed over what was left, so it was difficult for anyone to survive, but a few did, especially those who saw it coming.

There were survivors?

Millions of people lost their lives. There were a few survivors, and don't forget that there had been some migrations of people wishing to escape the war. They went in several directions to resettle.

Why didn't we think the other side would retaliate?

You underestimated the other side's ability to strike back. You and the others thought they would capitulate, but they did not. And you weren't aware they had developed weapons of mass destruction too.

How long had the war or hostilities lasted when my country bombed the other two?

Quite a few years, as the buildup did not happen overnight. There were many border clashes, including the attacks from the sea. Thousands of people had already perished.

Was there one explosion or a series of explosions that caused the continent to sink?

There was a series of explosions, as each country tried to wipe out the other after the first country attacked.

I would think those explosions would have been seen for many miles with clouds that would have swept across the oceans.

You are correct. It frightened many people living in the surrounding land-masses who had no idea what had just occurred.

When did the continent of Mu sink — 7000 BC or 7,000 years ago?

More toward the latter date. Don't forget, Mu existed 5,000 years longer than the Atlantean islands. I know it is a little confusing, but we are using general years here as, obviously, it did not take place exactly then, but that time is good enough for your purposes.

How did the sinking of the Mu continent affect the rest of the world?

There were giant tsunamis, which devastated coasts all along what is considered the Ring of Fire today.

Was there any event that occurred to raise the ocean levels after Mu sank?

No, that was the last time the ocean levels rose a significant amount. You must understand that most of the records that were kept at that time were destroyed by the rapid rise of the ocean levels. As we discussed long ago, there were many people who lived in low-lying areas, such as the land connecting England to the European continent, who lost their lives.

Then, yes, as you were going to ask, the boot of Italy connected to Oz (or Africa, as it is now called). It just happened earlier than records indicate today, as this was passed down verbally through generations, finally appearing on modern maps, such as the one in the 1500s. But that map was constructed based on very old maps that have disappeared over the ages. Even today, old parchments from just 1,500 to 2,000 years ago disintegrated unless they were kept in perfect conditions.

Was Italy still connected to Oz (or Africa) until Mu sank, or had the waters already overrun the land when the Third Destruction of Atlantis occurred?

Yes. Most of the land connection was already lost at that time. The sinking of Mu simply widened the Mediterranean to the approximate shape it is today.

Would you say the estimates of the Mediterranean and the ocean levels rising approximately 1.5 feet per one hundred years would be incorrect?

No, those estimates were based on modern calculations that considered coastal towns, saw how deep into the sea they went, and tried to calculate when they were above sea level based on how old they thought those settlements were. It was actually much slower after that last major event of Mu sinking. Keep in mind that it was slightly larger than Australia is today, so it displaced an enormous amount of ocean. Your modern calculations are erroneous, but they will someday be corrected when you learn more about your history from ET visitations.

Does the large Asian population have anything to do with Lemuria?

Yes, to a certain extent it does. There were immigrants to these lands in ancient times, so there was a budding population from the beginning. Although small in number, these tiny enclaves eventually grew and spread out across the continent of Asia and elsewhere. They, the Lemurians as a whole, were the seed populations. They are even more ancient than they realize.

I had previously read somewhere that the sinking of Lemuria was more about the collapse of the landmass than what I was told was because of war.

Yes, there was some sinking of the landmass itself over a number of years, but the major upheaval and the resulting sinking came from the warring nations or countries using colossal bombs that fractured the very heart of this continent.

So there you have it — the second sinking of a whole continent.

Chapter 10

INNER EARTH
Gaia, Theo, and Adama

Gaia, was there any connection between the Atlanteans and the Inner Earth?

There was some connection between the two, sort of like ambassadors, but that is all. The people who inhabit the planet underground really wish to be left alone, for the most part, with the exception of the Lemurian colony at Mount Shasta. They are assisting with your people's growth and will make an appearance after the shift to a higher dimension.

Are there Lemurians living underground in western Arkansas?

There were, but few if any exist today. They have the ability to travel vast distances through tunnels constructed eons ago, but their stay in that part of the country was brief. The ancient mines are there, of course.

How far down are the caverns where people live? Are any third dimensional?

The caverns are at various depths, but the closest ones to the surface are down approximately one mile. They range from there down to ten miles deep into my belly, I will say. There are those living lives in the third dimension, but for the most part, they are higher in focus than you — fifth-dimensional focus for the majority. Then there are a few with even higher focuses — seventh to ninth. There are a wide variety of peoples inhabiting my interior, and most wish to be left to their own pursuits, and I allow, as they are of a higher-dimensional focus.

Did they take over caverns that were already in existence, or did they work with you to ask for space?

In most instances, they simply asked to use certain unoccupied spaces within me that had light — of which you'll discover the source one day, plus

Figure 10.1: Carlsbad Caverns National Park located in southeastern New Mexico.

rivers, streams, lakes, and so on, needed for their sustenance. They, for the most part, live much simpler lives than you do on the surface, as they are not part of the Earth experiment.

Are there any beings living in the Carlsbad Caverns (see fig. 10.1), and if so, at what focus?

Yes, much farther down in the yet-to-be-explored regions of this maze of caverns are several sets of beings who make use of the space. But they are at higher focuses — not just five but seven to nine as well. They live their lives and wish to be left alone. You will not discover them anytime soon.

At the higher focuses, do they build towns or cities?

Yes, at the five focus they do, but none are really needed above that, as they can create anything they wish.

Why did Dianne Robbins (author of Telos*)[1] receive the information that Atlantis destroyed Lemuria, compared to what you told me?*

It was given to her that way so that she would not have to delve into the reasons for Lemuria's destruction. That was not her purpose, you see. It was to give the public information about Telos. Had she been given the actual information about them destroying themselves, she would have naturally wanted to explore that in more detail, and that was not what her soul contract called for her to do.

---

1.   Dianne Robbins, *Telos: 1st Transmissions Ever Received from the Subterranean City beneath Mt. Shasta* (Create Space Publishing, June 2015) p. 27.

What advice can you give us for progressing at this time?

That's an easy one: Love and respect one another, and accept and allow others to be different from you. If you are able to accomplish that even on an individual basis, you will assist all on Earth to raise their vibrations and become more loving.

• • •

INNER WORLDS

Theo, is there a tribe of Inner Earth people living under Mount Shasta, Mount St. Helens, and the Atlas Mountains called Agartha or Agharti?

There are Inner Earth people living under all three of these areas but at a slightly different focus or dimension than you, as we have discussed before. The Lemurians live under Mount Shasta, and there are the Aghartis who live under the mountains but at a slightly different focus, slightly higher, so that they can live their lives peacefully.

• • •

Gaia, is there such a place in the Inner Earth as Agartha, or is this perhaps a combination of the different inner worlds or inner societies you have spoken about before?

There is some confusion here. There are over twenty societies living beneath the surface, most of them at focuses different from yours on the surface. None of them are part of the Earth experiment, and there have been just a few times when those on the surface have stumbled across them. This was not by chance, you understand, but to create mysteries to introduce you to the concept that there can be civilizations living beneath the surface of any planet you reach in the future. Agartha is but one of these societies and is forbidden from contacting you except during dream times, such as you do with the Lemurians at Mount Shasta.

What about the depiction [by Gerardus Mercator in figure 10.2] of the whole Inner Earth as one gigantic world unto itself?

That's overdramatized. Certainly there are some enormous caverns with their own light from crystals; however, it's not as depicted in the artist's drawing.

How long have the societies occupied the interior of Earth, and have any of them, except the Lemurians, lived on the surface?

The figures are all different, according to which society you examine, as they came at different times. None of them were on the surface except for short periods on arrival, with the exception of the group from Lemuria. You have to understand that many societies all over the universe live underground, so

Figure 10.2: Map of the Inner World created by the Flemish geographer and cartographer Gerardus Mercator in 1569.

this is nothing unusual for them. They were attracted to Earth because of my immense caverns with light and water and all the things they would need to live. As you travel the stars, you will encounter many societies who live underground because the conditions on the surface are too hot or too cold for life there, but the interiors can be quite pleasant.

How can the readers get in touch with these societies in the dream state?

Most wish to have nothing to do with you on the surface. Only the Lemurians signed up to assist those of you who reach a certain vibrational level to conduct classes during your dream times to assist you in raising these vibrational levels. So your duty is to raise your vibrational level to that point through your actions. Naturally, this includes requesting most benevolent outcomes and benevolent prayers. Doing so assists in raising your vibrational levels. Also, show compassion and truly be gentle and nice to all you meet in this life.

Earth is going through a sort of birthing process right now in adjusting to the new energies, and there is great resistance from those following a violent path, which is not sustainable in the fifth focus. Many more people will exit in the next few years. Your readers can assist in this process through requests for MBOs and constant benevolent prayers for peace, assistance to those in harm's way, and for world leaders to make decisions in the best interests of all the citizens, not for just themselves and their thirst for power. You will be successful, I promise you. Though things may appear dire at the moment, this will not last.

Is it common for there to be many societies in the interior of planets, such as Venus and Mars?

No, it is not common. This planet has many attributes, or assets, that make life possible compared to other planets in this solar system — even in thousands if not billions of other systems in the universe. Earth is much more unique than you know. There are a great number of other water planets in the universe, but they do not have the makeup of the interior that this planet has. There are underground lakes and rivers and streams, which you humans know just a little about. There are large caverns in my interior with their own light that is almost as bright as the Sun but less intense. So the interior of this planet is just as attractive for life as the exterior is.

I would assume the societies would cover the gamut of possible life forms?

Yes, for the most part, that's true. Sorry to be a little vague here, but I'm asked to keep it vague by those societies who do not wish to be visited by humans based on your writings. A number do not wish to be known at all by Earth surface dwellers, so I respect their wishes and do not allow information to be given out about their existence. They each have their own desires and experiences about what they wish to do with their lives in the interior.

There are great varieties of humanoids beneath my surface, some so strange that you would have a hard time conceiving that they are earthlings like yourself. You would think they must be alien, but they are not. To answer your next question, there are several hundred alien species here to study. It is a very crowded place, but you are not allowed to see it yet. Some will be revealed to you in the next few years, so enjoy the experiences.

Are most of these societies living at the same level vibrationally as the rest of the universe compared to Earth humans who are now close to 5.0² — close to the 5.3 or 5.4 for the rest of the universe?

That's true. I'm glad you made the connection. They are not taking part in the Earth experiment, so they can be at the same level as their universal brothers and sisters.

• • •

2. According to what I've been told, each dimension — or "focus" — has many frequencies, so as an example the Explorer Race is now at the bottom of the fifth focus at 5.0. In the next hundreds and, yes, thousands of years, we will increase our vibrational levels to 5.3 and 5.4.

Theo, am I supposed to contact one or more of the underground dwellers, such as the Lemurians?

Yes, they are open for contact from you.

I would think the book on Atlantis and Lemuria would be the primary purpose or no?

Yes, they are willing to assist you with their history.

Is the contact Adama or one of the several hundred other souls making up the group?

Adama would handle the connection, as you and he have met several times in the past. He sends you his regards right now.

I send mine too and wish him a good life. It looks as if I'll have to come up with some questions for him.

That's fine.

I assume the other timelines — upper — are already in touch?

You guessed it, but don't let that stop you. He can fill in the blanks.

• • •

MOUNT SHASTA AND TELOS

Gaia, when I sent white light this time to Earth's interior, I thought I heard a response: "Thank you." Did I imagine this?

No, you did not imagine the response. One of the beings in Earth's interior responded to your wish of sending light and love to them. They appreciate you thinking of them, and they wish you well too.

What dimension are they on?

A higher fifth dimension.

Was it one of the Lemurians?

Yes, exactly. You've been in touch with them before. So it was not a hard connection to make.

Now that our focus has risen, will the Lemurian people who live in Mount Shasta soon be visible to us? When will that happen? Are they already visible to the upper four timelines?

They are not yet visible to the upper timelines, as you call them. They will see them first, but it has not been deemed the time for them to make their appearance known, at least not publicly. They will, as was the case during your trip, come in ones and twos to explore the world and allow a few people to see them to continually keep everyone talking about them, at least in the Mount Shasta area.

Did Lemurians live at Castle Crags, California³, south of Mount Shasta, and what is its history?

---

3. Castle Crags, just south of Mount Shasta, bears petroglyphs chiseled in its coarse granite rocks up Castle Creek. The artistry of these symbols shows greater skill and symmetry and a higher degree of culture than others found elsewhere in the southwestern United States.

Nice question. Yes, the children of Mu have lived in that region before and even currently reside there in a higher focus. They put out a vibration that extends to the third focus. Its history extends many thousands of years back to the time when the Lemurians were active in setting up outposts or colonies. This was one of the places they were drawn to.

Will the Lemurians make a public appearance similar to the ETs, or will they remain at a slightly higher focus?

They will remain inside the mountain for some time to come. There will be a time in the not-too-distant future when they will wish to show themselves, but society is not ready for this to occur yet. They will begin to make more appearances and will tell their story to you. But don't expect them to come running out en masse to greet you. It will be after the ETs make their public appearance, and it will not be such a big deal as it would be to happen now. So let's say within the next fifty years or less, depending on how people accept the idea of ETs and certainly after they give you your history of Atlantis and Lemuria.

They're not veiled as we are and are not part of the Earth experiment?

That's correct.

Are they in touch with ETs?

Yes, they're in touch all the time.

• • •

Theo, when did the Lemurians leave Mu for Mount Shasta?

They left not long before the two factions blew up the continent. These were gentle people who could see where things were headed, and they were advised in their meditations to leave.

How many migrated?

Just very few migrated. Not more than one hundred or so souls made the trip.

Were they in the fifth or the third focus when they moved?

They were in the third focus when they migrated. Through energy work, they raised their focus to the fifth focus. They were quite adept at energy work and were ahead of the rest of the Lemurians in this area. It is somewhat the same now. You have certain people who vibrate at a higher level than the rest of the population. These people, as we have discussed before, are yogis and other spiritual men and women, such as shamans, who can access the fifth focus at will. But it takes much work and a lifetime of dedication to achieve such results.

What is the size of their population in the fifth focus now in (or under) Mount Shasta?

They have kept their population at a steady few hundred. As you are about to ask, they have extremely long lives at their level of the fifth focus, and they are not taking part in the Earth experiment, so they do not have the stress and difficult lives that you as a human have. I'm speaking about Earth humans as a whole. They are not the only ones living on this planet who are not taking part in the Earth experiment. As you have been told before, there are over twenty groups in Earth's interior who live at different focuses and are not part of the Earth experiment. They should be of no concern to you, as in many cases, they do not even have human form. Gaia welcomes these people, as they contribute in their own way.

Is Lemurian DNA different from Earth humans'?

It definitely is quite different. They do not have the genes that cause diseases like the Earth population does. They handled any problems with genes long ago through energy work.

What is their home planet?

They are not from one of the Federation planets. They assist us in energy work by holding energy classes during your sleep time, for those who wish to take them. But interacting physically with humans is a ways down the road. It will just be a little at a time, as they are able to lower their frequency to this one when they so desire to walk among you.

They are quite tall.

Yes, both the females and males are around seven feet tall.

But what about the instance when I spoke with a woman who was married at a Kryon Summer Light Conference (June 17–19, 2005) at Mount Shasta who was told a Lemurian appeared at the foot of her bed one night and asked her to marry on that stage?

Yes, this was part of their assistance to us by creating an energy for all those who were in that audience at that time. If you could have seen that ceremony from our perspective, it bathed the audience in a higher level of energy, plus you and your wife were in the audience to meet those two. We naturally knew you two would sit near them at the conference.

What planet are they from, as you say they are not from a Federation planet?

No, but one we have energetic contact with.

They were never part of the Earth experiment?

No. This may be hard to understand, but they were allowed to be there during the time the Earth experiment was taking place and to have lives during that time. They chose not to enter the program and agreed, on a soul level, to assist humans in the future who wished to learn about energy work, as they are (and were) well versed in these abilities. You could compare it to a group of shamans and women.

Did the one hundred or so Lemurians have a leader when they migrated to Mount Shasta?

Yes, of course they did — Adama. He transitioned and returned more than once to continue — a sort of Dalai Lama as you have today.

Did they all leave at one time, or did a few prepare and the others followed?

They all left at one time. And to answer your next question, they went by boat.

Had they already chosen their landing place before departure?

Yes, they did this through their meditations.

What about the local people, or were there none?

There were a few, but they did not interfere with them. The tribes in the area considered them holy men and women with their tall statures.

Of the group of one hundred that migrated to Mount Shasta, how many were adults, as I assume there were children too?

There were children of different ages when they departed Mu. It was almost evenly split between adults and children.

How old was Adama when they migrated?

He was already over 200 years old at that time. This was quite unusual, as the residents of Mu did not have such long lives. But all the Mount Shasta Lemurians did.

How long did he live after arriving at Mount Shasta?

He lived another 200 years.

How long did it take them, after arriving at Mount Shasta, to raise their energy levels to the fifth focus?

Not as long as you might think, as they concentrated and had many meditative sessions, we will call them, to achieve that level — so less than one hundred Earth years.

Do they have their own schools and hospitals?

Yes, of a type. Healing is done through colors. Schooling is elective.

Do they have planned birth control?

Not as you know it. Keep in mind that life is much easier there, so they conceive when they want to conceive.

Since they are a small community, what do they do for food and nourishment?

They have their own farms, and water is plentiful where they are.

What about clothes?

Their clothes are lovingly made by those who enjoy that service.

What do they do for recreation?

They play simple games. Keep in mind, they teach classes for those in the third dimension who visit them during their sleep time. This keeps them very busy. Also, they do not need currency.

Do they have spaceships?

No. If they wish, a scout craft can be provided at their disposal for any length of time, but this is only when they wish to explore. They also interact at times with people in the third dimension who live in or visit Mount Shasta.

How did they keep up with the progress of humans after they arrived?

That was easy. They simply went into meditative states, and they could keep track of your long return back to your present-day level.

• • •

THE EARTH EXPERIMENT

Okay, now I wish to speak with Adama.

Adama here. Good morning.

Good morning — or day — to you, Adama. Nice to make the connection again.

Yes, I've been waiting for this day for some time. As you heard, your higher timeline selves have already been in touch, so it is good to make the connection with you.

Great. Sorry I was so slow.

No problem. You are admired for your willingness and determination to cut through the energy levels, we will call them.

Where have we met before? Was it all nonphysical, or did we actually meet in person in times past?

Actually, it was both. We met in the olden days, in your lives in Atlantis and then of course in a couple of lives on the continent of Mu.

I'm surprised we would have met during my times on Atlantis. How was that accomplished?

It was quite easy, as I had the ability to visit Atlantis. It was not so much that you visited me, you see. A vehicle was presented to me for my use when I needed it. I would simply put out the call and one of the ET vehicles would pick me up.

How did you know about me?

It was quite easy, as I tuned into your meditations and saw the good work you were doing, especially in the life you had when you were inspired to create the Gentle Way. That was a very significant life for you. Therefore, I reintroduced myself to you, as we had met in a life there once before. As you know, my lives are quite a bit longer than the typical Earth life, so I can span generations.

Were the lives on Mu times when I was just the bad guy, or did I have lives during which I would have been classified as a good guy?

That's a good question. No, you had lives as both a good and, we will we say using your language, a bad guy. I understand you still feel a sense of shame, but it was part of your soul contract, and like millions of others, you strayed off the path — your soul contract.

How long before Mu sank into the sea did you and your group leave Lemuria?

It was quite some time — about 300, as I know numbers can be a little difficult for you.

But that would have been well before I was born.

Yes, but again, I have access to transportation when I need it.

Adama, everyone living on Mu was involved with the Earth experiment except your group, am I correct?

Quite correct. All continued with the Earth experiment after the continent disappeared from the face of Earth.

How were you and your people able to be on Earth during the time of the Earth experiment and not be caught up in it or become part of it, as I think you are the first and only people I've heard who were not?

Yes, it was because we agreed to assist those souls who needed to work or study during their sleep time. We perform a service that you and many others have taken advantage of. To more fully answer your question, we communicated with the Creator's emissaries who told us this service would be needed and asked whether we would be interested in assisting. As Theo and Gaia have told you before, when Creator asks you to do something, you can refuse, but we don't know of anyone who has.

Then you were on a planet already in this universe?

Oh yes, we were small in number but had these interests and capabilities.

How were you able to be birthed on Earth?

It was not an immaculate conception. A few others and I came with human-type bodies first and slowly developed the population.

Were you and your people always quite tall?

Yes, fairly close to the height we have now, which as you know is around seven feet.

You really stood out in the crowd back in the Lemurian days, then.

It was understood and accepted that we were there for a purpose, and we were known as very peaceful people. Most of the population did not understand that we were not some offshoot, as there were a number of different-looking people during those times.

Have you and I met physically since you migrated to Mount Shasta?

No, it was only during your sleep time when you came for our classes.

I understand you traveled by boat to the West Coast and not by spacecraft?

It was easier by boat and was not very noticeable to the general population. I had already scouted out the area, you could say, using one of the spacecraft, so I knew where to go and that there were few people in the area on the route we would take to Mount Shasta. We were considered holy men and women when we encountered anyone who allowed us to pass peacefully.

Did you immediately enter the caves, or did you live above ground for some time?

No, it was immediate. We did not want to have to cut trees or take stones to make houses, so we immediately went into the cavern system.

How long did it take you to raise your vibrational levels to the point they are today?

It was less than one hundred Earth years. We were quite adept at doing that, dating all the way back in time to before we arrived on Earth.

How many countries were there on the continent when you were there?

There were three primary countries with a couple of smaller ones. Those three were the most powerful, dangerous, and greedy.

How many languages were there?

There were five. Not as many as you might have imagined.

How do you generate light in your caverns for your life there?

The light is generated by certain crystal formations. It is not the rocks but the crystals that generate light, as heat in the deep interior is translated into light for the caverns. The heat is transferred to light, and the caverns remain at a steady temperature.

Are there crystals that automatically generate light on their own?

No, there are no crystals that automatically generate light. The light has to come from somewhere, and here the heat of the earth generates light and also gives the caverns a mild, steady temperature. There are no fluctuations as there are on the surface.

Adama, back in 2010 I received that you did not reach your seven-foot height until you had been at Mount Shasta for a long time. Which is correct: Your people were tall during your many years living in Lemuria, or you developed this height when you settled in your new home in Mount Shasta?

Yes, the former is correct. We were tall for those times in Lemuria, around six feet, but did not allow ourselves to stand out too much from the population. We did anyway, you see, but after we settled in Mount Shasta, we had no need to be shorter. Again, you were having a little problem with reception that day, but you are able to correct it today.

That is part of the receiving process, Tom, and why you remind your readers that your reception can waiver at times, not only due to fatigue, but also due to circumstances beyond your control, such as planetary alignments. It was decided long ago for you to receive all the time and not worry about whether there was a full moon or heavy alignments such as squares and oppositions of planets, as they have energy largely dismissed by your scientists. This will change in time.

You said you were taller than the average Lemurians — around six feet in height? That would be closer to average today.

That's correct. The average male Lemurian was between five feet and five feet five inches in height, so even our females, who were just slightly shorter than our males, were taller than the Lemurian men, and they were much taller than the Lemurian women who were typically less than five feet tall. This was very common back in those days and even extended to your modern times.

Adama, how do people enroll in your dream classes, and what is taught there?

Not the easiest question to answer, but I'll try. These are energy classes, and although that sounds like a general statement — and of course it is — pupils are taught how to be more open to reception and how to raise their vibrational level. You would consider this very esoteric information, but it is needed for those who wish to progress. Therefore, this is done on a soul level according to the vibrational level you have reached.

Those who are consistently requesting MBOs are raising their vibrational levels so that they become eligible for advanced studies, which our clan agreed to conduct millions of years ago. All souls have different interests, but our souls have this interest, and we are quite happy assisting others. They can request MBOs to take part in our classes, and we will work with their GAs to make the classes available to them when they are ready.

Would you say you have had millions of souls take your classes over the years?

That's quite true, but we have been doing this for thousands of years, and the number can vary according to how the individual souls are progressing.

LIFE IN TELOS

Did Mu sink all at once, or was there a series of destructions?

There was a series of destructions very close together.

Did you observe this happening from the air on board a scout craft?

Yes, I did, as I was informed it was taking place, and I called for a ship to be made available to me. It was a scene I will not soon forget. Neither I nor anyone in my group had ever seen such destruction.

How long did the destruction take?

It took just a few short days. Not in one day but certainly much less than one month, just a few days, since it was as if dominoes were falling, to use your terminology.

Adama, was your first incarnation on Earth on the continent of Mu, and when was this?

Yes, we never had lives anywhere on Earth before we came to Mu. It was earlier than 40,000 BC, as keep in mind Mu was populated well before that and our group appeared not too long after that — perhaps a thousand years or so — so that we could be accepted, even with our strange appearance.

Did you reincarnate again shortly before the time Mu sank, or how old were you in Earth years then?

I did not need to regenerate my body. I was still young in Earth years at that time.

How many lives did you live before migrating to Mount Shasta?

Less than one hundred as, even with the long lives I lived, it adds up to more than 50,000 years.

Have you had any incarnations elsewhere on Earth, other than in Telos?

No, this is the duty we volunteered for, and there is no need for us to be caught up in the Earth experiment of having lives as you do.

What did we discuss when you visited me in the Gentle Way life on Atlantis?

It was for me to warn you that events were transpiring that would result in the rest of the continent — what was left of it, you see — sinking.

Why wouldn't I have received that in meditation?

You received that information, but I was able to suggest a place for you to take your flock, as Theo has called it, and of course that was Egypt. I simply suggested a direction, and you agreed.

Did you take me up in the ET ship to show me?

Yes, I did. I'm glad you made that connection. We had a quick scouting trip, you could call it, to see where you would go. We weren't gone but a few hours.

Santa Cruz Island (off the coast of California) was once known as LeMu (or LiMuw) by the Indians. Did they know of Mu's existence, or was that a coincidence or just a similar name?

No, there were some refugees, we will call them, who made their way there. They were few in number and did not last long.

When I was an American Indian shaman in the mid-1600s, did I study with you?

Yes, you might call yourself one of my regulars, as that was a significant life of study for you.

Why are your classes not something I would have already learned in my lives as a spiritual leader on the water world?

Good question. The simplest explanation is because we offer advanced studies not even taught or known on your home world. This is knowledge you are able to access when you return to your home planet. This is difficult for me to explain to you since you have no remembrance of what you knew back then. Trust me when I tell you we have added to your knowledge, which you will be able to access at any time in future lives not only on Earth but also on your home planet. That is the service we provide.

Did you meet with any of the priests or leaders of Atlantis, and if so, what was the purpose and results?

Yes, we tried to convince them that their actions would continue to lead to their destruction, but they refused to believe me. They were very obstinate men who have already been described to you as selfish and greedy. We thought it was worth the effort as I visited both factions, but I came away knowing I had had little effect on their thinking of that time.

What are your future plans for assisting humanity?

We are performing what we came to do, and that is assisting the Explorer Race during your sleep time.

How often do the citizens of Telos interact with the humans who live around Mount Shasta?

There is a slow but steady stream of contact. Some of the Mount Shasta area citizens have seen and spoken with us numerous times, but they do not publicize this. Then there are the tourists who see a couple of seven-foot people and think they must play basketball somewhere.

Is it true several extinct species of animals live with you in Telos?

Just a few — very few; here you would have to know more about extinct species for me to discuss this with you, but for the most part, this was quite limited.

There will be no surface people visiting you in the near future in Telos?

No, our city is at a different vibrational level than you, so that will not be happening in the next few hundred years.

Adama, when your people interact with those on the surface, how are they able to lower their frequency, I'll call it, and for how long are they able to do this?

That's an excellent question. This is something they are trained to do. We do not use any props or devices. This can be accomplished internally. It just takes great concentration, which they have learned over many years. Don't forget that we lead much longer lives than those of you on the surface, so what appears to be young people to you might be people who have already lived one hundred or more years here — Earth years.

Regarding how long?

Just as long as we need for a short foray on the surface in order to perhaps mingle with the local population. We are able to judge the overall vibrational level of the population when we do these appearances. And this constant contact solidifies our existence with the local population and, at times, tourists whom we feel will not be any danger to us. We have the ability to read auras, so we can steer away from anyone who might pose a danger to us.

Are you able to cloak yourselves in some way so that you can't be seen?

Yes, in a way. We simply raise our frequency just a little and "poof!" we cannot be seen. But it's as if we are looking through a transparent screen and are still able to see you. This is something taught to our children at an early age. It ensures we remain safe when we venture out for these contacts.

Did you have the same appearance on your home planet as you do now?

No, we adapted this appearance when we first came to Earth. We look very different. In a way, it is the same for the majority of people alive today. Almost all of you, with the exception of the people who came from one section of the Pleiades, have quite different appearances on their home planets like you do on your home planet. The Earth experiment would not have worked if everyone had a completely different appearance.

Will you return to your home planet at the end of the Earth experiment?

Most likely, we will — unless the Creator wishes for us to take on some other task. We are quite happy here in Telos. We have very gentle lives and are able to work with all of those who are raising their vibrational levels in dream time. We have the capability to handle almost unlimited numbers of people in these classes. There is no magic or set number that would be beyond our capacity and ability to do this work.

How are you able to work on the quantum level with people in a dream state?

It is second nature to us to achieve that level when we desire to. It is obviously done in a meditative state. There is someone always on duty, to use that expression, to greet those who are able to take these classes. It would not help you to describe them to those who read this, as it is very esoteric in nature and would leave them scratching their heads. It is sufficient to say that on that level they absorb what they need to from the classes. Even you have attended these in the recent past. You have just progressed over time to graduate studies, we will call it. When you awaken, your mind simply translates it into attending a university.

Did your people chisel the petroglyphs at Castle Crags or was it people indigenous to the area or perhaps some survivors from Mu?

We instructed the local people how to do so. We wanted there to be mysteries as to what the petroglyphs mean. The symbols, part of the pictographs, are a sort of calling card. If it attracts tourists, that is good, as people will be exposed to a lot of energy in this area. They return home energized in more ways than they know or understand.

Did Lemurians live at Castle Crags, and if so, was it your group, as you had previously stated that you went in immediately to the cavern system of Mount Shasta?

You're correct. We did not linger on the surface. Castle Crags became home for a short time to other Lemurian migrants before it sank. They eventually moved on, as the people indigenous to that area did not welcome them.

Are there any general subjects about which I should be asking specific questions?

No, I think for your purposes, this is sufficient for us. We want to introduce ourselves to a new group of people while encouraging them to begin following your Gentle Way and begin raising their vibrational levels. If they do, they may possibly be at a level to take our classes one day. It could be a few months for some people and several years for others, but it's all part of their journey of learning on Earth.

Adama, I thank you for our conversation, and I look forward to more in the future.

I know we will meet again. Keep up your work, as you will find what you are doing will contribute to world peace, and it will happen much faster with you involved.

Chapter 11
EVIDENCE OF THE
LOST CONTINENTS
Gaia and Theo

Gaia, did the Mayan temples connect to the akashic hall of records?

Not really in the way it is asked. Certainly there were Mayan priests who had the ability to tap into the akashic records, but the majority of the Mayan priests could not. This was considered forbidden territory for them. So the temples acted as their form of worship for the most part.

The small group of Atlanteans took with them records of the Atlantean civilization dating back as far as their records went. They are still in Guatemala waiting to be discovered, yet it will be quite some time before they are located. The akashic records exist as crystals in a cave, but they are not accessible in the third or fifth focus. Your souls pass by them on their way to birth and then as they depart Earth.

Was I aware of the group from Atlantis that traveled to the Yucatán during that time (200 years before the islands sank)?

No, they left soon afterward. They too could see what was coming. Their GAs warned them, and they left.

Can the akashic records be accessed for benevolent purposes?

Yes, they are available for all those who have reached a certain vibrational level to access them. That typically prevents anyone of a lower vibration from accessing them.

Therefore, we cannot say the akashic records are in Egypt, can we?

No, not really. There are records of the Atlanteans and their history that have not been discovered.

SIGNS

Where did Plato learn about Atlantis — from manuscripts or just verbally?

The records he viewed had been kept elsewhere when he discovered them. One day these records will be discovered. They are stored in an archive; they are buried among a number of others. A researcher will find them one day.

Did Plato or his father or grandfather bring back manuscripts recounting the Atlantean times from travels to Egypt?

It was his grandfather. He brought them back, fascinated with the story, but Plato was the one to write about it, based on a limited number of manuscripts available for his review.

Then the documents are not in the Vatican Archives, are they?

No, they're in another in Greece.

I read that in my life as Strabo (from 64 BC to AD 24)[1] that I believed the stories about Atlantis. Did I find manuscripts or records of some type, which I wrote about in the history of the world, that have been lost in time?

Yes, he (you) read manuscripts. That was another reason for them to be lost. We did not want that information out quite yet. Now sufficient time has passed for you to write about those times again.

Is the city recently discovered by archaeologists in a marsh in Spain[2] the fabled Poseidia central city, or is it one that perhaps was modeled after the original city and constructed in an outlying area?

This city they have discovered was modeled after the central city, just as here in the United States you have several capitals and even houses or mansions modeled after the Washington, DC Capitol building and the White House. Naturally, there was a reason for this alignment, we will call it, in energetic terms. Let them have their fun in their discovery. This was not the main city but a smaller duplicate of it.

Did it sink as the result of the tsunami, or was it flooded due to a rise of sea level?

A combination, as certainly there was a great tsunami caused by the sinking of the remnants of the continent — plus the sea level rose appreciably.

Ruins off the coast of Cuba were discovered recently. Did the ruins off Cuba's west coast sink or get flooded after the Second or Third Destruction of Atlantis or after the sinking of Mu?

---

1. Strabo was a Greek geographer, philosopher, and historian who lived from 64BC to 24AD. He traveled widely, and his descriptions of that ancient time are still read and studied today. Theo first told me about him when I asked if I had ever visited the Hanging Gardens of Babylon, and he confirmed I had — both as Strabo and in another life.
2. National Geographic Channel, *Channel Finding Atlantis*, "Looking for the Lost City." Information about this television episode can be found at http://natgeotv.com/uk/finding-atlantis/galleries/looking-for-the-last-city, accessed May 21, 2015.

It was after the Second Destruction when the waters rose 150 feet or so. Then they were covered with more water in the next two events, but there were few survivors after the first event. They were right on the coast at that time, so there were few survivors who were living closer to the interior. Almost all lived somewhere on the coast.

Why are there not more traces of Atlantean technology? Is it being withheld?

Not really. Bear in mind that this continent existed over 28,000 years ago, and look at what it takes to excavate towns and villages that existed only 3,000 years ago as you can see when watching NOVA.[3] Everything is covered in dirt over centuries, so much is hidden below the surface of the earth. But a few remnants of their civilization are starting to appear, such as the one in the marshlands of Spain. There will be more discoveries, but most will never be found.

When were batteries used in Mesopotamia, and how did they learn to use them?

A good question! They were used quite a few thousand years ago, and this knowledge had been passed down from generation to generation even at the time these particular batteries were discovered. Naturally, this knowledge originated in Atlantis, but when the continent sank, only those away from the coasts of Europe and Africa survived. So it was mostly farm folk who survived, and the knowledge of the electricity was passed down, eventually disappearing.

Was the Bimini Road off the coast of Nassau human-made, and if so, was it constructed during the Atlantean times?

Most agree that this road — yes, it was a road — was constructed during Atlantean times. It was at the far reaches of this continent, but they had developed this area to a certain extent. There were some villages in the area, long since covered by the ocean, that will probably never be found. So it is another of the enigmas for people to ponder and explore. You need these mysteries to slowly learn about how old and how long humans have inhabited Earth — millions of years.

Is Easter Island a remnant of Lemuria?

No, not exactly. It was on the outer band of an island chain. It was visited many times by the Lemurians, and it also had its own population.

Do the Hawaiians date all the way back to Lemuria?

Yes, in a way, but more from a point of view when other islanders visited them who were direct descendants.

---

3. NOVA is a long-running, award-winning documentary series broadcasted on PBS that focuses on science, its many applications, speculation, history, and researchers.

Please comment on the symbols found on the columns in Italy. Were they made up, Atlantean, or ET?

No. The builder was channeling the Atlantean times, and the symbols were from then.

Was the cold period known as Younger Dryas[4] around 12,900 BC caused by the last islands of Atlantis sinking?

Yes. Although it took just a little time for these events to manifest after the sinking, it caused the weather systems to be interrupted and changed, and the oceans rose from the displacement of the islands. It caused the weather systems to change course and eventually cold air to be released from the arctic, dropping the average temperatures for those years. Naturally when that occurs, you have snowpack that does not melt, causing the temperatures to drop further to the south. This was quite evident to your meteorologists and geologists.

Did the sinking of the continent of Mu cause the Mid-Holocene Optimum[5] around 7000 BC to 5000 BC?

When you have a great displacement of land anywhere in the world, it disrupts ocean currents and air currents, and the sea levels rise dramatically. There has to be a cause and effect from this kind of displacement, so it resulted in the period known to your scientists as the Mid-Holocene Optimum. You will see smaller examples of this as your oceans rise the two feet I promised. It will change the weather patterns around the world. There will be cooler temperatures as more rain is generated.

What were the Baigong pipes[6] used for in China, which seem very ancient?

It's an interesting question that seems quite unsolvable. Advanced societies slowly disappeared from China. I am referring to the continent of Mu, which had mining interests in this area. The pipes were used for these purposes, but what was being mined, I will leave for future archaeologists to determine. Needless to say, these pipes dated back over thousands of years to that period when Mu was an active society with broad needs and interests. Much more will be discovered in China in the coming years, some by accident and some by studying satellite images.

---

4. Also known as the Big Freeze, the Younger Dryas is one of the most well known examples of abrupt climate change. Learn more at the National Climatic Data Center: https://www.ncdc .noaa.gov/paleo/abrupt/data4.html.
5. Paleoclimatologists have long suspected that the Mid-Holocene period was warmer than present-day temperatures. Learn more at the National Climatic Data Center: https://www .ncdc.noaa.gov/paleo/globalwarming/holocene.html.
6. The Baigong pipes are a series of pipe-like features found on and near Mount Baigong in China. To learn more, see http://en.wikipedia.org/wiki/Baigong_Pipes.

• • •

Theo, who constructed the Money Pit on Oak Island?[7] Was it Atlanteans?

Good guess! Yes, its location made it ideal for a small group to hide treasure due to the instability and warring among the islands that remained of the Atlantean continent. Alas, they went down with the ship when the islands sank. So the treasure to be found in the future will provide some solid evidence.

How long before the mystery will be solved?

It will be solved in a few years — no more than, let's say, ten to fifteen years.

• • •

THE THERANS AND THE ISLAND OF DELOS

Gaia, were the Therans descendants from the Atlantean colony or continent?

Yes, some of them were. At one point, the Atlanteans had a colony in the area, not necessarily Thera. When Atlantis was going through the throes of war and destruction, there were those who said, "Enough is enough," and they left Atlantis. Some of them migrated to what is now known as Santorini,[8] just as your group migrated to Egypt. The Therans were already there, and they reluctantly accepted the Atlanteans who professed they were in no way interested in taking over the island.

Did they predate the Minoan civilization?[9]

Yes, somewhat. This was another group who added the Atlanteans.

Were the Theran females on an equal basis with the males?

Yes, at that time they were. Later, over a long period, this equality eroded.

Did the Therans influence other civilizations?

Yes, to a certain extent, but they were influenced by other civilizations too, you see, as there was great trading back and forth around the Mediterranean area. So there was certainly a little mixing going on over the years.

Was the island of Delos[10] occupied before 500 BC, and if so, how much earlier?

---

7. Oak Island in Nova Scotia, Canada, is noted as the location of the so-called Money Pit, a site excavated for treasure for over 200 years. Learn more about this fascinating tale at http://www.oakislandmoneypit.com.

8. Santorini is one of the Cyclades islands in the Aegean Sea southeast of Greece. The whitewashed, cubist houses of its two principal towns, Fira and Oia, cling to cliffs above an underwater caldera (crater). Learn more at http://en.wikipedia.org/wiki/Santorini.

9. The Minoan civilization was an Aegean Bronze Age civilization that arose on the island of Crete and flourished from approximately 2000 to 1450 BC.

10. According to Greek mythology, Apollo was born on the small island of Delos in the Cyclades archipelago. Apollo's sanctuary attracted pilgrims from all over Greece, and Delos was a prosperous trading port. See more at http://whc.unesco.org/en/list/530.

Yes, quite a bit earlier. It dates back to the days of Atlantis, so quite a few thousand years of being inhabited. It's just that they have not dug deep enough in the ruins to discover an even earlier time. As you saw when you and your wife, Dena, visited the island, dirt has slowly covered up much of the island over thousands of years.

As you read about your life as Strabo, you visited Delos several times and wrote about it. You even wrote about its history, but those writings have been lost forever.

The port of Delos runs into the Mediterranean and then under it. Was there another time when the Mediterranean rose up to cover the port after Atlantis?

Of course! It was Lemuria, which lasted 5,000 years more than Atlantis and caused the waters to rise almost a couple hundred feet more when it sank. Again, hundreds of thousands of people lost their lives all around the world due to the sudden sinking of the continent.

So there was not some other event that caused the Mediterranean to rise after Lemuria?

No, there was a slow rise after that simply due to silt being deposited from rivers flowing into this sea but only inches.

What about when a large portion of Thera sank into the sea?

Yes, that contributed to it but not to the extent of Lemuria's sinking.

What percentage of the present population of Earth has had Atlantean lives?

A rather large percentage, about 64 percent. You should also ask what percentage of the population had lives on the continent of Mu, and the answer is almost the same, 62 percent. Both continents destroyed themselves, so there are plenty of souls around that had previous lives on either or both of them to ensure it does not happen again. That includes you, my friend.

Are the majority of people who had lives on Mu now having lives in Asia?

Yes. The majority of people who have had lives on the continent of Mu are in Asia, since that was the closest land mass near Mu for those who left before the Final Destruction. Millions of them also went down with the ship, as you say. Mu's population was less than that of Atlantis at its peak, as Mu was settled later than Atlantis.

What percentage lived lives on both continents?

About 70 percent.

I wish to clear up figures previously given to me. Are there 3 billion people on Earth now who have had lives on Atlantis or Lemuria, or is it more like 64 percent of the Earth's population?

Yes. The higher figures are correct. Keep in mind that in over 50,000 years for both continents, millions and millions of people lived and died. Some had just a few lives during those times, and others had many, although your 187 lives on Atlantis is at the upper limits, for sure.

There are no records now, so it is extremely difficult for people to imagine that there were thriving societies, highly advanced ones such as Atlantis. Just in the past few years, modern societies have passed them in knowledge, and there are still subjects, such as the use of crystals, which you have yet to discover. You have been able to accomplish this fast advancement because time was sped up for you. Time was much slower back in those days.

Are there descendants of Lemuria living on Earth today, as I would suppose there are many descendants of the Atlanteans?

Yes, in both cases. The Lemurians tended to migrate to the west, populating parts of Asia.

I wish to verify if it is possible for someone to have his or her next life back on the continent of Atlantis, even though it no longer exists?

That's quite so! Not many people today have lives that far back after this one, fewer than 10 percent, but if a life there is needed for a particular lesson, then off the soul fragment goes to live it. It does not matter that the continent does not exist today. Keep in mind there were many ancient cities and towns that were on the shores of such bodies of water as the Mediterranean that are now covered by water. They are all in existence during their time and exist right now in the loop of time. Therefore, it makes it easy for you to have your next life far in the past or even far in the future.

Yes, and those future lives are all taking place right now, Gaia?

Yes, but certainly with a very fluid future with many probabilities. Each day of your life affects those future lives — sometimes in very tiny ways and at other times in major ways.

So is it less than 5 percent of the population that will have a future life in Atlantis?

About 3 to 4 percent.

What type of lives would they need or decide to have during that time?

The possibilities are endless, as even 3 to 4 percent of the population is quite huge. It encompasses every possible scenario. I can't just narrow the possibilities.

What were the stone spheres used for that were found in Puerto Rico?

They were used as part of religious practices in the past; again, another mystery to be solved. They give little hints as to the level of expertise needed to form them. How could they be so precise?

What decimated the American Indians before the white man appeared?

Over thousands of years, they had their own cataclysmic events to contend with, several of which have been reported, such as the flooding when tsunamis struck the coastline. People have lived near the oceans for millions of years.

Are the underwater images shown by the Farsight[11] people actually remnants of Atlantis?

Yes, in this case, they actually found some remnants of this ancient civilization.

Then they were not just natural lines crisscrossing each other on the floor of the ocean?

No, people with underwater equipment should investigate these, and they will find remnants of structures.

How much of our DNA dates back to the Atlanteans?

Some, but not very much. The races have blended so much during the past 10,000 years that their DNA makes up only a small portion of your DNA today.

ANCIENT LORE

What was Edgar Cayce referring to when he said, "... entry of the Ram into India"?[12] And how far back would that be?

He was referring to a person and, of course, a period of time. Certainly this was over 100,000 years ago.

•   •   •

Theo, what truth is there to the story of King Rana and the army of the monkey men and also the Bear King?

These are ancient stories from India's past when there were such creatures. They later died out, as they were part of an experiment, just as there were many others around the world. There were many experiments with different kinds of bodies, including the Things, which abounded on the continent of Atlantis. So there is truth in this legend, which has been embellished quite a bit over the centuries, as it was handed down verbally over many centuries before there was writing.

There was a bridge that existed long ago when the oceans were lower — many thousands of years ago. But there were many creatures on Earth in those early days that were allowed to live out their lives but were not allowed to reproduce. It was decided that the Adam man and woman were best suited; therefore, the other possibilities died out.

---

11. The Farsight Institute is a nonprofit group that has been doing remote viewing research since 1995. Their website is http://www.farsight.org. The underwater images can be found under the Atlantis heading.
12. A.R.E. website, Reading 364-3, http://are cayce.org/ecreadings/Default.aspx.

Was Angkor Wat[13] built by Indian people and then moved to Cambodia by boat and reassembled there using elephants?

No, that is but one story passed down regarding its origin. It was built long ago — longer than previously estimated by people who lived in that area, and they had assistance. It is a colorful story about using elephants for the heavy work, but they used other advanced methods lost over thousands of years. Still, if people wish to believe this story, allow them to, as they are attempting to understand how this huge complex could have been built using ancient tools.

Who were the Anunnaki[14] — simply gods for the people who lived at that time? Or were they actually ETs, such as the Nibiruans?

Yes, that is exactly who they were. As scholars and scientists have no proof that they existed, they would rather assign the Anunnaki to some mythical beings made up by those who lived at that time. But as you have been told before, myths and legends are passed down from generation to generation by word of mouth until they are so embellished as to take on the qualities of gods and goddesses. Mr. Sitchin[15] wrote about them, but his translations were incorrect in many instances, leading people to believe that all his translations were suspect, but that was not the case. You and everyone else will learn much more about the Anunnaki in the future.

Was there a nuclear war fought anytime on Earth in the past involving ETs?

Yes, there was, a very, very long time ago.

Was it part of the Star Wars or perhaps a war between those on Nibiru?

Yes, it was the latter. It is another reason — and I might add, a major one — why they are on a sort of probation.

Are there remnants of this in what is termed Death Valley in Siberia?

Yes, that is the location. That was the only one.

•   •   •

Gaia, was Siberia the only place that suffered a nuclear-type device and explosion?

No, India was hard hit too, but the events happened at different times.

---

13. Angkor Wat is a temple complex in Cambodia and the largest religious monument in the world. Learn more at http://sacredsites.com/asia/cambodia/angkor_wat.html.
14. The Anunnaki were a group of deities in ancient Mesopotamian cultures. See details at http://en.wikipedia.org/wiki/Anunnaki.
15. Zecharia Sitchin (1920–2010) was a Soviet-born American author of books proposing an explanation for human origins involving ancient astronauts. Read more about Sitchin's postulations at http://www.sitchin.com.

It was not the Nibiruans?

No, it was a different war, one fought in ancient times by two warring factions.

• • •

Theo, was the nuclear war in India well before Atlantis and Lemuria existed, or did it occur during the time Atlantis and Lemuria were flourishing?

It occurred well before. This goes back much, much further than even those two ancient societies.

How far back did this occur?

About half a million years.

Am I correct about the Nibiruan war not being fought when the Adam man and woman were in existence?

Not exactly. But let's say the model was getting close to what became standardized. And you still had the Cro-Magnon and Neanderthal models.

Was there a nuclear-type war 500,000 years ago in India or Pakistan?

Yes, there was, but not between humans. The people who existed then were simply casualties.

• • •

Gaia, what happened to Mohenjo-Daro[16] 8,000 to 12,000 years ago, and who caused the explosion?

This was a violent explosion brought on by an ancient war. This conflict occurred much earlier than their instruments and other possible evidence suggests. It occurred in a very ancient time.

Was it part of the Nibiruan conflict?

That's true. This ranged all over the world, as you can imagine, as their spaceships did not limit them to just one area.

What about the crater near Bombay, India?

It was all part of the remnants of a great war. It took thousands of years for the land to be habitable again.

Were the explosions at Mohenjo-Daro and Bombay[17] caused by the same war or two different wars. This is confusing.

The explosions were caused by two different wars thousands of years apart.

---

16. Mohenjo-Daro is an ancient Indus Valley Civilization city that flourished between 2600 and 1900 BC. See more at http://www.mohenjodaro.net.
17. Review the theories of this event at http://www.bibliotecapleyades.net/ancientatomicwar /esp_ancient_atomic_12.htm.

Mohenjo-Daro was part and parcel of the Nibiruan war and the Bombay crater was part of the Eighteen-Day War.[18]

I thought you said previously that there was only the nuclear-type blast in Siberia.

There was more than that explosion, as the two feuding brothers traveled far and wide. They killed millions of people back then, and they were not the Adam man and woman. Then 18,000 years ago, you had the Eighteen-Day War between the two families, which caused great destruction. It was at the height of their development.

That area was demolished to the point of survival mode for several hundred years as it slowly recovered. But the story of the Eighteen-Day War, as was written about in the Mahabharata,[19] has lived to the present day. It was a very ancient war, dating back much further than any scholar has estimated. This legend was based on a true story.

Was the Eighteen-Day War a recount of some sort of nuclear type devices being used?

Yes, this was a bitterly fought battle and large weapons had been created at that time. It is why there is still scarring on the landscape in India after 18,000 years. Millions died in this great war.

Did any of the three continents — Atlantis, Mu, or Oz — send people to fight in the Eighteen-Day war in India?

No, none of the three were drawn into that war. The warring factions had developed superweapons, and there was no need to bring in fighting forces from the other continents. It was what you would call an internal affair.

What was the main inspiration for the concept of the Hindu gods Brahma (creator), Vishnu (preserver), and Shiva (destroyer)? Was it ETs or someone's inspiration or simply an evolving religion?

The Hindu Trimurti[20] was originally very loosely based on ET contacts, but it evolved over thousands of years.

Is Vishnu an aspect of the Creator, an embellished human, or an ET?

Here we do get into religious beliefs, and we say to allow whatever belief someone has about a higher power.

But the Earth Directive was in force then, so there should have been little influence?

Yes, but when you look at India's location, you'll see a place where there

---

18. The Eighteen-Day War is a Sanskrit epic detailed in the Mahabharata. Learn more at http://en.wikipedia.org/wiki/Mahabharata.
19. The Mahabharata is a collection of legendary and didactic poetry worked around a central heroic narrative. Read it here: http://www.sacred-texts.com/hin/maha/.
20. Hindu Trimurti: the three principle deities known as Brahma, Vishnu, and Shiva.

was a seeding of people not really caught up in the Lemurian influence but rather their own influences. There were wars dating back thousands of years. The ETs had to assist in cleaning up the mess. They were regarded as gods at that time. Their religion took on these aspects and simply grew.

Was Krishna a real person?

Yes, he was.

How long ago did he live?

Long before there were modern writings about him.

Was it more than 6000 BC or less?

More, as India was seeded about the same time as the rest of the world with the Adam man and woman models. The stories about him were passed down from one generation to the next and were embellished to the point he would be unrecognizable to his followers today.

Was it before 10,000 BC?

Now you are getting close to when he lived. You can use that number.

How many years did he live?

They had longer lives during those times, but not as long as they were after seeding. For your purposes, go with 125.

Did Krishna have the ability to view past and future lives during his life on Earth?

Yes, he developed that ability, as he had worked on it in previous lives. It was not his first rodeo.

Did Krishna have an effect on the politics or economics of Atlantis, Mu, or Oz?

It was more so those who traded with villages and cities established on the coasts before the waters rose and inundated those towns. Krishna was much more involved in the politics and economy of India — at least his portion of it.

When Krishna died, it was reported that the oceans rose. Was that connected to one of the destructions?

That's correct. His death was timed so that he would be connected to the Atlantean destruction.

Did Vyasa[21] actually exist?

Yes, he was a great scholar of his time.

Then was the Mahabharata written by just Vyasa or by multiple people?

21. Also referred to as Veda Vyāsa or Krishna Dvaipāyana, Vyasa is a revered Hindu figure traditionally credited with composing the Mahabharata. Learn more at http://www.britannica.com/EBchecked/topic/633543/Vyasa.

No, he was the scribe for this.

Has he written other stories in other lives that are known today?

Yes, he has, but they are on a wide range of topics. He was and still is a great writer.

Is he incarnated today?

Yes, but I will not name him, as it would cause undo attention by followers of the Hindu religion.

Was Mahavatar Babaji[22] immortal, or was he the reincarnation of Krishna?

He was not immortal, but yes, he was the reincarnation of Krishna. He was a very advanced soul, but he was not in the class of Jesus.

• • •

THE OLDEST RELIGION

Theo, there are varying reports of Mahavatar Babaji living from 200 BC all the way up to the 1930s. How long did he actually live?

Mahavatar Babaji extended his life, just not as much as people think. He also had the desire to reincarnate, similar to the Dalai Lama, so that he could continue his work. Therefore, those reports were somewhat accurate in their description. He was a great avatar — a guide for his people.

Did I have any lives during which I knew him or had some sort of daily contact?

You had lives both as a friend of Krishna's and then again of Babaji, as you were a close confidant of each. You were not a relative but an observer, a friend, and a confidant.

Is Hinduism the world's oldest religion?

Yes, it is, as the religion is based on people who lived much earlier in human existence. This religion evolved over thousands of years.

Was there the concept of Hinduism in either Atlantis or Lemuria?

There were some very slight similarities in Lemuria, but this religion grew over thousands of years after Mu sank. I must point out that every type of religion has been explored over thousands and thousands of years.

Did the Atlanteans or the Lemurians have contact with the ancient Vedic people?

This contact came more from the Lemurian side, as they were closer geographically. The Atlanteans did not have flying machines, due to the lack of

---

22. Mahavatar Babaji is a deathless avatar who has resided for untold years in the remote Himalayan regions of India, revealing himself only rarely to a blessed few. Discover more at http://www.yogananda-srf.org/lineageandleadership/Mahavatar_Babaji.aspx#.VV5bsuu7KfQ.

crystal boosters that could travel that far. In reality, this helped the three groups exist and operate on their own without much outside influence.

Someone sent me a Hindu text speaking about a time long ago when there was no hate, jealousy, violence, or disease, and no one labored because, I suppose, we could manifest everything we wanted or needed. So will we return to those times, and I have to ask, when were those times?

This is a very ancient text from and about people who lived even much earlier than the lands of Mu and Atlantis. These people lived at a much higher focus, so there could be a time when this happens again but not for thousands of years, as even in the fifth focus you will need to have many lessons before reaching this level of existence. Then the Earth experiment will be concluded. It certainly is a time to strive for — but again far in your future.

• • •

CLUES IN PHYSICAL ATTRIBUTES
Gaia, do people who had previous lives on Atlantis or Lemuria have lines on their hands?

No, that's an old wives' tale. That said, there are still many things to learn about your hands for those who enjoy studying them.

• • •

Theo, is there any truth to the idea that if the toe next to your big toe is longer that you have had a life on Atlantis?

No, it is not true. There are many people alive today with longer toes than their big toes. This is just a genetic condition, not a reminder of days past.

Yet there are, at times, reminders of the past, such as a birthmark I have that I understand was from being shot in a past life?

True, but toes are a different matter. There are people alive today who had lives on Atlantis and their second toes are shorter than their big toes.

Were later civilizations patterned after Atlantis?

Yes, of course there were. Stories were passed down first in writing and then, as the centuries passed, in stories so that there was always the desire to become a great nation again. This came from those who reincarnated too. Time took its toll, and although most were able to stay at civilized levels, there were those who chose the European continent and became farmers and hunters and settled into simpler lives. That's why there was little to find there.

Is there a reason why Atlantis is popping up with those who channel at this time?

Oh yes, you and the other channels are supposed to help people remember Atlantis for a variety of reasons. The most important is to remember that it was a place of great accomplishments before greed set in and brought down the house of cards, you might say. The revelations about things they were able to do that you haven't will encourage those who invent to set their sights on creating what is described.

Regarding Atlantis, keep in mind there's been over 12,000 years to cover up remaining artifacts. Just as a small example, go to Bath, England, where there's a Roman bath (now quite a few feet below ground) that was level on the surface. That much dirt has slowly covered it over the past 2,000 years or so.

How close did the Atlanteans get to the energy level of the Harmonic Convergence we experienced in 1987?

Not too close. Their demise occurred over hundreds of years, and it could have been reversed except for the greedy factions who wanted everything. They eventually destroyed each other, so, no, they never even came close. This is why you are so lauded across the universe for attaining such a high vibrational level in such a short time. None of you on the planet can appreciate what a significant achievement that was, as others had tried and failed.

• • •

TOM'S CLOSING STATEMENT

There you have it — three major catastrophes [destructions] and only one of them was a natural disaster. The other two were brought about by the greed and desire for power. But as you read numerous times in the preceding chapters, this will never happen again. We will never destroy ourselves; however, conflicts will continue for a number of years. We will eventually learn how to live with each other and respect the differences in our beliefs.

Theo told me: "Even when you do not fully receive an answer, it will inspire others to try to seek the correct answer. Please do not forget that you are a catalyst, Tom. You will cause many people to begin meditating, and some excellent people will be encouraged by your work."

If I'm to be a catalyst, one of my main goals is to encourage you to try the Gentle Way modality in your daily life. It is a simple and powerful way to lessen the "fear factor" and stress level to help you be more successful, all the while raising your vibrational level, helping you "ascend," as some people call it. It works perfectly!

In my three Gentle Way books, hundreds of people have contributed their inspiring stories from all over the world about how they use the Gentle Way in their own daily lives. Please read the appendix to learn more.

In the meantime, have a good life, everyone, and Expect Great Things!

APPENDIX

EASY STEPS FOR REQUESTING MBOs: A QUICK REVIEW

- Request the benevolent outcomes aloud, whispered, or in writing.
- Start with easy requests for immediate feedback.
- Be very specific with your request.
- Make requesting benevolent outcomes a habit.
- Requesting a benevolent outcome with emotion and feeling reinforces the request.
- Don't be afraid to ask for the impossible.
- You can request that the outcome be even "more than you can expect or imagine."
- Thank your guardian angel for fulfilling your request.

"I request a Most Benevolent Outcome for _____. May the outcome be more than I can expect or imagine! Thank you."

ABOUT THE AUTHOR

TOM T. MOORE is the author of the Gentle Way books, a speaker, and a frequent radio guest. For the past twenty-five years, he has worked as the president and CEO of his own international motion picture and TV program distribution business based in Dallas-Fort Worth Metroplex, Texas. During this time, he has traveled extensively as part of his business duties to international film markets held in Cannes, France; Milan, Italy; Los Angeles, California; and Budapest, Hungary. Tom was inspired to publicize the modality of the Gentle Way, which dates back to Atlantean times and is described as a giant step forward over the law of attraction. He says that requesting benevolent outcomes for the past fifteen years has resulted in leading a gentler, less stressful, and less fearful life — the Gentle Way!

Before becoming an international film distributor, Tom owned and operated an international wholesale tour company with his wife, selling tours through 3,000 travel agents nationwide. That business began out of his first successful venture, a ski club for single adults, which grew to be the largest snow ski club in Texas. Tom is still an avid skier and loves to ski in the United States, Canada, and Europe.

Tom graduated with a BBA in finance from Texas Christian University in Fort Worth, Texas, and served in the U.S. Army as a first lieutenant. He is a native of Dallas, Texas, and is married with two children.

Tom publishes a weekly newsletter and blog, and his articles have appeared in a number of international and regional magazines. You can read his monthly column in the *Sedona Journal of Emergence!* To book Tom T. Moore as a speaker at your next conference or event, email him at speaker@ TheGentleWayBook.com.

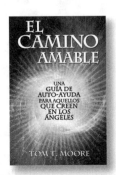

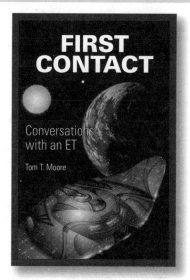

☦ *Light Technology* PUBLISHING *Presents*

Books by David K. Miller

Arcturians: How to Heal, Ascend, and Help Planet Earth

Go on a mind-expanding journey to explore new spiritual tools for dealing with our planetary crisis. Included in this book are new and updated interpretations of the Kaballistic Tree of Life, which has now been expanded to embrace fifth-dimensional planetary healing methods. Learn new and expanded Arcturian spiritual technologies.

$16.95 • 352 pp. • Softcover • 978-1-62233-002-7

Kaballah and the Ascension

"Throughout Western history, channeling has come to us in various forms, including mediumship, shamanism, fortunetelling, visionaries, and oracles. There is also a long history of channeling in Kaballah, the major branch of Jewish mysticism. I am intrigued by this, especially because I believe that there is now an urgent necessity for entering higher realms with our consciousness because of the impending changes on the planet. Through these higher realms, new healing energies and insights can be brought down to assist us in these coming Earth changes." — David K. Miller

$16.95 • 176 pp. • Softcover • 978-1-891824-82-1

Biorelativity: Planetary Healing Technologies

Biorelativity describes the ability of human beings to telepathically communicate with the spirit of Earth. The goal of such communication is to influence the outcome of natural Earth events such as storms, volcanic eruptions, and earthquakes. Through the lessons contained in this book, you can implement new planetary healing techniques right now, actively participating in exciting changes as Earth and humanity come together in unity and healing.

$16.95 • 352 pp. • Softcover • 978-1-891824-98-2

A New Tree of Life for Planetary Ascension

This is the second book David Miller has written about the Kabbalah. His first book, Kaballah and the Ascension, introduced basic concepts in the Kabbalah and linked them to the ascended masters and the process of ascension. In this second book, David has teamed up with Torah scholar and Kabbalist expert Mordechai Yashin, who resides in Jerusalem, Israel. This book is based on unique lectures and classes David and Mordechai gave over an eight-month period between 2012 and 2013. These lectures on Jewish and Hebraic lessons were held in open discussion groups and offer a truly unique perspective into the Kabbalistic Tree of Life and how it has been expanded.

$16.95 • 464 pp. • Softcover • 978-1-62233-012-6

Raising the Spiritual Light Quotient

The spiritual light quotient is a measurement of a person's ability to work with and understand spirituality. This concept is compared to the intelligence quotient (IQ). However, in reality, spiritual ability is not related to intelligence, and interestingly, unlike the IQ, one's spiritual light quotient can increase with age and experience.

$16.95 • 384 pp. • Softcover • 978-1-891824-89-0

Connecting with the Arcturians

Who is really out there? Where are we going? What are our choices? What has to be done to prepare for this event? This book explains all of these questions in a way that we can easily understand. It explains what our relationships are to known extraterrestrial groups and what they are doing to help Earth and her people in this crucial galactic moment in time.

$17.00 • 256 pp. • Softcover • 978-1-891824-94-4

New Spiritual Technology for the Fifth-Dimensional Earth

Earth is moving closer to the fifth dimension. New spiritual ideas and technologies are becoming available for rebalancing our world, including native ceremonies to connect to Earth healing energies and thought projections and thought communication with Earth.

$19.95 • 240 pp. • Softcover • 978-1-891824-79-1

BOOKS BY DAVID K. MILLER

Fifth-Dimensional Soul Psychology

"The basic essence of soul psychology rests with the idea that the soul is evolving and that part of this evolution is occurring through incarnations in the third dimension. Now, to even speak about the soul evolving is perhaps a controversial subject because we know that the soul is eternal. We know that the soul has been in existence for infinity, and we know that the soul is perfect. So why would the soul have to evolve?

The answer to this question is complex, and we may not be able to totally answer it using third-dimensional terminology. But it is an important question to answer, because the nature of soul evolution is inherently connected to your experiences in the third dimension. The soul, in completing its evolutionary journey, needs these experiences in the third dimension, and it needs to complete the lessons here."

—Vywamus

$16.95 • 288 PP. • Softcover • 978-1-62233-016-4

Teachings from the Sacred Triangle, Vol. 1

David's second book explains how the Arcturian energy melds with that of the White Brother-/Sisterhood and the ascended Native American masters to bring about planetary healing.

Topics include the Sacred Triangle energy and the sacred codes of ascension, how to create a bridge to the fifth dimension, what role you can play in the Sacred Triangle, and how sacred words from the Kaballah can assist you in your ascension work.

$16.95 • 288 PP. • Softcover • 978-1-62233-007-2

Teachings from the Sacred Triangle, Vol. 2

Our planet is at a dire crossroads from a physical standpoint, but from a spiritual standpoint, it is experiencing a great awakening. Never before have there been so many conscious lightworkers, awakened spiritual beings, and masters as there are on this planet now. A great sense of a spiritual harmony emanates from the many starseed groups, and there is also a new spiritual energy and force that is spreading throughout the planet.

$16.95 • 288 PP. • Softcover • 978-1-891824-19-7

Teachings from the Sacred Triangle, Vol. 3

Learn how to use holographic technology to project energies in the most direct and transformative way throughout Earth.

Chapters Include:
- Heart Chakra and the Energy of Love
- Multidimensional Crystal Healing Energy
- Healing Space-Time Rifts
- Integration of Spirituality and Technology, Space, and Time Travel

$16.95 • 288 PP. • Softcover • 978-1-891824-23-4

Enseñanzas del Sagrado Triángulo Arcturiano

Este paradigma es necesario para ayudar en la transición de la humanidad hacia la próxima etapa evolutiva. La humanidad debe realizar esta próxima etapa de la evolución, para asegurar su sobrevivencia por los cambios climáticos globales, la guerra y la destrucción del medio ambiente. ¿Cuál es la próxima etapa? Esta involucra la expansión de la consciencia del ser humano y está representada por el símbolo de este nuevo paradigma, el Sagrado Triángulo Arcturiano.

El guía de la quinta dimensión, Juliano, proveniente del sistema estelar galáctico conocido como Arcturus, trabaja junto a David en un papel prominente en esta introducción de la energía del Triángulo Sagrado en la Tierra. David le ofrece al lector un entendimiento del alma, su naturaleza evolutiva y como la humanidad esta avanzando hacia esa siguiente etapa evolutiva.

$19.95 • 416 PP. • Softcover • 978-1-62233-264-9

Expand Your Consciousness

Now more than ever, humankind is in need of developing its higher consciousness to heal itself and Earth and to experience life in a much more meaningful way. By expanding our consciousness, we can see the connections and unity that exist in all reality, and we might see objects with sharper colors, hear sounds with greater clarity, or even experience two sensations simultaneously! In this book, you will explore the fascinating multidimensionality that is yours for the taking.

$16.95 • 288 PP. • Softcover • 978-1-62233-036-2

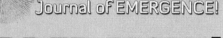